James Champlin Fernald, Godfrey Holden Pike

Charles Haddon Spurgeon, Preacher, Author, Philanthropist

With Anecdotal Reminiscences

James Champlin Fernald, Godfrey Holden Pike

Charles Haddon Spurgeon, Preacher, Author, Philanthropist
With Anecdotal Reminiscences

ISBN/EAN: 9783337729615

Printed in Europe, USA, Canada, Australia, Japan

Cover: Foto ©Thomas Meinert / pixelio.de

More available books at **www.hansebooks.com**

CHARLES HADDON SPURGEON

Preacher, Author, Philanthropist

WITH ANECDOTAL REMINISCENCES

BY

G. HOLDEN PIKE

AUTHOR OF "THE ROMANCE OF THE STREETS," ETC.

INTRODUCTION BY
WILLIAM CLEAVER WILKINSON
AND CONCLUDING CHAPTERS BY
JAMES C. FERNALD

FUNK & WAGNALLS COMPANY
NEW YORK
LONDON TORONTO

INTRODUCTION

By Professor W. C. Wilkinson, D.D.*

In every human generation there is a certain small number of picked men concerning whom public interest, beginning early, continues long to be so general and so vivid that everything proceeding from them, everything said about them, everything connected with them, is sure to engage the attention of mankind. Of this select class of men belonging to our generation, by eminence was Charles Haddon Spurgeon. It thus happens that, during many years, Mr. Spurgeon's biography has been, as it were, constantly written up to date, in the current periodical literature of his time. At his death, nothing, or almost nothing, remained of new to be told respecting him. There had long been simply the day's, or the week's, or the month's, addition to be made to the biographical bulletins that promptly advised an ever curious public what was the last thing of note that had befallen the foremost

---

* Requested by the publishers of the present work to furnish a brief general estimate of the genius, character, and career of the illustrious subject, I sought and obtained from the courtesy of the editors, respectively, of *The Examiner*, and *The Independent* (New York), permission to adopt and incorporate, in what I might write, parts of two articles, which I had contributed to these journals, one on occasion of Mr. Spurgeon's fiftieth birthday, and one on occasion of his death.

favorite preacher of the present time. This, however, is fully true only for Mr. Spurgeon's equals or superiors in age. A whole generation has grown up since he began to be famous, and, to the members of this new community of minds, the story of his career will be as novel as it is certain to be interesting.

In seeking some adequate expression for the imposing phenomenon presented in the life and labors of Spurgeon, I have myself been accustomed to distribute the mass of his achievement into three parts, and thus to find him by a threefold title deserving to be considered a truly great man. If he had never done anything but preach as he preached, he would assuredly remain, to all future time, one of the most commanding names that illustrate the annals of the nineteenth Christian century. For more than the full third of a century, he stood confessed, upon the whole, easily the first of contemporary preachers. His was indeed a sudden shooting up into the zenith, as of a meteor that might suddenly go out. But he took his station and held it steadily like a fixed star. The flash that surprised us was not a flash, but only the instantaneous beginning of a brightness to burn and to shine. A luminary, not a meteor, was the preaching eloquence of Charles Haddon Spurgeon. Nothing less meteoric, nothing more solar, in its quality of radiance, has ever been set by God among the merely human and uninspired lights of the world to shed illumination on any Christian age. Church history will always have to reckon Mr. Spurgeon as one of the greatest preachers of all times and of all climes. Such is his indefeasible heritage of fame as a preacher.

If, now, one were to disregard the thousands of sermons (in sober literal count, more than 2,200) from Mr. Spurgeon's tongue that, during his life, went into print, and were multiplied, each into uncounted numbers of copies—if, I say, one were to set all these aside and consider only what, apart from these and in addition to these, Mr. Spurgeon accomplished as a writer and maker of books, one would still have to acknowledge that, in the capacity of author alone, this fecund genius did enough to give him unchallenged rank among the most successful literary men of his generation. I must take no room here for statistics, but I may mention, by way of sufficient illustration and argument that his *John Ploughman's Talks* has reached a sale of 320,000 copies, while of a sequel, published a few years since, 100,000 copies have been sold. Each successive book of Mr. Spurgeon's—a considerable list the full number would make—would, I am sure, be accounted a marked publisher's success. So much for the literary part of Mr. Spurgeon's famous work.

But, once more, Mr. Spurgeon might never either have preached or have written, and yet, had he—could this be supposed possible—done nothing but found, establish, organize, administer the several great public institutions over which he presided, and to which, if one may so speak after the manner of men—he gave the breath of their life—

that work by itself, justly estimated, would entitle the prime human motor in it to be ranked a man of genius. Look at the church of the Metropolitan Tabernacle. Count out, as a thing not to be brought into the present comparison, that amazing missionary church in Ongole, and I suppose this to be by odds the largest Protestant church proper in the world. The exact present numbers are a little short of 6,000 members, and what a spectacle of organization and organized activity it presents! What a mother of churches it has been! Occasionally the pastor, in the full career of his ministry, would request the regular attendants and seat-holders to absent themselves from a preaching service, that the "unreached" masses of London population might have room to swarm in and fill the monster Tabernacle. Then hardly six or eight persons—and these amiably overcome, perhaps, by their half unselfish curiosity and joy to behold the animating sight—out of all the thousands that heard Mr. Spurgeon Sunday after Sunday, would be present. What discipline of love, and obedience, and self-denial! Then there, too, is the College for Pastors—an institution beyond, far beyond, anything in this respect to be paralleled with it, the creation of one brain and heart. And the Orphanage! And the Colportage Society! These organizations, I repeat it, with their already assured wise administration and abounding fruitfulness, would alone be a great and enduring monument to the name of their founder and chief manager.

Now roll the three, great preacher, great author,

great organizer, into one, and the result is a man for human nature to be—what shall we say?—proud of?—no; for the man is Charles Haddon Spurgeon—say rather to be glad of, to be unspeakably thankful to God for. "It is not, it is not," we seem to hear Mr. Spurgeon himself in almost pained deprecation say it—" it is not man's greatness, but God's grace."

In the physical man, Mr. Spurgeon's voice was his chief good fortune in endowment. But that good fortune would nigh have compensated for the lack of every other. The wonder of Mr. Spurgeon's voice grew upon me the more I considered it and compared it. He used it without *any* apparent effort, and it answered every purpose of his will. In its utmost violence, I never heard from it one note that grated harshly on the ear. It was virile, but it hid in its virile sweetness an effect of womanly winningness that was almost pathetic. In the mere matter of making people hear, Mr. Spurgeon accomplished with his voice feats probably never surpassed, I doubt if ever equaled. I was told, and I believe, that in Agricultural Hall, in London, a place described as being like uninclosed space for vastness, he made himself distinctly audible to 12,000 people. It is even credibly affirmed that, in the Crystal Palace, at Sydenham, he spoke, and was everywhere perfectly audible, to an assembly of 20,000 people. His voice, when he was speaking so as to be heard by such a number, would be no less agreeable to those persons nearest him than to those farthest removed, and hardly less distinct to those farthest removed than to those nearest. It was an instrument of speech that either needed no management, or was so perfectly managed that it seemed to need none. It was the perfection of nature; or else the perfection of both nature and art.

The thing most obvious and most striking in Mr. Spurgeon's mental endowment was his preternatural command of language, both vocabulary and syntax. For simple, lucid flow of appropriate speech, so uninterrupted and so easy that it seemed like lubricity itself become vocal and expressive, I never heard anything anywhere that even approached Mr. Spurgeon's habitual discourse. Mr. Beecher was great at this point; but he had fits of greater and less, was eruptive, sometimes explosive. Mr. Spurgeon *never* faltered. He never went faster than he wished to, for fear that if he went slower he might come not to go at all. He never went slow because he could not go faster. The fountain flowed because it was a fountain, and the nature of a fountain is to flow. Of course I describe what appeared. Doubtless Mr. Spurgeon had his subjective experiences of mental obstruction; but his frank, manly, womanly way was to make his hearers confidants of his moods, by telling them outright when his chariot wheels were driving heavily. No speaker was ever more sure of the sympathy of his hearers.

Perfect mastery of his own system of doctrine was another secret of Mr. Spurgeon's power. Perfect mastery of it, and perfect conviction of its truth, went hand in hand together with him. He never stood before his hearers like a reed shaken with the wind. He stood solid on the rock, with the whole balanced weight of his great personality.

The doctrine itself that he taught had the immense advantage of being a doctrine that could easily be made intelligible to average minds. And average minds composed the audience to which Mr. Spurgeon addressed himself. The character of mediocrity wrote itself legibly, unmistakably, over the aspect of the Tabernacle congregation. I say this to Mr. Spurgeon's praise. His church was essentially a mission church occupying mission ground. All the unequalled influence as a minister of the gospel that Mr. Spurgeon attained, he attained, let this be forever remembered to his honor, in the service of a church made up of "not many wise, not many noble." What his preaching did was to present to such hearers the one unchanging gospel of Christ in countless changes of form, each perfectly level to the comprehension of all. He turned and turned the kaleidoscope of the sermon, and exhibited to his hearers, never weary of beholding, the same precious truths over and over again, Sunday after Sunday, in displays that had nothing new to recommend them but the endlessly new combinations of things old that the magic of the preacher could produce. If the same combinations even were sometimes repeated, that did not make the pleasure of seeing them pall in the least upon the appetite of the beholders. The achievement was magnificent, of a magnificent aim—to preach the gospel to the poor.

It would be a capital omission not to make note of the blithe humor that enlivened the earnest temperament of Mr. Spurgeon, and broadened and quickened his touch with the people. This, and an instantaneous alertness of mind in him that served every useful purpose of wit, stood him many a time in good stead on oratoric occasions. These two qualities of his subsisted in a noble basis of Saxon common-sense, and, together with that, saved him remarkably, throughout his life, from serious practical errors.

The fundamental attribute, alike of his talent and of his character, was a magnanimous simplicity. His conduct and his speech were uniformly such as seemed comportable with the straightforwardness, the honor, the sense of personal responsibility, proper to a Christian gentleman.

But the thing to me most remarkable of all, about this remarkable man, I have thus far purposely reserved. It was not his magnificent gift of eloquence, that steady unfailing river of utterance, that winning, manly, pathetic voice, like a silver trumpet, like a flute, like an organ. It was not the inexhaustible fertility of his productive literary genius. It was not the matchless resource of organizing, sustaining, administering strength and wisdom that he displayed. It was no one of these things by itself, and not all of these things in their rare union and harmony. It was something other and higher. The most remarkable thing about Mr,

Spurgeon was this: the absolute, simple, single fidelity maintained by him throughout, maintained unintermittingly, from the juvenile beginning to the culminating maturity of his work—the serene, unperturbed, untempted fidelity of mind, of heart, of conscience, of will, of all that was in him, and all that was of him, to the mere and pure, unchanged, unaccommodated New Testament gospel of Jesus Christ, the same yesterday, to-day, and forever. That stands up and out, that lifts itself and is eminent, like a peak of the Himalayas, high regnant over all the subjected high table-land of this noble character and life. Blessed be God for it! There is comfort, there is strength left for us even yet, now that he is gone, in the backward contemplation. Look up at him. The wrinkled sea beneath him was crawling with its little waves of scientific guess, of new theologic shift and statement, of finical culture seeking to replace Christian ethics with pagan æsthetics. How, seen from that sun-bright, immovable summit of the gospel, the contorted sea beneath of human wisdom must have looked vain and small! Well might Christendom take part in celebrating with solemn joy the jubilee that struck its hour abroad, heard over all the world, in the fiftieth birthday of this faithful man of God. "It may be," Mr. Spurgeon at that time said of himself, "it may be, that we are only in mid-voyage," adding, "May that voyage end in landing our freight in port, and not as some life passages have terminated, namely, in an utter wreck of every hope!"

Somewhat farther on than "in mid-voyage" it proved that Spurgeon was, when he wrote those touching, prayer-laden words. But nothing of what he meekly so deprecated befell him to darken the end. All was peace and hope, triumphant over pain. With what heightening of the fine sense conveyed in Milton's words about Samson Agonistes dead, we may apply those words to Spurgeon!

> " Nothing is here for tears, nothing to wail
> Or knock the breast ; no weakness, no contempt,
> Dispraise, or blame ; nothing but well and fair,
> And what may quiet us in a death so noble."

That for Spurgeon himself. But for us that survive him! Alas, we feel how much light, how much warmth, how much life, as of a sun, withdrew from the world that Sunday night with the going hence of Charles Haddon Spurgeon.

CONTENTS.

	PAGE.
INTRODUCTION	. iii

CHAPTER I.
MR. SPURGEON'S EARLY DAYS 3

CHAPTER II.
REMINISCENCES OF WATERBEACH . . . 29

CHAPTER III.
THE FIRST SUNDAYS IN LONDON . . . 57

CHAPTER IV.
PERSONAL REMINISCENCES 89

CHAPTER V.
ANECDOTES, LETTERS, ANA, ETC. . . . 121

CHAPTER VI.
SOME SPECIAL OCCASIONS 159

CHAPTER VII.

TWO THOUSAND PRINTED SERMONS . . . 195

CHAPTER VIII.

THE PREACHER'S REWARD—ANECDOTES ABOUT THE SERMONS 219

CHAPTER IX.

MR. SPURGEON'S BOOKS 251

CHAPTER X.

THE BOOK FUND 269

CHAPTER XI.

REVIEWS IN "THE SWORD AND THE TROWEL" . 289

CHAPTER XII.

CONCLUDING THOUGHTS AND REMINISCENCES . 315

CHAPTER XIII.

LAST SCENES AND LAST SERMONS . . . 367

MR. SPURGEON'S EARLY DAYS.

"I will ask any sensible man, above all, any serious Christian here, whether there have not been certain times in his life when he could most distinctly see that indeed God did 'choose his inheritance for him'? . . . I do not know whether all of you can go with me here; but I think you must in some instance or other be forced to see that God has indeed ordained your inheritance for you. If you cannot, I can. I can see a thousand chances, as men would call them, all working together like wheels in a great piece of machinery, to fix me just where I am; and I can look back to a hundred places where, if one of those little wheels had run away—if one of those little atoms in the great whirlpool of my existence had started aside—I might have been anywhere but here, occupying a very different position. If you cannot say this, I know *I* can with emphasis, and can trace God's hand back to the period of my birth through every step I have taken; I can feel that indeed God has allotted my inheritance for me. If any of you are so wilfully beclouded that you will not see the hand of God in your being, and will insist that all has been done by your will without Providence; that you have been left to steer your own course across the ocean of existence; and that you are where you are because your own hand guided the tiller, and your own arm directed the rudder, all I can say is, my own experience belies the fact, and the experience of many now in this place would rise in testimony against you, and say, 'Verily, it is not in man that walketh to direct his steps.' —' Man proposes, but God disposes;' and the God of heaven is not unoccupied, but is engaged in over-ruling, ordering, altering, working all things according to the good pleasure of His will."—*The New Park Street Pulpit*, i. 255.

I.

MR. SPURGEON'S EARLY DAYS.

MANY hands have tried to do what I shall certainly not attempt in this volume—to write the life of Mr. Spurgeon. To accomplish such a task would be as impossible to-day as it will be in the future. No great man can be worthily preserved on paper—not even by the most perfect Boswellian mode of treatment; and what the Pastor has been heard to threaten he will do, should he ever be approached by a first cousin of Johnson's biographer, may well intimidate the boldest member of that inquisitive tribe. I am not a Boswell; I am not a biographer. I shall not impertinently pry behind the scenes of private life to annoy a worthy family on the one hand, and to gratify a morbid public curiosity on the other hand. All that is purposed to be done is, to produce a series of sketches different from anything which has, as yet, been put together in a volume, and which shall be sufficiently true to life not to mislead outsiders, and not to shock the sensibilities of friends.

In case any reader should need them for reference, I shall, in this opening chapter, put down a few commonplace facts such as are widely known and are everybody's property. Mr. Spurgeon was born at Kelvedon, in Essex, on the 19th of June, 1834; and, as the world is fond of comparing the events in the life of one great man with those belonging to the course of another great man, it may be remarked that on that auspicious day Thomas Babington Macaulay "crossed the frontier of Mysore." It was in that year, moreover, that the Houses of Parliament were destroyed by fire.

During several generations, the Spurgeons have been engaged in the Christian ministry. The Pastor's grandfather spent half a century among a flock at Stambourne, and this old worthy's son is a valued minister of the Independent denomination at the present time. One of the earliest custodians of the popular preacher was an affectionate maiden aunt, who, with others, could not fail to detect a precocious talent in her youthful charge. We have all heard how Richard Knill looked upon the boy with admiration, to express hopes in regard to the future which have not been disappointed.

A Puritan Veteran. 5

Some years ago the Rev. W. Osborne, who is now pastor of a flourishing Baptist Church at Eastbourne, supplied me with the following reminiscence of the Rev. James Spurgeon of Stambourne :—

The day preceding that on which he entered on college work in London, Mr. Osborne preached at Stambourne for old Mr. Spurgeon, who was then an octogenarian, and showed the strongest possible partiality for Dr. Watts's hymns. This deep-rooted prejudice on the part of the old gentleman was a trait in his character with which the neighbours and regular hearers were familiar; but it was something of which the young preacher had never heard even the slightest whisper. Mr. Osborne arrived at Stambourne, he entered the chapel, to receive the first intimation of a coming disagreement when a member of the congregation expressed a hope that the hymns were selected, and that all were of Dr. Watts's composition. On turning to the book it was at once seen that the unlucky youth had missed his way in each selection, every hymn being the production of an unappreciated poet, for none would suit the old gentleman but those of Isaac Watts. Time was pressing, however, and the hymns were allowed to pass ; but as the service went on, the effects of the strange verses on the mind of the old pastor were striking, and calculated to create trepidation in the heart of an inexperienced preacher. Like a master in Israel the old man took a seat in the table-pew, and, as occasion required, he cast a searching glance towards the pulpit. When the first hymn was announced he signified his disapproval by gravely shaking his head; when the second was given out, with no improvement, he expressed his disgust by simply closing the book; but when the third came, and was still by a forbidden author, he raised his fist as though he would chastise the offender. At the conclusion of the service there was an explosion, not of wrath, but of pent-up feeling. "Young man!" cried the aged pastor, with a genial twinkle of the eye, while he raised a stout stick to give emphasis to his words—" Young man! if you do not want your brains knocked out, you *must* sing Dr. Watts's hymns!" If he was not actually terrified into compliance with these forcible demands, Mr. Osborne took particular care not to repeat in the afternoon the mistake of the morning. At this second service hymns by Dr. Watts were quietly introduced; old Mr. Spurgeon according the preacher a nod of approval as soon as the first was announced. When the second and third hymns were such as could be commended, former chagrin gave place to extreme satisfaction.

A Child Preacher.

"Right, sir, right!" cried the pastor, after listening admiringly to a sermon on the fall of Jericho, "I am glad to see you can appreciate the best authors so quickly. Go now and get your ram's horn ready, like those men, and God may make you the means of hurling to the ground walls as strong and stubborn as those"—*i.e.*, of Jericho. On the following day Mr. Osborne removed to London, joined the Pastors' College, and thus got his "ram's horn ready" for future service in a manner that won the approval of his honest, outspoken preceptor.

It is generally understood that Mr. Spurgeon showed his ministerial proclivities almost as soon as he could walk and speak. His earliest recollections are of reading religious books; and in childish days he would address an audience, corresponding in age to his own years, with more force than some adults can command in the pulpit. Very strong tendencies in a certain direction in childhood are always interesting; they must have been doubly so in a case where the subject was endowed with one of the finest voices of which we have any example. Though thus piously brought up, he was not converted until he was sixteen, and the great change occurred at Colchester, in which town he purposed to visit one sanctuary after another in search of saving light. He turned into one of the humblest of chapels, and there heard a thin, pale man preach from the words, " Look unto Me and be ye saved, all the ends of the earth." The manner in which the preacher cried, " Look ! *Look !* LOOK ! " was peculiarly striking, and, what is better, relief came instantly, the simplicity of the Gospel being at once appreciated. The pulpit in which this memorable " Look " sermon was preached may now be seen at the Stockwell Orphanage.

On a certain occasion, Mr. Spurgeon's father, in speaking of his family to Dr. Ford, of America, is reported to have remarked :—" I had been from home a great deal, trying to build up weak congregations, and felt that I was neglecting the religious training of my own children while I toiled for the good of others. I returned home with these feelings. I opened the door, and was surprised to find none of the children about the hall. Going quietly up the stairs, I heard my wife's voice. She was engaged in prayer with the children. I heard her pray for them one by one by name. She came to Charles, and specially prayed for him, for he was of high spirit and daring temper. I listened till she had ended her prayer, and I felt and said, ' Lord, I will go on with Thy work. The children will be cared for.' "

Juvenile Literary Efforts. 9

Of his education after this date, little needs to be said. He plodded as a schoolboy at Colchester. He studied for a time at Maidstone, in an agricultural college of that town. He subsequently accepted an appointment in a school at Newmarket, the principal of which was a Baptist; but I am not aware that this fact in any way accounts for the change of sentiment— the transition from Pædobaptist to Baptist views —which about this time occurred. That change was brought about by a close study of the Bible; for Mr. Spurgeon's mind is of an independent cast, that would not brook the interference of any lower authority than Scripture. Thus early his mind was active, while his industry was great. A slight *brochure* of those days, called "Antichrist and her Brood," has never been published, although I believe that the MS. is still in the possession of the Rev. John Spurgeon. A poem called "The Fall of Jericho" was printed, and afterwards republished in the first number of *The Sword and the Trowel*.

Before his conversion, and as a mere youth, Mr. Spurgeon was tempted to become an unbeliever; and while preaching at Exeter Hall, on Sunday evening, March 18th, 1855, he gave some vivid reminiscences of that unhappy time, *e.g.*—" There may be some one here to-night who has come without faith, a man of reason, a free-thinker. With him I have no argument at all. I profess not to stand here as a controversialist, but as a preacher of things that I know and feel. But I too have been like him. There was an evil hour when once I slipped the anchor of my faith; I cut the cable of my belief; I no longer moored myself hard by the coasts of revelation; I allowed my vessel to drift before the wind; I said to reason, 'Be thou my captain;' I said to my own brain, 'Be thou my rudder;' and I started on my mad voyage. Thank God it is all over now; but I will tell you its brief history. It was one hurried sailing over the tempestuous ocean of free thought. I went on, and as I went the skies began to darken; but to make up for that deficiency the waters were brilliant with coruscations of brilliancy. I saw sparks flying upwards that pleased me, and I thought, 'If this be free thought, it is a happy thing.' My thoughts seemed gems, and I scattered stars with both my hands. But anon, instead of these coruscations of glory, I saw grim fiends, fierce and horrible, start up from the waters, and as I dashed on they gnashed their teeth and grinned upon me; they seized the prow of my ship and dragged me on, while I, in part, gloried at the rapidity of my motion, but yet shuddered at the terrific rate with which I passed the old landmarks of my faith. As I hurried forward with an awful speed, I began to doubt my very existence; I doubted if there were a world, I doubted if there were such a thing as myself. I went to the very verge of the dreary realms of unbelief. I went to the very bottom of the sea of infidelity. I doubted everything. But here the devil foiled himself; for the very extravagance of the doubt proved its absurdity. Just when I saw the bottom of that sea, there came a voice which said, 'And can this doubt be true?' At this very thought I awoke. I started from that death-dream, which God knows might have damned my soul, and ruined this my body, if I had not awoke. When I arose faith took the helm; from that moment I doubted not. Faith steered me back; faith cried, 'Away, away!' I cast my anchor on Calvary; I lifted my eye to God; and here I am alive, and out of hell. Therefore, I speak what I do know. I have sailed that perilous voyage; I have come safe to land. Ask me again to be an infidel! No; I have tried it; it was sweet at first, but bitter afterwards."

I will now briefly allude to the pastor's first sermon, and then return to some other things which were providentially overruled to produce the best results in after days.

On a certain day, between twenty and thirty years ago, two young men might have been seen walking out of Cambridge towards a village lying in the suburbs of that town, for the purpose of holding a cottage service. Neither of the two pedestrians had ever preached a sermon in his life; but more singular was the fact that each marched forward along the green level lanes while harbouring the comfortable mistake that the other was the preacher for the day. They talked as they travelled, and, after a time, the younger ventured to intimate to his companion that he hoped the Lord would bless his—the companion's—labours. Those words as they fell appear to have produced something akin to an electric shock. "Oh, dear!" cried the elder youth, eagerly, desirous of correcting an inconvenient error—"Oh, dear, I never preached in my life. I never thought of doing such a thing. I was asked to walk with you, and I sincerely hope God will bless *you* in *your* preaching." "Nay," cried the younger, apparently growing nervous, "but I never preached, and I don't know that I could do anything of the sort." The elder had thrown off the burden; the younger walked on, filled with fear and trembling. There was

A Child Theologian.

the cottage, there were the people assembled, and a sermon would have to be preached to them. The effort was made; the younger of the two novices made that effort, succeeded beyond his expectations—and his name was Charles Haddon Spurgeon.

For years before this eventful day in his history he had shown himself to be of a strongly inquisitive mind. Having once set his heart on knowing a thing, he would persevere until he came at the truth, nor would he allow his reasonable curiosity to be evaded either by the friendly "Pooh, pooh!" or by sterner rebuke. In an autobiographical article, published more than ten years ago, we are supplied with some juvenile reminiscences far too characteristic to be overlooked. When as a child he was living with his grandfather, it was the custom for Charles Haddon to read the Scriptures at family worship, and on every occasion he was allowed the licence of asking any question he chose on the portion for the day. On a certain morning the inconveniently-inquisitive reader came to the "bottomless pit" of the Revelation, and immediately asked, "Grandpa, what can this mean?" "Pooh, pooh! child, go on," replied the old man, regarding the question as too trivial to call for serious reply. To a child, however, every subject of interest is important; and in this instance Charles determined to read the same chapter morning after morning until a satisfactory explanation should be offered. "Well, dear, what is it that puzzles you?" asked the grandfather, after he had heard about the Beast, the Mother of Harlots, etc., etc., etc., as often as he thought desirable, or perhaps profitable. The question was then put in a more definite form, "If the pit aforesaid had no bottom, where would all those people fall to who dropped out at its lower end?" The query was too deep to be answered at once; it seems to have disturbed the gravity of the little circle, and to have been a sample of the "difficulties" that were propounded for elucidation at family worship.

The late sainted Mr. Knill, of Chester, was a friend of the family in those early days, and he happened to be drawn in an extraordinary manner towards the child whose singularities were sufficiently marked to make him an object of more than ordinary interest. One fine morning Mr. Knill awoke his *protégé* at an early hour, and for some time they walked together in the garden. They conversed about books and reading, and about the privilege of winning souls for Christ. Then they knelt together in the arbour, where the elder prayed for the younger, and did so in a manner that brought a blessing and left a lifelong impression. Afterwards, in the midst of the family circle, Mr. Knill placed the child on his knee, and remarked, "I do not know how it is, but I feel a solemn presentiment this child will preach the Gospel to thousands, and God will bless him to many souls. So sure am I of this, that when my little man preaches in Rowland Hill's Chapel—as he will do one day—I should like him to promise me that he will give out the hymn beginning

"'God moves in a mysterious way
His wonders to perform.'"

That rather striking prophecy was completely fulfilled; but Mr. Spurgeon is of opinion that the words themselves were instrumental in bringing about their own fulfilment.

The "first sermon" has been already mentioned. When the ice was once broken, the neighbourhood of Cambridge was the scene of the young Christian's evangelistic efforts. On arriving at a village on an unpropitious wintry night he has found the chapel empty, and has, lantern in hand, gone round to the houses to collect a congregation. It is quite a mistake to suppose that he was not popular before coming to London; for he was a favourite with the Cambridgeshire peasantry before he became so conspicuous a figure in the outer world and the leading member of his denomination. When stationed at Waterbeach, his services began to be in excessive demand, and invitations to preach were cordially responded to. The more shrewd even among the common people must have perceived that one who was something more than a rising man was in their midst.

In youth he did not altogether set his face against going to college, though in later life he has "a thousand times thanked the Lord very heartily for the strange providence which forced his steps into another and far better path." Truth to say, Mr. Spurgeon missed a collegiate training consequent on one of those singular mishaps which, at the time, are as annoying as they are unavoidable. While he was carrying all before him at Waterbeach his judicious seniors thought that the pastor would never become all he was capable of becoming unless he went to London and sat the prescribed number of times at the feet of a duly-qualified professor. This advice was listened to, and arrangements were made for a meeting of Dr. Angus on the one part and Mr. Spurgeon on the other part, the rendezvous appointed having been the house of the well-known publisher, Mr. Macmillan of Cambridge. The young pastor arrived at the time specified, was ushered into a drawing-room by the maid, and, after waiting for two hours, he rang the bell to learn the reason of the protracted delay. In the meantime, Dr. Angus had arrived, had been shown into another room, but not being so well able to exemplify the virtue of patience as his younger friend, the learned doctor departed for London, doubtless wondering why young aspirants to the ministry were not more eager to seize fleeting opportunities. Thus the two sat in adjoining rooms until patience had "had her perfect work," neither suspecting that the other was near. What momentous consequences sometimes hang on small matters! how much may occasionally depend on the remissness of a half-witted servant-maid! Still, the Church would have gained nothing by C. H. Spurgeon's admission into Regent's Park College.

Writing in 1881, Mr. Spurgeon thus referred to his own days of early plodding:—

"My college course was after this fashion. I was for three years a Cambridge man, though I never entered the University. I could not have obtained a degree, because I was a Nonconformist; and, moreover, it was a better thing for me to pursue my studies under an admirable scholar and tender friend, and preach at the same time. I must have been a singular-looking youth on wet evenings. During the last year of my stay in Cambridge, when I had given up my office as usher, I was wont to sally forth every night in the week except Saturday, and walk three, five, or perhaps eight miles out and back again on my preaching work; and when it rained I dressed myself in waterproof leggings and a mackintosh coat, and a hat with a waterproof covering, and I carried a dark lantern to show me the way across the fields. I had many adventures . . . but what I had gathered by my studies during the day I handed out to a company of villagers in the evening, and was greatly profited by the exercise. I always found it good to say my lesson when I had learned it. Children do so, and it is equally good for preachers, especially if they say their lesson by heart. In my young days I fear I said many odd things and made many blunders, but my audiences were not hypercritical, and no newspaper writers dogged my heels; and so I had a happy training-ground in which, by continual practice, I attained such a degree of ready speech as I now possess. There is no way of learning to preach which can be compared to preaching itself. If you want to swim you must get into the water, and if you at the first make a sorry exhibition, never mind, for it is by swimming as you can that you learn to

Youthful Discipline. 19

swim as you should. Hence we ought to be lenient with beginners, for they will do better by-and-bye. If young speakers in Cambridge had been discouraged and silenced, I might not have found my way here, and, therefore, I hope I shall be the last to bring forth a wet blanket for any who sincerely speak for Christ, however humble may be their endeavours. The fear of there being too many preachers is the last that will occur to me. I rejoice in that passage of the psalm, ' The Lord gave the word ; great was the company of those that published it.' Go forth, young man, and proclaim among the people of this vast city all the words of this life. Among these millions you will all be few enough. . . . Fill your baskets with living seed, and in due season bring them back laden with many sheaves. My heart is with you ; my soul rejoices in your successes ; and I look to the great Head of the Church, through your means, to gather in His blood-bought ones."

Speaking at the laying of the first stone of the Metropolitan Tabernacle, August 16th, 1859, the Rev. John Spurgeon thus referred to his son's early days :—

" I always thought my son did wrong in coming to London ; now you see that I was wrong. I always thought he was wrong in not going to college; I tried three or four hours with him one night with a dear friend that loved him, but it was no use; he said, 'No, I will never go to college, only in strict obedience to you as a father.' There I left the matter; and I see that God has been with him, though I thought it was a wrong step in him to go to London. And I thought it was a wrong step for me to come here to-night; but perhaps I may be mistaken again. I can tell you it is one of the happiest days of my life. I feel beyond myself when I think of the kindness that has been shown to him when but a youth. I ascribe it all to God's goodness and the earnest prayers of his people. He has been exposed to temptation from every source, and even now, my friends, he is not free from it. You have prayed for him, and God has sustained him. Oh! let me entreat you to continue your prayers. Every one here to-night, go home and pray for your pastor. A meeting like this is enough to carry a man beyond himself and fill his heart with pride; but the grace of God is all-sufficient. Several persons said to me—I do not know what their motive was—'Your son will never last in London six months; he has no education.' I said, 'You are terribly mistaken; he has the best education that can possibly be had; God has been his teacher, and he has had earthly teachers too.' I knew, as far as education went, he could manage London very well. Then they said his health would fail; but it has not failed him yet. He has had enough to shake his constitution, it is true, but God has been very merciful to him. I think if there is one thing that would crown my happiness to-day, it would have been to see his grandfather here. I should have loved to see him here. He said, 'Boy, don't ask me to go, I am too old; I am overcome with God's goodness and mercy to me.' He is always talking about him. Old people like to have something to talk about, so he always talks about his grandson. And next to that I should like, my dear friends, to have seen his mother here. I believe, under God's grace, his mother has been the means of leading him to Christ. You are well aware that I go and talk in the best manner I can to a few poor people on the Sabbath day, and God has blessed my labours. I thought, however, I ought not to go out on the Sabbath day, as God's people should train up their children in the best way they can; I thought I was neglecting my children, and as I came home one evening about seven o'clock, and went upstairs, I heard the voice of a mother pleading for her boy Charles, and talking to him and the others, and pouring her heart out in prayer in such a way as I never did in my life, and as I never heard before. It is for the encouragement of mothers that I mention this, that you may pray for your children, for God is a prayer-hearing and prayer-answering God."

Whilst taking a retrospect of a third of a century of work, we become conscious of feeling unwontedly curious about the youthful associations of one whom we may pronounce to be the first preacher of this age without fear of contradiction. What signs of unusual genius, of future distinction, were visible during youth? Who were his friends? where may we trace the footprints of his first travels as a preacher? Feeling more than ordinary interest in these minutiæ, I some years ago asked a friend, whose fortune it was to reside near " Ouse's silent tide," if he would collect such *ana* as he could relating to Mr. Spurgeon's early days in that vicinity.

I believe there are about a score of Houghtons in the British Empire; but to myself the one interesting member of a numerous family is that Houghton which lies low and snug among the tall trees luxuriating on the banks of the broad, slow-rolling Ouse, midway between Huntingdon and St. Ives. It is not a spot whereon one would at first expect to find any religious memories of more than common interest; but

The Guest of Potto Brown. 23

in this case appearances are, happily, deceptive. Near Houghton, Dr. Brooke, an able preacher, and father of the well-known Rev. Stopford Brooke, was for some time stationed. Here also laboured Mr. Edward Cressell, a minister of the Independent denomination, and whose ministrations were heartily appreciated by the homely village folk of the neighbourhood, and by lovers of good preaching farther away. Above all, it was at Houghton in his early days that Mr. Spurgeon became the guest of the eccentric Potto Brown, called by Elihu Burritt, in one of his books, "The Miller of Houghton." Mr. Brown was thoroughly eccentric, but he was still a kind-hearted man, who grew hot-house grapes for the sick poor, and who could commend the Wesleyans for saving souls at a cheaper rate than was done by any other denomination. On this question, as well as on others, the youth and the veteran were far from being agreed, and consequently some lively discussions came off between the two which for smartness would not have disgraced the Literary Club in its palmiest days.

I will now give what my Ouse-side friend says about Houghton, its famous miller, and the youthful preacher, C. H. Spurgeon :—

"It has been with much interest that I have

traced, by the aid of the memories of my acquaintances, the early teachings and appearance of one who has taken and maintained an honoured place in the vineyard of Jesus Christ, and one who has well borne the burden and heat of the day. A gentleman, whom I took to be a relative, informed me that he heard Mr. Spurgeon preach his first sermon when about fourteen years of age, and he then read, prayed, and expounded the Word, being attired in a round jacket and broad, turn-down collar, such as I remember to have seen in fashion at that period.

"Mr. C. D. tells me that he remembers C. H. Spurgeon preaching at Somersham about twenty-six years ago, and when he would be about seventeen years of age. He was then wearing a round jacket and turn-down collar. He remembers the words of the text, though not their place—'Fear not, thou worm Jacob.' The boyish voice of the preacher afforded a striking and impressive contrast to the tones of the aged minister who was accustomed to occupy the pulpit.

"Mr. Spurgeon was then living at some place near Cambridge, and his mode of preaching afforded promise that he would become a powerful and popular speaker. One old man, who was a Particular Baptist, and, I believe, difficult to please, went to hear him, and was careful to repeat the visit.

"One old minister, for whom Mr. Spurgeon preached, was plagued with a bad wife, and she must needs go to America; but with great patience the husband waited for her return, never fastening the door of the house nor suffering others to do so till she came back to him.

"Mrs. J. A. remembers Mr. Spurgeon preaching at Houghton when quite a lad. She remembers the sermon was a very impressive one, and could it have been heard without seeing the boyish preacher, any one would have taken it to be the discourse of a staid and experienced Christian. She believes this was one thing that led Mr. Potto Brown to look upon the youthful orator with less favour than he might otherwise have done, because he thought that the sermon could not have been his own composition.

"Mrs. B. appears to me to have a more vivid recollection of the impression of what Mrs. J. A. felt at the time above stated. There was much conversation between the youthful preacher and Mr. Potto Brown, and evidently much contention, too; for each would hold firmly to his own opinion.

"Mrs. C. tells me that her husband, who was the schoolmaster at the time, was struck by the precocious talent of the young preacher, and with his general style of preaching."

The above notes were collected for me by the late Edward Cressell, whose friendship I highly valued, and who, as pastor of the Congregational Church, Houghton, Hunts, was one of the best preachers in the neighbourhood. The information is now, I believe, regarded as common property by *quidnuncs* in both the Old and the New World.

In regard to Mr. Spurgeon and the late Potto Brown, the Pastor on one occasion himself referred to that memorable meeting—" How he shocked our Calvinistic propriety! . . . We recollect his telling us that our preaching was *very well for an apprentice boy*, which was no doubt a correct estimate, but after he had spoken in that style one felt quite at home with him, and gave him a Roland for his Oliver without the slightest compunction. It was a battle royal, and both the old gentleman and the 'prentice boy grew sufficiently warm ; but no scars remained on either combatant. Mr. Brown walked with us to Huntingdon in loving conversation, and afterwards sent us Haldane's *Life* as a present."

REMINISCENCES OF WATERBEACH.

I. THE VILLAGE AND ITS SURROUNDINGS.

II. RECOLLECTIONS OF MR. SPURGEON'S PASTORATE.

"When I think upon the all but infinite mischief which may result from a mistake as to our vocation for the Christian pastorate, I feel overwhelmed with fear lest any of us should be slack in examining our credentials; and I had rather that we stood too much in doubt, and examined too frequently, than that we should become cumberers of the ground. There are not lacking many exact methods by which a man may test his call to the ministry if he earnestly desires to do so. It is imperative upon him not to enter the ministry until he has made solemn quest and trial of himself as to this point. His own personal salvation being secure, he must investigate as to the further matter of his call to office; the first is vital to hims If as a Christian, the second equally vital to him as a pastor. As well be a professor without conversion, as a pastor without calling. In both cases there is a name and nothing more."—*Lectures to My Students*, i. 23.

II.

REMINISCENCES OF WATERBEACH.

I.—The Village and its Surroundings.

AS the village in which Mr. Spurgeon commenced his pastoral career, Waterbeach seemed to be worthy of a special visit, so that when the opportunity occurred I undertook the journey. The parish lies about five miles north. of Cambridge, the soil is remarkably rich, and on leaving the station the tourist will not fail to observe the tokens of more than average prosperity everywhere manifest; while the magnificent dome of sky presents that aspect of immensity which is particularly noticeable on great level areas such as the Cambridgeshire flats and the neighbouring fens. At the last census the population had been put down at sixteen hundred and nineteen, and one might despair of finding a more comfortable agricultural settlement. The in habitants eat the fruits of their luxuriant marshes while sitting beneath their own vines and fig trees; for, instead of belonging to one domineering autocrat, the land is divided into small proprietorships. The people are, consequently, as remarkable for their independence in religious matters as they are for their Liberalism in politics. They are an honest, hospitable folk, always ready to entertain a stranger, and while characterised by hereditary prejudices, know only of two hemispheres—Waterbeach and Mark Lane. Their prejudices are going one by one. The open sewer, for example, which formerly crossed and fumigated the village, has been covered over, though the older "Conservatives" battled bravely on behalf of a venerable institution; and a smithy, black and begrimed, still defiling the middle of the "Green," was said to be already doomed. Nonconformity was everywhere in the ascendant, and the vicar, who was a decided Evangelical, appeared to lead the pleasantest existence possible by simply preaching the Gospel instead of fighting the sects. Were his procedure less judicious he would wage unequal war, and would, besides, risk changing present friends into ecclesiastical wasps. Fully to realise the anomaly, remember that we were just ten minutes' ride from the University, and that though Waterbeach Church attracted one of the best congregations in the vicinity, yet the parish, as I understood, con-

A Congenial Sphere. 31

tained only one large farmer, and a few small ones, who were Churchmen; and then commend a vicar who, under such conditions, could command the loving esteem of every parishioner.

Such being the character of Waterbeach, we cannot wonder that in his youth Mr. Spurgeon found the village to be a congenial sphere, that he did his share in confirming the Puritan-like faith and politics of the people, while his own character may have taken a colouring from his associations. In a strain which a certain critic judges to be worthy of "The Complete Letter Writer," he referred to his charge, at the age of nineteen, as a "little Garden of Eden," and only poverty obliged him to sever the tie of union. Had Mr. Spurgeon's ministry commenced in these times, instead of at the date it did, Waterbeach would, undoubtedly, have held its own a year or two longer, in spite of the call to London. The people are immensely proud of their old connection; and still, in a manner, regarding their late pastor as one of themselves, always welcome him back into their midst with fervent enthusiasm. This regard would appear to be pretty general among high and low. At the best tables no guest would be allowed to speak words of detraction unchallenged; and no one, who is nice as regards consequences, would impugn Spurgeon's orthodoxy or good nature among the peasants at any one of the village lounges.

After alighting from the train, I had scarce advanced a hundred yards towards the village when it was my good fortune to encounter Mr. James Toller, of Winfold Farm. Mr. Toller is a pillar of the Nonconformist interest in Waterbeach, he is a liberal contributor to the institutions at the Metropolitan Tabernacle, and Mr. Spurgeon himself has, more than once, been a guest at the worthy yeoman's house. One piece of luck—the word is used by the compilers of the Prayer-Book—was soon followed by another; for the clouds, which had threatened rain, broke and lightened, so that we were even privileged to see Waterbeach in the autumn sunshine.

After paying our respects at the manse of the Baptist pastor, and looking in at the village news-room, we find ourselves on that eminently interesting site—the scene of Mr. Spurgeon's first pastorate. The old thatched chapel has, however, disappeared—we feel a sort of selfish regret that it should be so—it has given place to a handsome and more commodious meeting-house, the corner-stones of which were respectively laid by Mr. Spurgeon and Mr. Toller.

A Waterbeach Deacon.

Still, the site is the same, and that is enough for our present purpose. On this very ground, a generation ago, many honest country folk assembled for worship who already began to wonder whereunto the thing would grow. The then boy-preacher not only edified and surprised the people who crowded the little chapel; there were some hearers there who, though poor and unlettered, were yet sufficiently discerning to know that an uncommon genius was in their midst. "He astonished everybody at that time?" I inquired of an elderly deacon who well remembers every circumstance. "Of course he did!" was the quick, curt reply. "How, then, did he preach?" "Why," continued the old man, looking straight at me, as though I ought to know all about it, "like a man a hundred years old in experience!" That honest deacon afterwards visited London for the first time; he went the countryman's usual round of inspection in the capital, saw the Metropolitan Tabernacle, and sat down as a guest of the pastor in his house at Clapham. On his return he tried to tell the people what he had really seen; but memory grew confused. His unsophisticated mind seemed to retain but one thing, the lustre of which darkened everything else—"Mr. Spurgeon was very glad to see me."

Winfold Farm covers an area of nearly six hundred acres, and the residence is a mile from the village. The proprietor of this fertile inheritance is Mr. Toller's eldest son, a young gentleman who had then just come of age, and who resided with his father. In the opinion of Mr. Toller no man can be a landlord and tenant at the same time, and earn a competence—the shortest road to bankruptcy is over your own land as a gentleman farmer. There is more philosophy in this reasoning than a townsman can gainsay.

The admirer of fine breeds will find enough of entertainment at Winfold Farm; and by a little judicious selection from the bullocks in the straw-yard, and the sheep in the turnip-field, a very taking cattle-show might be put together —especially if the thing were supplemented with a few choice pigs, and with some more than admirable specimens of horse-flesh which would be available. But more akin to our subject is the acre of land which is annually set apart for the orphans of Stockwell, the produce of flour and potatoes being despatched to London every autumn. The best things on the estate are not deemed too good to bestow freely upon Mr. Spurgeon's Institutions; to be but a friend of the pastor is to carry a passport to liberal entertainment. Only a day or two before, a well-known gentleman, then in repute at the Metropolitan Tabernacle, had been down to Winfold for the purpose of enjoying "a little sport." Provided with the most perfect of breech-loaders, he started forth to bang and blaze away his powder at a prodigal rate, though from morn to dusk he did not even ruffle the feathers of a single native bird. Any stray rambler at whom this amateur might have directly aimed would have risked no bodily harm, the general opinion, as Mr. Toller explained, being that the marksman would not have hit the house had he levelled and fired with that intention. But still, ramblers abroad were seriously threatened by the stray shots which, for the time, whizzed hither and thither in wild irregularity. Such is the account Mr. Toller gave of his sporting guest, who, it scarce need be said, was not that ready marksman— but not with firearms—Mr. Spurgeon himself.

A walk before dinner being proposed, Mr. Toller conducted my companion and myself to Denney Abbey Farm, the estate adjoining his own, the dwelling-house and outbuildings being the remains of a pre-Reformation monastery, of which Mr. Richard Toller was found to be the master. Everything here is weird and antiquated to a degree which is sufficiently pleasing on a summer day, when the objects of interest can be seen and enjoyed ; but the effect is less pleasing when the shades of night are falling, and the winter wind, moaning around the tall, stout chimneys, seems to be Old Nature's funeral requiem over monks and nuns whose bones are thickly packed beneath the garden soil. It is as strange as true that owls, bats, and other night-birds find at Denney a congenial retreat wherein to screech and croak away the midnight hour. When the business of the day is hushed, one might easily associate the clanking of a horse's halter chain with the creaking of a Templar's armour, as he would once have ridden from the courtyard to join the First Crusade ; or the pattering of a cat's feet on the garden-walk might remind one of those light-treading maidens whose lives were consecrated to God and St. Clare. But as we are not superstitious, and the sun is shining, let us deal with sober fact.

In the year 1160, Robert Chamberlain, Earl of Richmond, became a monk at Ely, some ten miles distant, and being a man of enterprising piety, he gave an island in the surrounding mere for holy purposes. A cell for a few hardy brethren was accordingly erected ; but when repeated floods obliged them to remove they encamped on higher ground, bestowed by Aubrey Picot, at Denney.

After they had held the site for a few years, the Ely monks were superseded by those daring foes of Moslem infidels, the Knights Templars, to whose wealthy Order the manor of Waterbeach belonged. In the fourteenth century the society of Templars was abolished, when their forsaken cells were occupied by the nuns of St. Clare, twenty-five of whom resided here on an income of £172 a-year. After the dissolution of the religious houses, at the era of the Reformation, Denney passed from one owner to another; and in the reign of Elizabeth the farm was rented, I believe, by Hobson, the carrier of Cambridge, the first master who let out hired horses, and in whose stables the familiar proverb "Hobson's choice" is known to have originated. It is not probable that the property has undergone any great changes during the last century. The dwelling-house is a portion of the original Church, founded in 1160, and rebuilt by the Countess of Pembroke in the reign of Edward III. Some of the outbuildings appear to have been removed, or to have gradually fallen into decay, though for several generations the ancient refectory has served as a convenient barn. When the convent was in its prime a double entrenchment encircled its towers, and instead of traversing the country on foot, or by horse, as in after years, the monks plied their oars across the mere, which then spread its broad smooth surface between Denney and Ely.

We now return to Winfold to dine and to rest away the afternoon. When at last we finally take leave of our friends, we are conscious of having been entertained in a worthy Old English style, and also of having spent an agreeable holiday, on ground which will still be visited by summer tourists for its own sake, and also on account of its happy association with the first pastorate of Charles Haddon Spurgeon.

II.—RECOLLECTIONS OF MR. SPURGEON'S PASTORATE.

Some time after the adventure just related I determined on paying a second visit to the scene of Mr. Spurgeon's first pastorate.

It had been a wet night, and the damp, cold November morning was but the prelude to a soaking, tempestuous day, the wind and the rain having completed an alliance which was destined to hold good through another six-and-thirty hours. "Waterbeach must be a wet place," I remarked to the honest ostler who was driving through the High-street of the village, meanwhile eyeing somewhat despondingly the thick, leaden-coloured clouds which were unstintingly emptying their watery treasures over the flat, far-spreading country. "Yes, sir," replied the man, at once catching my meaning, "it ain't called Waterbeach for nothing." On further enquiry it was readily found that the notion of the district never having been known to suffer to any considerable extent from drought was generally accepted. One authority was heard to venture the opinion that the weather never *would* clear up any more; while another gentleman, who had been a frequent visitor, declares that it always rains when he is there, go when he will. It may be all very well to ask, What's in a name? but cavil as we choose, Waterbeach is exceedingly suggestive, and our ancestors who framed the double word doubtless took into account the local characteristics of the country. Be this as it may, people naturally seem to associate the village with mists above and water below. It is not so very long since that a genius of a student, who was commissioned to "supply" the pulpit for a certain period, arrived on the ground provided with a complete oilskin outfit. Though the knowing might smile, "Waterbeach" was redolent of water; and he showed the wit of a growing theologian by being prepared for contingencies. Without presuming to

speak as an authority, either one way or the
other, I may add to the testimony of others that,
having visited Waterbeach twice within the space
of two years, it rained more or less on each
occasion.

The object I had in view in visiting Waterbeach
a second time was to see a veteran Baptist elder,
named Robert Coe, who was a deacon of the church
more than thirty years ago, when Mr. Spurgeon
was pastor, and who then retained his honourable
office. If Mr. Coe was not the *beau ideal* of a
Nonconformist deacon, one's judgment must be
awry; for he was hardly less than this to an
unprejudiced Londoner interested in the "lions"
and folk-lore of Old Cambridgeshire. The elder
and his wife were found to be thorough country
people, of the old-fashioned type; and while they
were pious, thrifty, and well-to-do, they were so
far animated by the predilections of a former
generation that they were tempted to look askance
on some of our valued modern contrivances.
During the whole of their quiet, peaceful life
they had not travelled any great distance from the
family home; and, truth to say, they had never
become completely satisfied with railway locomotion. Waterbeach was their world; and limited as
the sphere might seem to natures of a more ambitious turn, Waterbeach had, under Providence, very

sufficiently supplied their simple wants. If any are disposed to doubt the happiness of such a lot, their scepticism would vanish after they had spent an hour at the veteran's fireside. Mr. Coe was a successful man because he had done well as regards both worlds; and the restlessness of his eye was not the restlessness of discontent; it was rather the habit of a keen observer who could see through a visitor at a glance. He not only knew all about what had happened at Waterbeach during one or two generations, but he was quite willing to be communicative.

"Oh, what a sight of times he did try to get me to London," he remarked, passing his hand across his forehead and looking straight into the fire. "You mean Mr. Spurgeon?" "Yes," was the reply; "and he said, 'If you will come I will present you with a new flagon, and it shall be engraved.'" It transpired that a common black wine-bottle had been used at the communion table of the chapel opposite; and as such a practice could hardly be said to be either "decent" or "in order," the presentation of something better was suggested. The flagon was earned in due time, and I was privileged to hold the treasure in my hand, and to read the inscription, "Presented to the Baptist Church, Waterbeach, by C. H. Spurgeon, 1876."

The first visit of an elderly man to the metropolis, after he has spent his life in the country, is a momentous event; it is a very agitating piece of experience. The strangeness of everything very naturally engenders a timidity such as he has never felt before. His uneasiness begins when he finds himself seated in the "London Express," and when the train attains its highest speed he feels a disposition to stand and hold on by the windows. The excitement increases before he has "done" a tithe part of the round of wonders he is expected to see; so that if at luncheon or dinner he is caught in the act of using sugar with potatoes, and salt with apple tart, the error is to be attributed to the exceptional nature of the surroundings. When Mr. Coe actually visited London he well survived a succession of shocks, until a life longing was realised as he stood, on a Sabbath morning, a unit in the great congregation at the Metropolitan Tabernacle. "Robert, is that you?" said the Pastor at the close of the service, without attempting to disguise his surprise and delight; "I thought I should never have succeeded, but you are here at last!" The visitor was entertained at Clapham; he returned home delighted with London, and more content than ever with the quiet prosperity of Waterbeach. Mr. Coe will never misinterpret these revelations of his private life. He perhaps remembered that his position in the world was an exceptional one; for, as one of Mr. Spurgeon's first deacons, thousands of people in both hemispheres were interested in his antecedents.

It appears that Mr. Spurgeon first went to Waterbeach in the fall of 1851, and ministered to the church during two years without having any fixed residence in the village. He succeeded Mr. Peters, who preached to the people for twenty-two years, the stipend through that period having been £5 a quarter. This venerable man was still living at Cambridge when I visited the neighbourhood; and on one occasion, at the chapel anniversary, he grew warmly enthusiastic while speaking about old times. On such occasions there appears to be only one drawback to act as a damper on the natives' satisfaction—the old meeting-house is no more. One day, during the hot, dry weather of 1861, some careless person threw a quantity of hot ashes on a heap of litter hard by, and the result was that not only the chapel, but one or two other buildings, including an old workhouse, were totally consumed. "If it had not been burned the place would never have been pulled down," said Mr. Toller, who supplied the information, "for there were people there who venerated the very smoke." Mr. Spurgeon himself laid the first stone of the present sanctuary, a few months after the catastrophe.

Although it was then twenty-seven years ago, my friend, Mr. Coe, still vividly remembered the occasion of Mr. Spurgeon's first visit to Waterbeach on an autumn Sunday in 1851, the young preacher having been commissioned to supply the pulpit by an association at Cambridge, which attended to the wants of neighbouring churches. "He sat on one side of the table-pew, and I on the other side," remarks the deacon, his face beaming with pleasure as he recalls the scene. "I shall never forget it. He looked so white, and I thought to myself *he'll* never be able to preach —what a boy he is! I despised his youth, you know, and thought all this while the congregation was singing. Then, when the hymn was over, he jumped up and began to read and expound the chapter about the scribes and pharisees and lawyers, and as he went on about their garments, their phylacteries, and long prayers—I knew that he *could* preach. All along I was fully persuaded in my own mind that he would not remain long at Waterbeach. I could see that he was something very great, and was evidently intended for a larger sphere. I could not make him out ; and one day I asked him wherever he got all the knowledge from that he put into the sermons.

A Village Revival.

'Oh,' he said, 'I take a book, and I pull the good things out of it by the hair of their heads.'"

Before its revival under Mr. Spurgeon's ministry the congregation at Waterbeach was very small, the chapel on ordinary occasions not being more than half filled; but a new era of prosperity at once commenced. The empty seats were immediately taken, the aisles were invaded, the doors were surrounded by rustic crowds for whom there was no accommodation. One of Mr. Spurgeon's first deacons, a worthy of whom little is now to be learned, was named King, and for a time Mr. King was the Pastor's right-hand man. He has long since gone home to heaven. In those days the village bore an evil name on account of the drunkenness and profligacy which abounded; now the inebriate appeared to be sobered, while transgressors of other sorts were awed into propriety. Because they could see that he was earnest and faithful, and had a kind heart, the most degraded of characters liked the new preacher, in spite of his terrible straightforwardness in denouncing all kinds of evil. Mr. Coe remembered the sermons of those days; and one especially—" How wilt thou do in the swelling of Jordan?"—with its terrific warnings and solemn appeals, could never be effaced from memory. According to our informant it was truly wonderful how, thus early, Mr. Spurgeon thundered judgment against the sinner. After he had mellowed a little he seemed to grow milder; but, taking him for all in all, the like had never been heard in Cambridgeshire before. Though a thorough Calvinist, whose doctrines some thought at times to be rather high, his views at the outset were substantially the same as those preached to-day at the Tabernacle. He was from the first as faithful to ministers as to ordinary people, telling those who preached nothing save Election, without ever warning the sinner, that he should not like to stand in their shoes.

In the meantime, Deacon Coe was passing through one of the most enjoyable experiences of his life; and his pleasure was only lessened by the consciousness that the sunshine could not last. If friends mentioned the matter to him, Deacon Coe would shake his head in his characteristic expressive manner, and remark, " He will not be here long. God has a great work for him to do somewhere. I don't know where, but he will not be here long." Probably this opinion was shared by others in the little community; at all events, the people seem to have made much of their youthful pastor, and to have hotly competed among themselves for the honour of according him a genuine hospitality. So numerous were the invitations to dinner that he never, during his tenure of office, went twice to the same place, the poor as well as the rich being allowed to take their turn. Thus, at a certain village lived a quaint worthy who was not despised on account of his poverty, and an invitation to take refreshment was accepted. At dinner a large pudding was placed on the table, and after the host had taken about a quarter of the same on his own plate he pushed the dish across the table with, " Now, friend, help yourself."

One or two of the Pastor's adventures during these early interesting years may be narrated. Much pleasure has been experienced in recovering them, and they will serve as material for a future biography.

At a certain date in the year 1852 Mr Spurgeon was appointed to preach the anniversary sermons at a village chapel in the vicinity of Waterbeach, where the pastor was an octogenarian, a fine specimen of the old-fashioned school of dry, respectable, and orthodox ministers. The old gentleman adopted this course because he had heard of his young brother's popularity, although he had not seen his face, and he desired to attract a full congregation. When the preacher of the day arrived on the ground his extremely youthful appearance created anything but a favourable impression on the white-headed pastor who had proclaimed the gospel in the neighbourhood during forty years. "How do you do, Mr. ——? I've come to preach your anniversary sermons," said the new comer, expecting the usual welcome. "Ugh!" replied the other, looking up somewhat disconcerted, "I'm none the better for seeing *you*." Thinking that he was in a dilemma, and that the anniversary would be a failure, the old pastor rose, and, pacing the room, gave expression to his impatience. "Tut, tut! a pretty kettle of fish; boys going up and down the country preaching before their mother's milk is well out of their mouths." To the visitor all this naturally sounded like somewhat strong language, and he inwardly resolved that the veteran should hear of the matter in another place. In the meantime the crisis appeared to be all the more serious on account of the numbers of people who were flocking into the village from all directions. As the venerable pastor remarked, they were coming in carts, they were coming in chaises, and they were coming in buggies; there would be an overflowing congregation. From Mr. Spurgeon's standpoint there was nothing that could be done other than for him to do his best, and to look for the blessing of God: but this was so far from being satisfactory to the pastor that he went about the village still expressing his disgust at the idea of boys being sent abroad to preach. The chapel was crowded at the time of service; but instead of yielding pleasure this fact seemed to make the occasion still more unlucky. At first the old pastor retired into the background, where he could not be seen. A hymn was sung, and the prayer was not quite what the judicious would have expected from a mere boy. Mr. Spurgeon read Proverbs xvi., and when he came to "A hoary head is a crown of glory," he showed that, Solomon or no Solomon, it was not always so. There were tongues in some hoary heads which could not be civil to the boy who came to preach. Rudeness gave no glory. Then reading further— *if it be found in the way of righteousness*—he showed that Solomon was right after all, for unless this were the case a man might as well have red hair as white for a crown. When the sermon was over, the aged pastor, who had long since come forth from his hiding-place, walked up the pulpit stairs, opened the door, and as the boy-preacher descended he received a smart, playful slap on the loins, accompanied with the complimentary remark, "You are the sauciest dog that ever barked in a pulpit." Instead of complaining of his "supply," Mr. —— now went, first to one and then another, expressing his wonder and delight, seeing such an extraordinary youth had appeared in their midst.

The above is an example of the mistakes that may be made by those who too readily despise a preacher's youth; and, according to Deacon Coe, Mr. Spurgeon's trials in this respect were exceptionally heavy; but neither in youth nor later on in life did he ever retaliate.

There were "characters" to be found at Waterbeach in those days, and among them was a man who, although he was worth some thousands of pounds, was at last buried in his own garden "to save expense." On a certain Sabbath morning this individual placed seven shillings and sixpence in the Pastor's hand with some such remark as, "Please accept this; you want a hat." On the following Sunday he brought an additional half-crown. "What is this for?" asked Mr. Spurgeon, surprised at receiving a supplemental offering. Then came a singular confession —"Last week the Lord told me to give you ten shillings; but I kept back half-a-crown, and there it is." The tradition in Waterbeach is, that a hat was purchased with this money.

On a certain summer evening Mr. Spurgeon had engaged to preach at Teversham, which lies a short distance from Waterbeach; but before he

An Adventure in a Storm. 51

could reach his destination the sky darkened, and a severe thunder-storm burst over the country. While passing a cottage on the road a woman was observed to be alarmed and in sore distress on account of the tempest; and not liking to pass on and leave a fellow-creature in trouble, Mr. Spurgeon entered the house, read a few verses, then prayed, and so comforted the woman while the storm continued. Having done this piece of service, he proceeded to Teversham to fulfil the engagement; but found that the chapel was closed and dark, for people were not expecting a sermon on account of the tempest. Mr. Spurgeon wore a waterproof coat, and on entering the village he divested himself of this, because the smooth surface seemed to reflect the vivid flashes of lightning in a way that might alarm the timid. He then went round from door to door, and told the people there would be a service, and advised them to assemble in the meeting-house. The summons was obeyed with alacrity, the sermon was preached, and when all was over the young pastor started on his homeward walk to Cambridge, a distance of four miles.

"A Wesleyan Minister," writing about twenty years ago, in speaking of Mr. Spurgeon's early days, remarks: "He removed from Newmarket to Cambridge in the capacity of usher to his old friend and former tutor, Henry Leeding. Here both his earthly comforts and religious privileges were increased. He now began publicly to exhort, and united himself with a society called the Lay Preachers' Association, connected with the church in St. Andrew's Street, formerly under the pastorate of the illustrious Robert Hall. At a little village called Teversham, in a cottage some miles from Cambridge, he preached his first sermon, when only sixteen years of age. His preaching from the beginning was highly acceptable, and his sermons were illustrated by geography and astronomy ... and, to his praise be it recorded, the common people heard him gladly. But he was pre-eminently liked by the members of a small church at a village called Waterbeach, who, perceiving this germ of uncommon talents, invited him to become their pastor. And here, in a rude chapel made out of a barn, with a high pitched roof, he preached every Sabbath in the forenoon and afternoon. When requested to preach also in the evening, he modestly replied, "I cannot always preach three times, for I am not so strong as a man."

It would have been a satisfaction to many who are now interested in taking a retrospect if the sermons of Mr. Spurgeon's earliest days had been preserved. There was a time when he himself

.thought of presenting the public with a selection, for in 1857 he wrote: "I shall soon issue a volume of my earliest productions while pastor at Waterbeach, and would now bespeak for it a favourable reception." We are not aware that this publication ever appeared.

Such are a few of the things associated with Waterbeach which I was enabled to recover through the kindness of friends on the spot and from others. The church was found to be in a flourishing condition, and the stipend of the pastor was probably double what it was in Mr. Spurgeon's time.

To these, however, may be added the following, relating to these times, and told by Mr. Spurgeon himself in *The Spare Half Hour*:—

"Having to preach at one of the village stations of the Cambridge Lay Preachers' Association, I walked slowly in a meditative frame of mind over Midsummer Common to the little wooden bridge which leads to Chesterton, and in the midst of the common I was startled by what seemed a loud voice, but which may have been a singular illusion; whichever it was, the impression was vivid to an intense degree: I seemed very distinctly to hear the words, 'Seekest thou great things for thyself? Seek them not!' This led me to look at my position from another point of view, and to challenge my motives and intentions.. I remembered the poor but loving people to whom I ministered, and the souls which had been given me in my humble charge, and although at that time I anticipated obscurity and poverty as the result of the resolve, yet I did there and then solemnly renounce the offer of collegiate instruction, determining to abide for a season at least with my people, and to remain preaching the Word so long as I had strength to do it. Had it not been for those words, in all probability I had never been where and what I now am. I was conscientious in my obedience to the monition, and I have never seen cause to regret it.

"Waiting upon the Lord for direction will never fail to afford us timely intimations of His will; for though the ephod is no more worn by a ministering priest, the Lord still guides His people by His wisdom, and orders all their paths in love; and in times of perplexity, He makes them to hear a voice behind them, saying, 'This is the way, walk ye in it.'"

THE FIRST SUNDAYS IN LONDON.

"*Before any great achievement,* ome measure of . . . depression is very usual. Surveying the difficulties before us, our hearts sink within us. The sons of Anak stalk before us, and we are as grasshoppers in our own sight in their presence. The cities of Canaan are walled up to heaven, and who are we that we should hope to capture them? We are ready to cast down our weapons and take to our heels. Nineveh is a great city, and we would flee unto Tarshish sooner than encounter its noisy crowds. Already we look for a ship which may bear us quietly away from the terrible scene, and only a dread of tempest restrains our recreant footsteps. Such was my experience when I first became a pastor in London. My success appalled me; and the thought of the career which it seemed to open up, so far from elating me, cast me into the lowest depth, out of which I uttered my *miserere* and found no room for a *gloria in excelsis.* Who was I that I should continue to lead so great a multitude? I would betake me to my village obscurity, or emigrate to America, and find a solitary rest in the back woods where I might be sufficient for the things which would be demanded of me. . . . I felt myself a mere child, and trembled as I heard the voice which said, 'Arise, and thresh the mountains, and make them as chaff.'"—*Lectures to my Students,* i. 173.

III.

THE FIRST SUNDAYS IN LONDON.

WHAT people call accident is frequently the course of events as pre-ordained by God; and the truth of this remark was strikingly proved in the manner of Mr. Spurgeon's general rearing. The more carefully we look into the surrounding circumstances of his early life, the more clearly shall we see that all things were working together for good to equip the child and the youth for his arduous life-work that lay beyond. His parents, and the generation preceding them, were not only Christians of an old-fashioned type, they were professors who made no secret of their Puritanic sympathies. Even the prophet Samuel could hardly have enjoyed more tender nurture and careful training to fit him for future service in the Lord's house. The father was a preacher, so also was the grandfather; and one of Mr. Spurgeon's earliest recollections belongs to his sitting on a hassock in the study of the latter, looking at the missionary pictures in *The Evan-*

gelical Magazine, not ever presuming to make a noise, lest grandfather should be interrupted in making his sermon, and thus be unable to preach, when no good would be done, and Charles would be the offender. On account of the uncompromising old-fashioned notions entertained by the family in religious matters, the opinion that the Pastor commenced work as a lame scholar may have gained currency. The truth is, that at a very early age his scholarship was not only far above the average, but very conspicuous to all who had eyes to discern. This happens to be a subject on which we can speak with authority; for some time ago Mr. Spurgeon made some passing remarks relating to his former tutor, which were quite new and conclusive. During some years past the gentleman in question had resided in a southern suburb, unknown to his former scholar; and, like some others of his profession, found the new Board-schools serious drawbacks to his day-school. He is, however, a thoroughly able teacher, who would be invaluable to anyone who should seek out and obtain the benefit of his instructions. This gentleman, who may be regarded as a thoroughly competent judge, held very clear and decided views in regard to the attainments of his quondam pupil. He was in a position to set those right who went about retailing the news that Spurgeon was no scholar; for in point of fact, the said Spurgeon, as a mere youth, was one of the most competent scholars in the neighbourhood of Cambridge, and one who could easily have taken a degree at the University without undergoing the process of cramming. While he spoke like a man who was reasonably proud of his former charge, the venerable tutor was not of the genus which can tolerate cross-examination or interviewings.

Perhaps it never occurred to those who spread the report about Mr. Spurgeon being no scholar, that at the time of his first coming to London he was very competently earning a livelihood by his scholarship. In addition to the Waterbeach church he received a salary as usher in a school at Cambridge, and afterwards salary as tutor to a couple of youths in the same neighbourhood. Very few indeed of our Nonconformist students at seventeen could show the same amount of knowledge; and his habits of reading, in pulling the best things out of books " by the hair of their heads," enabled him to rapidly increase his stores.

It should also be generally known that Mr. Spurgeon was popular even as a boy; for when in his turn he would address the Sunday-school at Newmarket, many members of the church would secrete themselves in any convenient hole or corner within earshot, and there eagerly listen to his earliest efforts. On the other hand, there were those among the Nonconformists of the town who, through being unable to see excellence in any form, supposed that the young preacher was not only not a genius, but decidedly below the average in every respect. When he first came to New Park Street Chapel there arose a great chatter among the Baptists of a certain important town. Said one leading elder to a brother officer of a similar calibre to himself, " They have invited Charley Spurgeon to London, and they are actually going to pay him £150 a-year!" A more curious misjudgment never came out of Essex; and to add to its impressiveness, the words were drawn out to unnatural length, as though the speaker's vocabulary were as elastic as his notions were modest.

A good deal has been said at different times about Mr. Spurgeon's conversion; and some ingenious endeavours have been made to trace the preacher of the sermon which was the means of bringing peace to his soul. All that is really known, however, about the preacher is, that he was a Primitive Methodist in Colchester, and a working man. The things spoken about were the end of all things; the most unlikely people to be saved ; the most despairing ; the most sinful ; and then it was shown that salvation is not by works, but by faith—the soul must look at Christ, and do so in a way corresponding to the perception of natural objects by the natural eye. After hearing this sermon he experienced the peace of God which passes all understanding, and went forth in strength to begin his life-work.

How Mr. Spurgeon first came to London is a question that has not always been correctly answered, and the causes which worked together to bring about the Pastor's removal to an enlarged sphere of labour are known only to a few persons. Let me narrate the circumstances as concisely as possible.

There can be no doubt that Waterbeach was a very comfortable sphere of labour for a young man like Mr. Spurgeon. Though the people were homely they had warm hearts, and they cordially appreciated their pastor's energy and eloquence. It is not impossible that some among the good farmers and simple peasants who crowded the chapel may have reckoned on a life-long union. At any rate, it is unreasonable to suppose that everybody detected in their accomplished pastor the surprising talents that he really possessed. Others were more far-sighted ; they were happy ; their church flourished ; but, alas! it was contrary to the ordinary run of things for the great outside world—a selfish world, as it must have appeared to the Baptists of Waterbeach—to allow so unequal a union to exist for lack of a suitable opening being found elsewhere.

The fact was, that an ancient church, and formerly a congregation of some importance in the capital, was in great straits for want of a pastor. Two centuries before, that church had been formed by a band of Puritan Baptists, the first pastor of whom we have any account being William Rider. The divines who afterwards successively held the pastorate, during a great number of years, were all men of power and celebrity: Benjamin Keach is still kept in remembrance by his *Metaphors;* Benjamin Stinton was equally worthy; John Gill was a celebrated commentator; John Rippon was the compiler of the hymn-book named after him; Joseph Angus is a successful tutor and author of our own times; James Smith was an uneducated genius of fervent piety. In the chequered history of this old church it has been a favourable omen for the pastor to be chosen at the age of nineteen. It was so with John Gill, and also with his successor, John Rippon, who were the only pastors during the unusually long period of one hundred and seventeen years. Mr. Spurgeon was of this same auspicious age of nineteen when some one carried word to the despairing deacons at New Park Street Chapel that there was a young man making some stir at Waterbeach, and it was just possible he might resuscitate their cause.

The church at this date was slowly dying a natural death, and it was worth while to grasp at a straw if, thereby, the threatened death could be averted. It so happened that Mr. Olney, one of the deacons at New Park Street thirty-three years ago, was acquainted with a gentleman of the name of Gould, and on a certain occasion Mr. Gould's nephew happened to look in at a Baptist Chapel in Cambridge, at which a meeting was being held. On the platform were a couple of elderly ministers and a full-faced youth of more tender years. In due course the younger man made a speech, and, because he spoke as a Calvinist, what he said had the effect of highly displeasing those who considered that they were his elders and his betters. They had not even the good sense to keep their anger to themselves, but each had his say. One thought that Mr. Spurgeon should tarry at Jericho till his beard was grown; the other wished to know why the young Baptist had left his few sheep in the wilderness; he had surely come up to see the battle. A reply was made, and one which was very characteristic of the speaker at that time, but unfortunately this has not been recovered.

In course of time the news spread that a young Baptist minister had been snubbed down in Cambridgeshire; and, as the declining church at New Park Street was then in want of a pastor, here was an opportunity to secure a promising man. "I wish you would send for him, I believe he would suit you," remarked the informant, and the deacon at once felt disposed to make the experiment recommended. Mr. Olney wrote at once to Mr. Spurgeon, who, however, manifested no particular anxiety to visit the great metropolis. When he first received the letter he thought a mistake had been made, and thus sent on the epistle to another pastor of the same name; but it was at once returned with the intimation—"It is not a mistake: you are the man intended." Still he was in no hurry to settle in London. Only a short time before, while walking near Chesterton, he had been startled by what seemed like a voice speaking, "Seekest thou great things for thyself? seek them not;" and this remarkable circumstance, which fixed the young preacher's determination not to enter Stepney College, may have checked the rising of any ambitious aspirations connected with a London settlement. At all events he did not consent to preach at New

Park Street Chapel until an application for him to do so had been repeatedly made; and when at length he came forth from the seclusion of Cambridgeshire, he came in no very sanguine mood. Nor was this a matter for surprise. The Church at New Park Street was not so flourishing as it had been; and in the estimation of outsiders, who were disposed to take a desponding view of the situation, nothing very far short of a miracle could save the cause from ultimate decay. There were deacons of piety and substance, and a congregation of a hundred or more; but, notwithstanding, what man of common prudence, or of common sense—especially at nineteen years of age—would be likely to hazard leading the forlorn hope of filling twelve hundred empty seats, or of imparting life to a cause which was richer in illustrious memories than in present resources? But Mr. Spurgeon was invited, and, to the great delight of the church, he accepted the invitation. When he entered the vestry he asked which was Dr. Gill's chair, and on seating himself in that interesting relic he exclaimed, "He must needs go through Samaria." This showed the Calvinistic tendencies of his mind, and also the desponding view he took of a London settlement. "I knew that I should be of no use to you," he added, "but you would have me come."

On the Sabbath morning of Mr. Spurgeon's first preaching at New Park Street, only the average congregation was present, and many, when for the first time they cast their eyes on his youthful features, were not cheered. " What a boy!" was the thought uppermost in the minds of not a few judicious souls. His first text was James i. 17: " Every good gift and every perfect gift is from above," etc. Was it to be expected that a boy could turn that valley of dry bones into a garden of the Lord?

In the evening the congregation had very perceptibly increased, but even then it was only by degrees that the staid members gained confidence. When he turned to Revelation vii. and began to read, and then to expound, thoughts of misgiving arose in the hearts of some. What an absurd thing, mused one experienced Christian who was present, for such a boy to turn to such a passage as that of the hundred and forty and four thousand, who were sealed unto everlasting life. He became reassured, however, as the preacher proceeded with his comments. Then came the text and the sermon: " They are without fault before the throne of God." It would be impossible to describe the emotions of the congregation as the discourse proceeded, and the preacher warmed with his subject. One who was present assures us that the effect was amazing. Nearly all the members of the old church were at last raised from their condition of despondency; although it is possible that some were present who could not all at once become reconciled to the preacher's bold departure from pulpit conventionalities. From the first the commenting struck people as being even more extraordinary than the sermons.

After the service was ended, the congregation were too excited to leave the chapel and go home. In all parts of the building they were seen in groups conversing about what they had heard, and of Mr. Spurgeon's eligibility for the pastorate. The deacons had to come forth from the vestry and promise that they would use their endeavours to secure the young preacher. I have also been informed that a church meeting was arranged for to be held as soon as possible when an invitation to Mr. Spurgeon to accept the pastorate was adopted. The invitation was unanimous with the exception of one dissentient an elderly deacon, who quietly left immediately after the pastor's settlement.

One other reminiscence of that memorable day must be recorded. Mr. Thomas Olney, the senior deacon, and his wife Unity—whose name is kept in remembrance by one of the Orphanage houses at Stockwell—at that time resided at Croydon; and, partly because she was an invalid, it was not Mrs. Olney's practice to attend New Park Street Chapel when no one save a "nobody" was to preach. On the occasion of Mr. Spurgeon's first coming Mrs. Olney did not undertake the journey from Croydon to Southwark, on account of what she judged to be very valid reasons. Who was the preacher for the day? Oh, nobody but a young man from Waterbeach, in Cambridgeshire—a little village, and the last place under the sun likely to have an attractive preacher for its pastor. When Mr. Olney returned home in the middle of the day his face beamed with pleasure, and the sparkle of his eye told that his heart was filled with gladness. At last when he spoke he said to his wife, "We have such a wonderful young man come to preach to-day; you must come to chapel to-night." The old lady went to New Park Street as desired, and the good impression produced on her mind was as deep as it was lasting. "He will do," she said, on her return to Croydon, and, with her own peculiar emphasis, "*He* will do." Was not Mrs. Olney right?

In addition to the above we must not overlook the reminiscences which Mr. Spurgeon has himself given in *The Sword and the Trowel* for

January 1879. The article is entitled "Twenty-five Years Ago," and the following are its opening paragraphs, which directly refer to the first visit to London in the last days of 1853:—

"*Twenty-five years ago* we walked on a Sabbath morning, according to our wont, from Cambridge to the village of Waterbeach, in order to occupy the pulpit of the little Baptist Chapel. It was a country road, and there were four or five honest miles of it, which we usually measured each Sunday foot by foot, unless we happened to be met by a certain little pony and cart which came half way, but could not by any possibility venture further, because of the enormous expense which would have been incurred by driving through the toll-gate at Milton. That winter's morning we were all aglow with our walk, and ready for our pulpit exercises. Sitting down in the table-pew, a letter was passed to us bearing the postmark of London. It was an unusual missive, and was opened with curiosity. It contained an invitation to preach at New Park Street Chapel, Southwark, the pulpit of which had formerly been occupied by Dr. Rippon,—the very Dr. Rippon whose hymn-book was then before us upon the table—the great Dr. Rippon, out of whose Selection we were about to choose hymns for our worship. The late Dr. Rippon seemed to hover

over us as an immeasurably great man, the glory of whose name covered New Park Street Chapel and its pulpit with awe unspeakable. We quietly passed the letter across the table to the deacon who gave out the hymns, observing that there was some mistake, and that the letter must have been intended for a Mr. Spurgeon who preached somewhere down in Norfolk. He shook his head, and observed that he was afraid there was no mistake, as he always knew that his minister would be run away with by some large church or other, but that he was a little surprised that the Londoners should have heard of him quite so soon. 'Had it been Cottenham, or St. Ives, or Huntingdon,' said he, 'I should not have wondered at all; but going to London is rather a great step from this little place.' He shook his head very gravely; but the time was come for us to look out the hymns, and therefore the letter was put away, and, as far as we can remember, was for the day quite forgotten, even as a dead man out of mind.

"On the following Monday an answer was sent to London, informing the deacon of the church at Park Street that he had fallen into an error in directing his letter to Waterbeach, for the Baptist minister of that village was very little more than nineteen years of age, and quite unqualified to occupy a London pulpit. In due time came another epistle, setting forth that the former letter had been written in perfect knowledge of the young preacher's age, and had been intended for him, and him alone. The request of the former letter was repeated and pressed, a date mentioned for the journey to London, and the place appointed at which the preacher would find lodging. That invitation was accepted, and as the result thereof the boy preacher of the Fens took his post in London.

"*Twenty-five years ago*—and yet it seems but yesterday—we lodged for the night at a boarding-house in Queen Square, Bloomsbury, to which the worthy deacon directed us. As we wore a huge black satin stock, and used a blue handkerchief with white spots, the young gentlemen of that boarding-house marvelled greatly at the youth from the country who had come up to preach in London, but who was evidently in the condition known as verdant green. They were mainly of the evangelical church persuasion, and seemed greatly tickled that the country lad should be a preacher. They did not propose to go and hear the youth, but they seemed to tacitly agree to *encourage* him after their own fashion, and we were encouraged accordingly. What tales were narrated of the great divines of the metropolis, and their congregations! One we remember had a thousand *city* men to hear him, another had his church filled with *thoughtful* people, such as could hardly be matched all over England, while a third had an immense audience, almost entirely composed of the *young men* of London, who were spell-bound by his eloquence. The study which these men underwent in composing their sermons, their herculean toils in keeping up their congregations, and the matchless oratory which they exhibited on all occasions, were duly rehearsed in our hearing, and when we were shown to bed in a cupboard over the front door, we were not in an advantageous condition for pleasant dreams. Park Street hospitality never sent the young minister to that far-away hired room again, but assuredly the Saturday evening in a London boarding-house was about the most depressing agency which could have been brought to bear upon our spirit. On the narrow bed we tossed in solitary misery, and found no pity. Pitiless was the grind of the cabs in the street, pitiless the recollection of the young city clerks whose grim propriety had gazed upon our rusticity with such amusement, pitiless the spare room which scarce afforded space to kneel, pitiless even the gas lamps which seemed to wink at us as they flickered amid the December darkness. We had no friend in all that city full of human beings, but we felt among strangers and foreigners, hoped to be helped through the scrape into which we had been brought, and to escape safely to the serene abodes of Cambridge and Waterbeach, which then seemed to be Eden itself.

"*Twenty-five years ago* it was a clear, cold morning, and we wended our way along Holborn Hill towards Blackfriars and certain tortuous lanes and alleys at the foot of Southwark Bridge. Wondering, praying, fearing, hoping, believing,— we felt all alone and yet not alone. Expectant of Divine help, and inwardly borne down by our sense of the need of it, we traversed a dreary wilderness of brick to find the spot where our message must needs be delivered. One word rose to our lip many times, we scarce know why —' He must needs go through Samaria.' The necessity of our Lord's journeying in a certain direction is no doubt repeated in His servants, and as our present journey was not of our seeking, and had been by no means pleasing so far as it had gone—the one thought of a "needs be" for it seemed to overtop every other. At sight of Park Street Chapel we felt for a moment amazed at our own temerity, for it seemed to our eyes to be a large, ornate, and imposing structure, suggesting an audience wealthy and critical, and far removed from the humble folk to whom our ministry had been sweetness and light. It was early, so there were no persons entering, and when the set time was fully come there were no signs to support the suggestion raised by the exterior of the building, and we felt that by God's help we were not yet out of our depth, and were not likely to be with so small an audience. The Lord helped us very graciously, we had a happy Sabbath in the pulpit, and spent the intervals with warm-hearted friends; and when at night we trudged back to the Queen Square narrow lodging we were not alone, and we no longer looked on Londoners as flinty-hearted barbarians. Our tone was altered, we wanted no pity of anyone, we did not care a penny for the young gentlemen lodgers and their miraculous ministers, nor for the grind of the cabs, nor for anything else under the sun. The lion had been looked at all round, and his majesty did not appear to be a tenth as majestic as when we had only heard his roar miles away."

So far as I have been sufficiently fortunate to recover them, the incidents related are those which were associated with Mr. Spurgeon's first Sabbath-day's work in London in the fall of the year 1853. The congregations immediately increased until the chapel was densely thronged at every service; and the building was then enlarged to accommodate some eighteen hundred people. The more they knew of their Pastor the more did the church and congregation learn to appreciate his public service and personal worth; but it was otherwise with outsiders of the same denomination, who were either too undiscerning or too jealous to see and acknowledge the truth.

There were many who were still partial to old-fashioned ways, and these had misgivings. Could they only get another Rippon all might yet be well—the tide of prosperity would return; but what could be made of the bold Essex youth of nineteen, whose daring originality was shocking to people who had beheld the propriety reflected in the portraits of Gill and Rippon?

It is an interesting question, What did the preacher appear like at this time? The query is thus answered by an American quarterly for the year 1859: "He was unpractised in either the art of oratory or of preaching, his public efforts having consisted of addresses before Sunday-schools, and a very brief but successful pastorate over an obscure Baptist church at Waterbeach. In personal appearance he was not prepossessing; in style he was plain, practical, simple; in manner, rude, bold, egotistical.

approaching to the bigoted ; in theology, a deep-dyed Calvinist ; in church relations, an uncompromising Baptist. We could scarcely imagine a more unpromising list of qualifications, or rather disqualifications, for public favour."

Such was the man, as viewed by a discriminating judge at a distance ; what were his associations at home and his prospects in the metropolis ? The chapel in New Park Street seated twelve hundred persons, and for some time past a sixth part of that number made an average congregation. The revival was, of course, immediate. The good souls who were present at the first scantily-attended service, and who, according to their nervous temperament, professed to be shocked or edified, carried the news of the altered aspect of affairs to others, and thus helped to bring together ever-increasing crowds. Ever after this day of small things the aforesaid good souls were sorely inconvenienced by having less elbow-room, and a more limited supply of pure air, than they had been accustomed to enjoy in olden time. The chapel became suddenly crowded as no other London chapel had ever been known to be—that is to say, the throng, which weekly filled aisles and pews, manifested a determined sort of eagerness to see and hear the preacher. This was the aspect of affairs in

London when the deacons said, "Come amongst us for six months."

Waterbeach was, at least, a sufficient contrast to all this excitement and popularity for Mr. Spurgeon to call it, on his return, "this little Garden of Eden." He loved his people; he experienced uncomfortable sensations in being called upon to leave them; and, had not poverty denied him freedom of action, he would "have turned a deaf ear to any request to leave them." As, however, the little church was unable to afford him adequate support, he was impelled forward by necessity. The engagement at Waterbeach could be terminated at any time by either party after the expiration of a three-months' notice; but pastor and people were bound together in closer union than could ever have been effected by legal forms. At the outset, he showed no symptoms of being carried away by that amazing popularity which immediately confronted him. In a letter to Mr. Lowe, he commended the people on account of their prudence in allotting an ample term of probation, while at the same time he declined to bind himself for longer than three months. If all progressed well, the engagement could easily be prolonged; if otherwise, he "would only be a 'supply'—liable to a fortnight's dismissal or resignation." The deacons at London said, "Come at once;" those at Waterbeach were quite averse to so sudden a termination of their connection, and in this respect carried their point. The regular pastorate of Mr. Spurgeon in London may be said to have begun on the 27th of April, 1854. He immediately achieved an unexampled popularity for one so young; but neither pastor nor people could have had even a faint idea as to what lay before them in the future.

As this is not a complete history, it will not be necessary to give a connected account of subsequent events. These are told by Mr. Spurgeon himself in his book on the Tabernacle, and anything which is included in that volume is not likely to be news to readers of these pages. How the old chapel at New Park Street became crowded so as to warrant an adjournment to Exeter Hall, and subsequently to the Music Hall at the Royal Surrey Gardens, where an appalling accident saddened the church and prostrated the preacher, are things too well known to need recapitulation.

In "The Treasury of David," under Psalm xci., there is a less-known reminiscence of the eventful first year in London, which is too characteristic to be omitted. The country, it will be remembered, was stricken with the fever engendered by the Russian war, when the sickness referred to was raging :—

"In the year 1854, when I had scarcely been in London twelve months, the neighbourhood in which I laboured was visited by Asiatic cholera, and my congregation suffered from its inroads. Family after family summoned me to the bedsides of the smitten, and almost every day I was called to visit the grave. I gave myself up with youthful ardour to the visitation of the sick, and was sent for from all corners of the district by persons of all ranks and religions. I became weary in body and sick at heart. My friends seemed falling one by one, and I felt or fancied that I was sickening like those around me. A little more work and weeping would have laid me low among the rest. I felt that my burden was heavier than I could bear, and I was ready to sink under it. As God would have it, I was returning mournfully home from a funeral, when my curiosity led me to read a paper which was wafered up in a shoemaker's window in the Dover Road. It did not look like a trade announcement, nor was it; for it bore in a good bold handwriting these words :—'*Because thou hast made the Lord, which is my refuge, even the Most High, thy habitation, there shall no evil befall thee, neither shall any plague come nigh thy dwelling.*' The effect upon my heart was immediate. Faith appropriated the passage as her own. I felt secure, refreshed, girt with immortality. I went on with my visitation of the dying in a calm and peaceful spirit; I felt no fear of evil, and I suffered no harm. The Providence which moved the tradesman to place those verses in his window I gratefully acknowledge, and in the remembrance of its marvellous power I adore the Lord my God."

That a special Providence watched over the youthful pastor during the trials of that first terrible summer in London, no one will doubt after reading of the above adventure. Only a man with a large admixture of heroism in his nature could have faced the ordeal to come off in the end a conqueror.

When Mr. Spurgeon first settled in London in the spring of 1854, the news of his success soon reached the ears of quiet-living folks in every rural nook in England. Well do I remember how his fame found its way into the secluded Somersetshire village where I was then residing, when of course the village politicians each formed an independent opinion. What a talk there was about his work, and about the daring originality of his manner of doing it! The sermons were read with avidity; for neither the young, who were ready to welcome something new, nor the more elderly, who still venerated William Jay and John Angell James as models of pulpit propriety, had ever seen words put together in such a way before. When Macaulay first appeared in *The Edinburgh Review* the question was, "Where did he get that style?" and a similar query might have been started when the new preacher suddenly burst upon the world in 1854. In a certain instance a pastor went to one of his brethren who served a church four miles away, and, having mentioned the fact that he had read one of Mr. Spurgeon's latest sermons, he added, "but he can never keep on like this." The reference was to the prodigality of thought and to the number of illustrations diffused throughout the discourses; and as the publication proceeded the old worthy thought he had discovered a falling off, as he had predicted there would be.

Persons of strong sense and penetrative judgment were enabled at once to see Mr. Spurgeon's worth, but weaker men required a longer time for their opinions to become settled. What was most surprising was the singular behaviour of one or two leading Baptist ministers in London, whose open hostility to the man who was manifestly raised up for a great work had the effect of making both themselves and their clique ridiculous. As it was with individuals, so was it with the newspapers. The weaklings hesitated—they were neither supporters nor detractors of Mr. Spurgeon ; but stronger natures, such as the *The Morning Advertiser*, assumed a bold front, and gained considerable credit in the long run for the sagacity which enabled them to arrive at a common-sense decision.

Though he differed on many doctrinal points from Mr. Spurgeon, the late Dr. Binney was able from the first to perceive the great talents of the young preacher. On a particular occasion, as I have learned, when he was visiting one of the Independent colleges for the purpose of giving a lecture to the students, the Weighhouse pastor happened to hear some disparaging remarks concerning Mr. Spurgeon from certain of the students. The lecturer asked them to be quiet, to listen to what he himself had to say on the matter, and addressed them in such words as these : " I myself have enjoyed some amount of popularity; I have always been able to draw together a congregation ; but in the person of Mr. Spurgeon we see a young man, be he who he may, and come whence he will, who at twenty-four hours' notice can command a congregation of twenty thousand people. Now, I have never been able to do that, and I never knew of anyone else who could do it." Mr. Spurgeon could do greater things than Dr. Binney, or all the efforts of the students combined could do, and on that account there was wisdom in remaining quiet, and withholding railing words.

One of the earliest sermons preached by Mr. Spurgeon in London was from the text, "Fear not, thou worm Jacob." It was a discourse of great power, and was one which seemed at once to establish the preacher's fame. It was, moreover, one of the series which were to have been probationary sermons; but, in reality, it can hardly be said that Mr. Spurgeon ever preached any probationary sermons at all. His very first Sabbath day's work in the metropolis settled the matter of his unanimous call to the pastorate.

I have heard it said by one of its oldest members that the church at New Park Street was as much prepared for the reception of Mr. Spurgeon by providence as Mr. Spurgeon was prepared for the position. The church was in a low condition, however; and although there were two hundred members, no one knew where to find them. There was a good chapel, and there was a staff of well-to-do deacons to second the efforts of the pastor; but had Mr. Spurgeon been an optimist the outlook would have been discouraging to the last degree.

When he suddenly became popular in London

applications for Mr. Spurgeon's services began to pour in from the provinces. His days were, accordingly, days of travel and adventure, and his own words, spoken in 1855, give a more vivid picture of his experience at this time than any other description. Referring to a northern tour he said: "Many persons know that on my road home I was exposed to very imminent danger. I crossed the river Clyde in a ferry: the man who had the management of the boat had taken 'a wee drap o' the cratur,' and was not able to manage it at all, and had put twenty-six persons into a boat that ought to have contained far less. I have been informed by one or two ladies that report was current that I was thrown into the water, and fished up by the hair of my head. Now, that was not so. We were simply in danger, but by a little management and expostulation, which was resented by oaths and curses, we came safe to land. Thanks to that God who both on sea and land cares for His people! I had engaged to preach in Bradford, in Yorkshire. I first made a journey to Lake Windermere, round which I sailed, and greatly enjoyed the beauties of its scenery. I went to Bradford, and on Sabbath morning I found they had engaged the music-hall, which holds, they say, a thousand persons more than Exeter Hall. Instead of being able to contain the crowds who came on Sunday, about as many had to go away as were accommodated. In the evening the streets presented a solid blockade of men and women. The place was crammed to excess, and I had scarcely room to walk about to deliver what I had to say to the people. . . . I went to Stockton-on-Tees, and there again preached the word of God to a very numerous congregation. I journeyed on still further, to Edinburgh, and in Queen Street Hall, notwithstanding the most pouring rains, more crowds were assembled." Thus in one town after another great crowds were attracted, and on one occasion, in Glasgow, it was said that twenty thousand persons went away unable to obtain admission.

It was not long before the crowds in front of New Park Street Chapel filled the street. Then Exeter Hall and Surrey Gardens' Hall were successively taken, but more because they afforded a larger sphere of usefulness than from any other reason. The profits from the services of the last-named place aided in some considerable degree the Tabernacle building fund. It is not generally known that the Tabernacle very narrowly escaped being erected on leasehold land ; and that what would have been a real disaster was prevented by certain of the deacons refusing to sign the building contract on such conditions. The site was in possession of the Fishmongers' Company; and Mr. Joynson, of St. Mary Cray, became a main instrument under providence in obtaining the freehold. Thus, as we hope, THE METROPOLITAN TABERNACLE can remain until the end of time as a monument of the sanctified genius and earnest life-work of C. H. SPURGEON.

PERSONAL REMINISCENCES.

"Our life has been mainly spent in *direct* religious teaching, and to that work we would dedicate our main strength; but men need also to hear common every-day things spoken of in a religious manner, for to some of them this roundabout road is the only way to their hearts. Theology is dull reading to the unconverted; but mixed with a story, or set forth by a witty saying, they will drink in a great amount of religious truth and find no fault. They like their pills gilded, or at least sugar-coated, and if by that means they may be really benefited, who will grudge them the gilt or the sugar?"—*Preface to The Spare Half-Hour.*

IV.

PERSONAL REMINISCENCES.

WHAT others say about a man must be estimated according to the personal worth and sympathies of the speakers; but what a man says about himself is sure, one way or the other, to be a revelation of character. While no one will defend egotism, it is possible for conceit or spurious humility to conceal itself in a reticence, foolish because studied and unnatural. He must be a shrewd judge both of himself and others who can constantly make capital of himself, while it is still evident that self is not mentioned for the sake of glorification. It must be evident to every observer that from the first Mr. Spurgeon has been to himself an exhaustless book of illustration, many of the most telling things in his sermons and lectures being personal reminiscences. Anecdotes of childhood and of later age are continually appearing, without any sign of the stock becoming exhausted.

People are naturally interested in the childhood

of remarkable men; and shrewd observers, like John Foster, are glad to recover, so far as recovery is possible, those early mind impressions which came and went like fleeting clouds in the fresh spring-time of life's opening days. Our first impressions of the world are for the most part lost; but on this account we value more highly than we should the fragments which remain. If he had not himself narrated the fact, who could have supposed that Mr. Spurgeon was ever fascinated with the exciting sport of the hunting-field? Yet so it was; the dogs, the horses, the horn-blowing, the riders in red coats, constituted a picturesque paraphernalia which had irresistible charms. Had we, as inquisitive well-wishers, enquired in those days what occupation Master Charles Haddon Spurgeon would prefer as a life profession, the reply would have come with smart readiness, "A huntsman! a huntsman!" Well may the man exclaim as he looks back on such childish preferences, "A fine profession truly!" but then there is the unvarnished fact,' as a child he "always felt a natural taste for that sort of business." Whenever the hounds were descried, they were invariably followed at highest speed over fields, hedges, and ditches, regardless of hazard. The indulgence of this propensity once cost dear; for, executing a market commission, the contents of the basket—rice, mustard, etc.—were shaken together into "one awful mess." As anecdotes, such things are interesting contributions; but as anecdotes merely they would never be told by Mr. Spurgeon. Everything must point a moral or serve as an illustration to clinch a religious truth. The childish predilection for field sports warns young men not to be too readily drawn into the Christian ministry by outward things, and thus resemble children who are captivated by the holiday trappings of sportsmen. The adventure likewise shows the value of a clear arrangement of ideas. Due care should be exercised so that good things are not heaped together "all in a muddle." It is obvious that "people will not drink your mustardy tea, nor will they enjoy muddled-up sermons, in which you cannot tell head from tail, because they have neither, but are like Mr. Bright's Skye terrier, whose head and tail were both alike."

Happy is the child to whom the season of school discipline comes with pleasures which are remembered with satisfaction in after life. Mr. Spurgeon met with good masters, and he drank in their teaching until he became himself a tutor with pupils taller than himself; Colchester, Maidstone, and Newmarket all being associated with those early days. In connection with Colchester we once heard him relate this characteristic anecdote. On a certain very cold morning the tutor, without design, so arranged the class that the lower boys sat in proximity to the school stove, the comforting glow of which it was hardly worth while to surrender for the passing honours of priority. After he had asked sundry questions with unsatisfactory results, the schoolmaster suddenly, as he thought, discovered in the genial fire the one cause of Master Spurgeon's unusual dulness. The order was accordingly instantly given to wheel round, the head, instead of the bottom, of the class being now placed nearest the stove. The effect was exactly what the sagacious leader expected; for when warmth as well as honour could be gained by proficiency, a few correct answers presently reinstated Master Spurgeon in his former place near the fire at the head of the column

A child in whose susceptible heart the Old Adam so far predominated that he was carried off his head by the fascination of hunting would not in the natural course of things appear to everybody as a subject likely to succeed in the pulpit. A dame who was "as godly a Christian as ever breathed" thought that no good was ever likely to come of young Mr. Spurgeon's meddling with sacred things, and like a woman of conscience, if

Advised not to Become a Preacher. 93

not of sense, she advised according to her light : she steadfastly dissuaded her young friend from assuming a calling for which it was so manifest that neither nature nor grace had fitted him. We cannot any of us afford to laugh at the judgment of this simple soul : for if it is hard to judge of a literary work in manuscript, how much more difficult is it to say what a preacher in embryo will achieve. If there were those living in the Puritan age who would have burned the manuscript of *The Pilgrim's Progress* to do God service, their descendants, in 1850, would act after the example of their fathers. The Fathers advised John Bunyan not to scandalise the church by printing a silly book ; the children, by shutting his mouth, would have made a tutor or a clerk of Mr. Spurgeon. In one case as in the other, a better judgment prevailed. It is, nevertheless, the Pastor's opinion that the young should show a deference to the counsel of their superiors in age and experience. The first sermon from the text, " Unto you, therefore, which believe He is precious," was preached unexpectedly and without preparation, and the work has ever since continued.

Probably Mr. Spurgeon has preached a greater number of sermons than any other living pastor of the same age ; and hence we are prepared for the admission that all along, he has been careful of his throat. His advice to all public speakers is to discard once and for ever "horehound, ipecacuanha, or any of the ten thousand emollient compounds." His experience has taught him that for the voice there is nothing like astringents. When he removed from New Park Street to Exeter Hall he discovered that his voice was none too strong for a place so difficult to speak in; but he found relief in Chili vinegar mixed with water, which he sipped occasionally during the service. He still finds a panacea in beef-tea "as strong with pepper as can be borne."

A preacher of such varied experience will necessarily have met with various entertaining adventures in connection with the business of choosing a text; and Mr. Spurgeon ingenuously confesses that he is "an odd man." While residing at Cambridge, in the days of his village preaching, he on one occasion vainly endeavoured to collect his thoughts for a sermon, which had to be given in the evening. Do what he would "the right text" could not be found. After remaining some time in a somewhat anxious condition he happened to walk to the window, when on the roof of a house opposite were seen a company of vindictive sparrows worrying a solitary canary, which had been unfortunate enough to escape from its cage. After looking for a few moments, the words of Jeremiah xii. 9 stole into his mind: "Mine heritage is unto me as a speckled bird, the birds round about are against me." "The text was sent to me," says the preacher, "and if the ravens did not bring it, certainly the sparrows did." Why do not the birds, or other agents in nature, more often than they do bring our teachers their texts? Because all have not the eye to utilize what they see. After he had seen the sparrows and their victim, Mr. Spurgeon "walked off with the greatest possible composure; . . . and preached upon the peculiar people and the persecutions of their enemies."

While Mr. Spurgeon held the pastorate of Waterbeach the inconvenient, old-fashioned custom of holding three services on the Sabbath was still in vogue. This usage, now in a great measure obsolete, was one which a young pastor would not find reason to admire; for, leaving out of the question the extra labour imposed, "roast beef and pudding lie heavy on the hearers' souls, and the preacher himself is deadened while digestion claims the mastery of the hour." On a certain Sabbath, during the happy days of youth, all went well at morning service, and at dinner the preacher ate sparingly, in order that he might wear well through the afternoon. The sermon had been thought out beforehand, without the aid of ink and paper; but in the hour of need, when the people were fast assembling in the meeting-house, the train of ideas suddenly vanished, leaving a dark vacuum, which occasioned some commendable trepidation in the mind. The fact was related to the farmer in whose house the dinner had been served; but not having to preach himself that hospitable worthy made light of the mischief. It is all very well for farmers to say, "Oh! never mind, you will be sure to have a good word for us," and so on; but such commonplaces are only cold comfort, and they do not point a way out of the difficulty. Just while the two were conversing a piece of wood, blazing and smoking, fell from the fire. Here was the missing link. "Here was a text, an illustration, and a leading thought as a nest-egg for more." The hearts of one or two were reached on that afternoon.

The above are interesting examples of their kind; but a more extraordinary instance of a change of text having taken place, and not through any mishap, once occurred in the chapel at New Park Street on a Sunday evening. The preliminary parts of the service passed off in the usual manner; the Bible was opened at the text selected and previously studied, when another passage hard by not only attracted attention, but seemed to spring up "like a lion from the thicket." The preacher tells us that he was " in a strait betwixt two." In imagination he seemed to listen to a dispute between the rivals; and when one pulled importunately at his skirts the other answered, " No, no, you must preach from me." The new comer had its way, and the first and second heads were proceeded with while the third head had not yet suggested itself. Immediately after the second division was closed the gas went out, and as the chapel was crowded with people the danger was considerable. The people were providentially saved from panic by hearing Mr. Spurgeon's voice, and the assurance that he could speak to them as well in the dark as the light. Two persons were reached and converted on that evening. " I cast myself upon God," says the preacher, " and His arrangements quenched the light at the proper time for me."

In his time Mr. Spurgeon has encountered many interesting specimens of the species called eccentric people. An uneducated genius in the pulpit has always something for the observant hearer in the pew. One of these persons referred to was a worthy who could found a sermon on such a text as " The night hawk, the owl, and the cuckoo." The text was, of course, ingeniously selected, but where were the divisions? Divisions? The birds had a head a-piece, and after wringing their necks there they were. The hawk was a sly rogue, the owl was a drunkard who was most lively at night, the cuckoo was one who harped on the notes and sucked the eggs of others. And yet because the matter corresponded with the quaint instrument it "did not seem at all remarkable or odd." This man was a godly rustic who was great at spiritualizing; and though long since laid in the grave his memory lives in "Lectures to my Students."

Pastors should cultivate the art of conversation, they should be masters of the knack of turning to profitable account the thousand and one every-day incidents of ordinary life. This was illustrated by an adventure on Clapham Common some years ago. A common porter was pushing along a large truck, and in the middle of the commodious carriage lay a small parcel, perhaps looking more diminutive than it really was by contrast. "It looks odd to see so large a truck for so small a load," remarked Mr. Spurgeon. "Yes, sir, it is a very odd thing," quickly replied the man; "but do you know I've met with an odder thing than that this blessed day. I've been about working and sweating all this 'ere blessed day, and till now I haven't met with a gentleman that looked as if he'd give me a pint of beer, till I saw you." What was the result of this delicately-worded appeal we are not informed ; but the ready earnestness with which the man sought to turn the occasion to profit carried home a lesson such as the interrogator was not slow to learn. The opinion may be hazarded, however, that in this instance the natural acuteness of the importunate porter was overrated. From what we know of the working classes of London we dare affirm that there are hundreds who would have manifested a corresponding smartness, the wit and the repartee being second-hand, and thus common property. Working men often speak with great ease and drollery ; but then the witticisms thus admirably rendered may have existed for generations.

Interested as we may be in all that we know about Mr. Spurgeon's habits of study, ministers and public speakers would do well to give some extra attention to what he says concerning his own efficiency in extempore speech, how he acquired and how he sustains the coveted art. The too common notion is that when a man does anything remarkably well he does it without taking trouble ; but the experience of real life dispels such an illusion. It is through incessant hard work alone that men succeed, and are able to maintain their prestige when they have worked their way to the front. This is strictly true of

Mr. Spurgeon; for he has worked as hard as any man in England. In one sense, unfortunately, the position occupied by such a man is not without its drawbacks. The ceaseless pressure of work does not allow of the popular minister enjoying life like other people. Holidays are always scarce; he may even be precluded from walking round his garden once in a week. He has a gift, and to maintain his standing the practice which is said to "make perfect" must be sustained.

As regards the manner of working, Mr. Spurgeon thinks it unsafe for those who retain their powers unimpaired to indulge in sticks, crutches, or spectacles. The preacher above every man should be self-reliant, and keep his natural faculties bright with constant service. Mr. Spurgeon's experience proves that those who would excel as extempore preachers must trust to memory and not to notes. Only make your notes a few lines longer this Sunday, and soon you will "require them longer still." He goes further, and assures us that if there is an increased trust in the pre-arrangements of memory, it is naturally followed by "a direct craving, and even an increased necessity for pre-composition." If the art of speaking well be encompassed with so many difficulties, which even a Spurgeon must overcome, the lessons of his experience speak to all.

To a public speaker a liberal supply of fresh air is of vital importance, and this is especially the case with the Pastor of the Tabernacle. Occasionally, in the middle of a service, he will ask for *more air*, and he counsels all pastors not to be afraid of opening their chapel windows, because " the next best thing to the grace of God for a preacher is oxygen." He will not tolerate having comfort in breathing sacrificed to architecture ; and soon after settling at New Park Street the officials found out to their cost the predilections of the Pastor. There was a window in the chapel whose iron bars would not allow of its being opened, and, after repeated suggestions had been vainly made that a glazier should take out the panes, they were one morning found to be broken. The Pastor suggested that a reward of £5 should be offered, and that the money should be given as a testimonial to the offender ; and, although he never informed, he went so far as to confess that he had walked with the stick which let the oxygen into a stifling structure.

A considerable weight of responsibility once devolved on those who kept Mr. Spurgeon's vestry-door, which after every service was surrounded with a goodly array of persons, one and all having wants or whims to be satisfied. From time to time many "characters" appeared in the throng. Women with wild fancies, men with some chronic trouble weighing them down, or others who had visionary projects they would talk about to a sympathetic friend, might there have been encountered. Now and then the fire of insanity was to be detected in the eye of a new comer, and the arm of the sentinel deacon would be raised to hinder the ingress of a doubtful character. Among the more extraordinary specimens were found those who applied for admission to the Pastors' College. The college is Mr. Spurgeon's best-loved institution; and it is generally known that candidates for the ministry may reckon on receiving patient attention. There are, of course, bold pretenders who come forward to turn liberty into licence, and to take advantage of good nature. One such was a young man whose face "looked like the title-page to a whole volume of conceit and deceit." The man had enough assurance for a hundred adventurers, and because his case was so remarkable he wanted to be admitted at once. His private opinion was that his attainments were immense, and that no such application had ever been received before. He testified that he had thoroughly explored the field of ancient and modern literature, while his preaching was exceptionally eloquent. When his application was declined, this upstart retired with dignity, supposing that an " unusual genius " and a "gigantic mind " showed the cause of failure.

Some references should be made to Mr. Spurgeon's editorial troubles, and to the offence which is necessarily given in some quarters through strict adherence to principle. All editors receive manuscripts of the most extraordinary description. A journalist once remarked that all persons suppose themselves to be competent writers, and the general experience of editors teaches that the assertion is not very wide of the truth. The absence of talent and education never damps the ardour of literary aspirants, whose sole ambition is to secure the honours of appearing in print. Who shall estimate the amazing amount of doggerel with which editors and publishers are still pestered ? The plague is a cross to bear, and shows signs of increase rather than of diminution. Although *cacoethes scribendi* may be a prevalent and incurable disease, we believe that general readers have little conception of the extent to which it prevails. There appears to be no class without its writers, or without those who suppose themselves to be capable of handling the quill.

As an editor, Mr. Spurgeon's adventures are sure to be singular, proportionately with the eminence of his position. Because his name is known to everybody, the eccentric will not be wanting in endeavours to take him into their confidence. The poets are always a source of trouble; for not only do the doggerel traffickers claim attention, a batch of rhymes was once received from one who claimed to be divinely inspired by the Holy Spirit! Instead of being inspired, however, all the pieces bore the mark of imposture; and did so because the editor's shelves could "show many poems as much superior to these pretended inspirations as angels are to blue-bottles." What fool is to be compared with your "inspired" fool?

Mr. Spurgeon is very partial to open-air preaching, and in his lectures on that subject gives many interesting incidents from his own experience. His favourite pitch is the front of "a rising ground, or an open spot bounded at some little distance by a wall." Mr. Duncan's garden at Benmore is a favourite site—"a level sweep of lawn, backed by rising terraces, covered with fir-trees." He also tells us of "a grand cathedral" once provided for his accommodation in Oxfordshire. "The remains of it are still called Spurgeon's Tabernacle, and may be seen near Minster Lovell, in the form of a quadrilateral of oaks. Originally it was the *beau ideal* of a preaching place, for it was a cleared spot in the thick forest of Wychwood, and was reached by roads cut through the dense underwood. I shall never forget those 'alleys green,' and the verdant walls which shut them in. When you reached the inner temple it consisted of a large square, out of which the underwood and smaller trees had been cut away, while a sufficient number of young oaks had been left to rise to a considerable height, and then overshadow us with their branches." He once preached in the time of haymaking from the appropriate text, " He shall come down like rain upon the mown grass, as showers that water the earth," but during the sermon a storm of rain passed over the ground. His general advice to open-air preachers is all valuable. Certain trees are to be avoided on account of their " rustling sound." The sun must not be directly in the speaker's face ; nor are they to attempt to preach "against the wind."

Such is a selection of personal reminiscences collected from his own works, which a future biographer of Mr. Spurgeon will be able to utilize. I could easily add other anecdotes which have not appeared in print ; but the insertion of these would unduly lengthen this chapter. I will, however, give one that comes from a trustworthy friend concerning an English judge, now dead, but who in his lifetime was very generally esteemed, and who was deacon of a congregation in London, a member of the Baptist denomination, and, therefore, well acquainted with Mr. Spurgeon. When out of court, or when in the ante-rooms, both the justice and his learned associates converse familiarly among themselves, so that on one occasion the Pastor of the Metropolitan Tabernacle became the topic of the hour. Of course differences of opinion were freely expressed ; and it is possible the brilliant coterie were a little surprised on hearing from their friend the judge that they should have an opportunity of deciding for themselves the merits of the case, as he intended to invite all of them, and also Mr. Spurgeon, to a friendly dinner. "Do you mean it?" cried the lawyers, in expectant tones. "Yes." "Then agreed!" The bargain being thus concluded, the worthy justice fulfilled to the letter his part of the contract. Mr. Spurgeon accepted the invitation, knowing nothing of the previous arrangements ; and, as Dr. Johnson would have said, the time passed well with some "good talk." When the judge and counsel next met in the robing room, the exceedingly hearty manner in which the latter expressed their thanks showed that they were not speaking in the dialect of mere compliment. Mr. Spurgeon was all that he was said to be, or even more ; and all confessed how well they had been entertained. The confession went even further ; they acknowledged that they had conspired together to test his knowledge by arranging beforehand a number of questions, and the answers received surpassed expectation. In point of fact, Mr. Spurgeon's table-talk is in itself good fare; and hence we are well able to estimate the quality of the banquet which the lawyers enjoyed, and acknowledged with a *bonhomie* characteristic of their order when out of court. Indeed, this table-talk is too good to be lost, but there are difficulties in the way of its collection ; for, as I remarked at the outset, " what the Pastor has been heard to threaten he will do, should he ever be approached by a first cousin of Johnson's biographer, may well intimidate the boldest member of that inquisitive tribe."

On December 1st, 1880, Mr. Spurgeon gave some reminiscences of his earlier days which may very properly close the present chapter :—*

After thanking his people " from the bottom

---

* The report of what the Pastor said on this interesting occasion is that which appeared at the time in *The Christian World*.

of his soul" for the hearty way in which they had ever worked with him, Mr. Spurgeon said he was afraid they were getting old together. Speaking for himself, however, he felt young about the head, but quite old down below. His life had been specially interesting, and he was not likely to grow tired of it. He verily believed that had he the power of a novelist he could produce a three-volume novel from the events of any one day of his life, so singularly had that life been crowded with interesting incidents. Indeed, if he were ever dull, it must be from something within, for he could not get gloomy from the outside. He had promised to tell them a few stories of things he could recollect; and a face he saw before him reminded him of a visit he once paid to Tring. He was regarded as being too *high* for one chapel there, too *low* for another, but in a third he was permitted to preach. The pastor of this chapel was in receipt of only fifteen shillings a-week, and Mr. Spurgeon had some misgivings about drinking the poor man's tea. During the meal he noticed that his host wore a very shiny alpaca coat. At the close of the sermon Mr. Spurgeon said, addressing the congregation—" Now I have preached my best to you. 'Freely ye have received, freely give.' The minister of this place looks as if he wants a new suit of clothes. I will give half-a-sovereign, my friend down below will do the same, and plates will be held at the doors for your contributions." The effort was successful. After the service the poor pastor, addressing Mr. Spurgeon, observed that ever since he became a minister of Jesus Christ his Master always sent him his livery, and he was beginning to wonder where the next would come from. The same day and in the same place Mr. Spurgeon addressed a gathering of children, and was subsequently severely taken to task by some good men for telling the little ones that God heard his prayers before he was converted. The grave men gathered around, exclaiming that the prayers of a sinner were an abomination to the Lord. The victory was, however, won by an old woman in a red cloak. "What are you battling with this young man about?" she inquired, squeezing herself into the circle. "What do *you* know about the Scriptures? You say God does not hear the prayers of unconverted people, why, have you never read that He heareth the young ravens when they cry? and there is no grace in them. If God hears the cry of the ravens, don't you think He will hear the cry of a man made in His own image!" The objectors suddenly vanished, and Mr. Spurgeon walked away with the old lady.

His earliest recollections, Mr. Spurgeon went on to say, gathered around his grandfather, who was for sixty-four years pastor of a congregation at Stambourne, in Essex, and at the age of eighty-eight was wont to rub his knee and complain that rheumatism was shortening his days. Mr. Spurgeon acknowledged that he owed a great deal to the teaching of his early youth. When a boy, and while staying at his grandfather's house, he met the Rev. Richard Knill, the missionary, who would take him into an arbour and pray with him. On one occasion Mr. Knill lifted him on to his knee, and said that he felt persuaded the child would grow up to preach the Gospel to more people than any man living, and that he would one day preach in Rowland Hill's Chapel. Mr. Knill gave him sixpence, in return for which he was to learn the hymn, "God moves in a mysterious way," and at the same time extracted the promise from little Spurgeon that he would have this hymn sung when he occupied Rowland Hill's pulpit. On coming to London the preacher was taken ill, and Mr. Spurgeon was asked to take the service in Surrey Chapel. He did so, and redeemed his promise by letting the congregation sing the hymn suggested by Mr. Knill. Strange things came about in the working of God's providence. It was through Mr. Knill

Baptised in a River.

daring to preach in a theatre, that led Mr. Spurgeon to conduct services in the Surrey Music Hall. He became a Baptist through reading the New Testament, especially in the Greek, and was strengthened in his resolve by a perusal of the Church of England Catechism. He was baptised at the age of fifteen in a river. Two women, who were immersed at the same time, desired him to lead them into the water; but he was such a timid, trembling creature that he needed all the strength he possessed for himself. But his timidity was washed away. It floated down the river into the sea, and must have been devoured by the fishes, for he had never felt anything of the kind since. Baptism also loosed his tongue, and from that day it had never been quiet. When Mr. Spurgeon became pastor of the church of Waterbeach they held their baptisms in a neighbouring river. There was to be a baptism one day, and it was raining "cats and dogs." The service was to be undertaken by Mr. Elvin, a man of enormous size, who said he must decline, for if he got wet through there was not a waistcoat within forty miles that would fit him. One day when Mr. Elvin was preaching for Mr. Spurgeon at Park Street, an old lady put her head in at the door, and, perceiving Mr. Elvin, withdrew, remarking that "no good could possibly come from a man who had so much of the flesh." Mr. Spurgeon went on to remark that he recollected most distinctly hearing Mr. Jay preach at Cambridge. The text was, " Ever let your conversation be as becometh the Gospel of Christ." And he remembered with what dignity he preached, and yet how simply. Ladies, Mr. Jay said, in the course of his sermon, were sometimes charged with dressing too costly. He did not know much about it himself, but if they told him what their income was he would tell them how many yards of ribbon they could afford. His recollections of Mr. Jay were such as he would not like to lose.

On another occasion he made a journey to Birmingham to hear John Angell James, for he was most anxious to be able to say that he had heard Jay and James. Mr. James's text was, " Ye are complete in Him." And what a delicious sermon it was! Years afterwards, on being in Mr. James's company, Mr. Spurgeon told him that he went all the way to Birmingham to hear him preach. On his mentioning the text, Mr. James replied, " Ah! that was a Calvinistic sermon. You would get on with that, but you would not get on with me always." Dr. Brock, when dining with Mr. James on one occasion, asked him if he recollected preaching at a certain place for two hours. "I do," replied Mr. James, "but the clock did not indicate it." "No," said Dr. Brock; "I was in the gallery, and stopped the clock whenever I liked, and thus made you preach for two hours instead of three-quarters of an hour." At this Mr. James observed, "Mr. Brock, you always were at your fun, and I daresay you would do the same again." "But I wouldn't," retorted Dr. Brock, to the great surprise of Mr. James, who expected the Doctor would still be desirous of hearing a sermon from him extending over two hours at least. Dr. Brock's tone suggested pretty plainly that if he happened to be a listener again, he would rather make the hands travel unusually quick in the orthodox direction.

When Mr. Spurgeon commenced preaching at Waterbeach he was sixteen years old. The people could do but very little for his support; hence he also filled the post of an usher at Cambridge. After a time he gave the latter occupation up, and trusted to the generosity of his people, who raised about £45 a-year for him. Out of this he paid twelve shillings a-week for two rooms, and his congregation did for him what he wished country congregations generally would do for their pastors. Whenever they went to Cambridge they carried him vegetables, and any quantity of loaves of bread, and at no time did any member of his flock kill a pig without his receiving some portion of it. Once young Spurgeon was invited to preach for Mr. Sutton, who, on perceiving the youth for the first time on his arrival, exclaimed, "You can't preach. What is the world coming to? A parcel of boys preaching who have not got their mothers' milk out of their mouths!" Mr. Sutton was a quaint old man, who, after being a shepherd of sheep for forty years, became shepherd of men for a similar period, and was wont to remark that his second flock "was a deal more sheepish than the first."

Mr. Spurgeon went on to observe that his (Mr. Spurgeon's) acquaintance had been most varied and extensive. He had enjoyed the friendship of most of the noblest persons that had passed over the history of his own time. He just happened to have the least possible connection with Christmas Evans, having found his widow nearly starving, and it was his great joy to support her till she died. A friend, now gone, however, on hearing of it, insisted upon having shares in the pleasurable undertaking. Mr. Spurgeon remarked that if he had not washed the feet of Christmas Evans, he had done what he could for any relic there was left of him.

Then he enjoyed, too, the most intimate friendship of Daubigné, author of the "History of the

Reformation," who once gave an address at the Tabernacle. Mr. Spurgeon also preached for Daubigné on the continent, and the same day occupied Calvin's old pulpit. In the evening he met two hundred of the greatest preachers of Switzerland, and before departing, one after the other kissed him on both cheeks. It was his pleasure to have the personal friendship of Mr. Sherman, also that of Dr. Hamilton, whom it was always a real joy to meet in his own home. Then he well knew glorious old Tom Guthrie. "What a man he was to be with!" said Mr. Spurgeon. "And he could tell a story or two. When we were together we were happy." And Dr. Candlish it was his delight to be acquainted with. He well recollected addressing the General Assembly of the Free Church of Scotland, and Dr. Candlish was all over the place—now in the gallery, now to the moderator's right, now to his left. Dr. Candlish was made of quicksilver, and, though his body was not very large, it seemed to partake of the quicksilver of his nature. Mr. Spurgeon regarded Candlish as one of the greatest men of modern times. And then he knew Arnot, and. should not soon forget the good old man. "All honour to these men," added Mr. Spurgeon. "They did not come to England, but they did exceedingly well in Scotland, where they were burning and shining lights." He owed much to the Scotch, for when his Tabernacle was being built, a considerable portion of the money came from the North. Whenever he went to Scotland —it was not "Blue-bonnets over the Border," but wide-awake over the Border—he came back loaded with money. He just passed over the skirts of the Claytons, and everybody who lived in Walworth recollected what gentlemen the Claytons were. Without a doubt they were the most gentlemanly race of preachers that ever lived. Mr. Spurgeon did not lament that such dignified brethren had passed away, though they did good in their day. He had been told that souls were saved by the white bibs ministers wore. Then John Howard Hinton had a good word for him when very few had anything to say in his favour. He called in at the Tabernacle one day, and said to Mr. Olney, Mr. Spurgeon's senior deacon, "Take care of that young man; he is an old Puritan bound in morocco." "But I maintain," added Mr. Spurgeon, "that I am bound in calf, for I belong to Essex." Then that good old Dr. Campbell, editor of the *British Banner*, was a very dear friend of his. Whenever he went to preach for Dr. Campbell he had always to take his wife and boys with him. When writing to invite them Dr. Campbell would say, "Our cat has had kittens on purpose for the boys to play with." And the day before their arrival the good old man would be out buying toy horses and carts for the juvenile Spurgeons. This showed that while he was a stern man he stooped down to do a kindly action, and took a pleasure in delighting children. Dr. Binney once went to hear Mr. Spurgeon, and remarked of the sermon in the presence of some of the preacher's friends—" It is an insult to God and man. I never heard such a thing." Twenty years afterwards Dr. Binney visited the Pastors' College and related the incident, observing, "Well, you know, your minister has so much improved since those days. I denounced him then most heartily, and even refused to preach where he preached, but I very soon found out my mistake." "And the grand, great man," added Mr. Spurgeon, " was perhaps right in his first observation ! " After mentioning a few other incidents, Mr. Spurgeon brought his chat to a close, promising to resume it on a future occasion.

When Dr. Binney took exception to the style of the young preacher, he was not so singular in his prejudices as some might now be disposed to think. In 1851, when Mr. Spurgeon commenced work, the world may not have been unprepared to greet something new—to condone some departure from the old and beaten ways;

but it was hardly ready to welcome a preacher of such thorough originality, that he ignored time-honoured conventional pulpit fashions to follow methods of his own; even his most uncompromising detractors did not attempt to deny that the preacher was original; but the world did not find in such an admission a passport to its favour. This was partly accounted for by the fact, that in great measure people spoke and acted as their fathers had done before them. A Latinised rhetorical style was still regarded as eloquence; and the "great" sermons of popular orators at important anniversaries were marvellous examples of painstaken elaboration. The success of Mr. Spurgeon meant a total change of fashion; but the world does not change its ways at the bidding of a provincial youth without some growls and warm protests. Elderly people did not know that what they thought to be so proper was doomed to become obsolete; and they could not be expected all at once to apprehend that the youth whom they accused of so many improprieties was really a reformer, such as the pulpit and the world had long wanted.

ANECDOTES, LETTERS, ANA, ETC.

"Gentlemen of the press have an eye to the amusement of their readers, and make selections of all the remarkable anecdotes, or odd sayings, used by a speaker, and when these are separated from their surroundings the result is anything but satisfactory. No man's speeches or lectures should be judged of by an ordinary newspaper summary, which in any case is a mere sketch, and in many instances is a vile caricature."—*Preface to Eccentric Preachers.*

V.

ANECDOTES, LETTERS, ANA, ETC.

TRUTH *versus* FICTION

LIKE Rowland Hill and some other celebrated preachers of wit and wisdom, Mr. Spurgeon has had many apocryphal stories told about him, and the manner in which these piquant fictions are circulated is well illustrated by the following letter, which the Pastor received in the year 1883:—

"As I see that you are still occasionally put to the trouble of answering enquiries as to the truth of various anecdotes, etc., concerning yourself, I thought the following brief statement might interest you, or some of your numerous readers, if you think it well to publish it. About seventeen years ago I was for some time at a well-known health-resort on the south coast. At the *table d'hôte* I sat next to a young married lady, who was, alas! consumptive; and of that temperament which is so common in such cases, *très spirituelle*, and very learned and accomplished. You may be sure she never lacked auditors for her lively conversation. At dessert one day she was 'telling stories,' in the juvenile and literal sense of the phrase, about yourself. I let her go on for some time, until I thought the fun was getting a little too fast; and then I said, 'I hope, Mrs. ——, you do not believe the stories you are detailing, because I assure you I heard nearly all of them in my childhood, before Mr. Spurgeon was born, and that most of them were then attributed to Rowland Hill—doubtless with equal lack of authenticity.' She looked me calmly in the face, with a very comical expression, and replied, 'Oh, Mr. ——, we never ask whether such stories are true; it is quite sufficient if we find them amusing.' 'Well,' I said, '*so long as that is understood all round*, by all means keep on.' The poor, brilliant, thoughtless woman, and her husband also, have many years since passed away; but she has many, many successors, who are without her wit, and not quite so good-humouredly candid as to their practice. If only you can get it 'understood all round,' that such folk really do not consider whether their 'anecdotes' are true or not, it might save you some trouble." In reference to this, Mr. Spurgeon himself remarked: "This is quite true, but it is a pity that people should lie in jest. The lady was let off very easily. Our friend has touched the root of the matter. It is not malice, but the passion for amusement, which creates the trade in falsehood, which never seems to decline."

CLAPHAM AND WESTWOOD.

The *North British Daily Mail* once remarked that those who have visited Mr. Spurgeon at his home in Nightingale Lane, from which he lately removed to Norwood, will recollect having seen in the pleasant garden the old pulpit stairs that were used at the great preacher's first London chapel— the old meeting-house in New Park Street, where he was preceded as pastor by a long line of worthy ministers—Dr. Gill, the learned Hebraist; Dr. Rippon, the editor of the old Baptist Hymn-book; Dr. Joseph Angus, the Bible Reviser, and Mr. Smith, of Cheltenham. When the chapel was sold Mr. Spurgeon removed the pulpit stairs to his garden, and fixed them to the trunk of a huge willow tree. " Here," says Mr. Spurgeon, " the observer can see those very rails down which we did *not* slide to illustrate backsliding, and he may be sure of that negative fact, because the story was told of us when the pulpit was fixed in the wall and the entrance was from behind; and more than that, the same story was told of another preacher before we were born." Mr. Spurgeon has not taken the stairs with him to his new home at Norwood. He has left them attached to the great willow in Nightingale Lane. "The purchaser of our former abode," he says, "will preserve the staircase quite as carefully as we have done, and we hope his children will for years ascend by them to the pleasant seats, where they may in the summer sit and enjoy themselves beneath the willow's shade."

AT HOME AT WESTWOOD.

Before leaving England for America, Dr. Theodore Cuyler visited Mr. Spurgeon at his new home near the Crystal Palace, and in a letter to the New York *Evangelist* describes his villa as "a rural Paradise." "The great preacher," writes Dr. Cuyler, "with a jovial countenance, came out of his door with both hands outstretched to give us welcome. Saturday afternoon is his holiday. For an hour he conducted us over his delightful grounds and through his garden and conservatory, and then to a rustic arbour, where he entertained us with one of his racy talks which are as characteristic as his sermons Mr. Spurgeon's study is a charming apartment opening out on his lawn; the view extends for twelve miles to Epsom Downs. His parlour, too, is lined with elegant volumes. He showed us with great glee a portfolio of caricatures of himself; and then, by way of contrast, a series of translations of his sermons in various foreign tongues. His comely wife—for a long time a suffering invalid—presided at the table with grace and sweetness. Their twin sons have already entered the ministry, one in London and the other now in New Zealand. It was six o'clock on Saturday when we bade him 'good-bye,' and he assured us that he had not yet selected even the text for next day's discourses! 'I shall go down in the garden presently,' said he, 'and arrange my morning discourse and choose a text for that in the evening: then to-morrow afternoon, before preaching, I will make an outline of the second one.' This has been his habit for many years; he never composes a sentence in advance, and rarely spends over half-an-hour in laying out the plan of a sermon. Constant study fills his mental cask, and he has only to turn the spigot and draw."

THE PASTOR AT PLYMOUTH.

While at the Baptist Union Meetings at Plymouth in 1875, Mr. Spurgeon told the following anecdotes:—

Unaired Drawing-rooms.—I was at a minister's house the other day, and he said, looking at the drawing-room, "Well, you see this drawing-room looks a little seedy." I said that I did not think it did. "Well," he said, "my wife has a Bible-class here every Sunday, and she generally gets it once in the week. In my study I always have a young men's Bible-class on a Sunday afternoon." Oh! good friends, your houses were not meant to be half shut up as they are. When I call on some of my people, if they happen to be a little upper-crust, they put me up in the drawing-room in the winter even, when there has not been a fire there for three months, and I get the rheumatism, and I go out of the room saying to myself, "I wish to goodness those people would have a service there every week, for if they did that the room would be aired, and there would be an incidental blessing to me, and I do not doubt it would be so to them."

The Rose of Sharon.—I met the other day a lady who had lost the sense of taste and the sense of smell; I had never met with a person before in that condition. The sweetest fragrance of a rose was lost upon her nostril, and the choicest delicacies had not the slightest flavour to her. It was a painful loss, in some measure; but, oh! what a wretch a man must be who has lost the power of smelling the fragrance of the Rose of Sharon, and lost his taste so that he does not perceive any sweetness in the fruit which came down from heaven, even Jesus Christ. I feel in a pitying mood as I look at you that do not love Him. Oh, what perverted tastes you have got! what strange judgments! for you love this painted Jezebel of a world; you love this witch of sinful pleasure; but my Lord, who is altogether lovely, who puts the angels in amazement every time they get a gaze upon Him—you do not love. Oh! what has happened to you? What strange madness has come over you?

The Newfoundland Dog.—I read in the "Guide to Kingsbridge" a pretty story about the Start Bay villages, where the Newfoundland dogs are kept to go out to sea to fetch in a rope. The story is that one of these dogs saw a child in the water and swam in and brought the child out. He could do that, and as he laid the child down on the sand it was nearly dead, and he licked its face to try and bring it round; and when he found that his licking would not revive it, he went up to a village, and he caught hold of people's coats, till at last he induced some to come down, and by their care the little flame of life in the child, which was almost extinct, was made to burn up again. As I read the story, I hoped to be something like that dog. I will go into the water after souls and try to bring them out; and, if I could, I would kiss them into life with loving words; but as that is out of my power, I will go and tug the skirts of Jesus, and ask Him to come and give them life, and raise them up, and I do not doubt that He will do so. That was a dog's work. Christians, do something more than dogs can do, or, at least, attempt to do as well. God grant you may; and though you cannot quicken them into life, you can bring Jesus to them, and He can give them life and strength that they may be saved.

The Power of Kindness.—One day an old man shook me by the hand with a firm grasp, and he said, " Sir, one Sunday night you said, ' Every one of you do something to-night for Jesus such as you never did before.' Now," he said, " my son had been a great trouble to me. He was a very wicked youth indeed, and he had left me for some time, and he had brought himself to death's door by his ill habits. I had, therefore, given him enough to live upon; but I thought to do nothing else. But that night," said he, " I went home and looked out of my larder the best things I had got, and I put them in a basket, and I sent them round to my son to tell him that I had forgiven him all, and that I had sent him a little something extra that night, and I meant to do it continually, and I hoped that he would get well. Now," said he, " I never could speak to him of religion till

I did that; and the next morning I went round and we were able to converse about the things of God, and he died with a comfortable hope; whereas, before, I had been afraid that he would die far from God."

The two following letters were also printed for the first time about sixteen years ago in my History of the Tabernacle Church. Of course they have been copied by others, so remarkable are they when read in connection with what has since happened.

"No. 60, PARK STREET, CAMBRIDGE,
"*January* 27*th*, 1854.

"MY DEAR SIR,—I cannot help feeling intense gratification at the unanimity of the Church at New Park Street, in relation to their invitation to me. Had I been uncomfortable in my present situation, I should have felt unmixed pleasure at the prospect Providence seems to open up before me; but having a devoted and loving people, I feel I know not how.

"One thing I know, viz., that I must soon be severed from them by necessity, for they do not raise sufficient to maintain me in comfort. Had they done so, I should have turned a deaf ear to any request to leave them, at least for the present. But now my Heavenly Father drives me forth from this little Garden of Eden, and whilst I see that I must go out, I leave it with reluctance, and tremble to tread the unknown land before.

"When I first ventured to preach at Waterbeach, I only accepted an invitation for three months, on the condition that, if in that time I should see good reason for leaving, or they, on their part, should wish for it, I should be at liberty to cease supplying, or they should have the same power to request me to do so before the expiration of the time.

"Now with regard to a six months' invitation from you, I have no objection to the length of time, but rather approve of the prudence of the Church in wishing to have one so young as myself on an extended period of probation.

"But I write after well weighing the matter, when I say positively that I cannot, I *dare* not, accept an unqualified invitation for so long a time. My objection is not to the length of the time of probation, but it ill becomes a youth to promise to preach to a London congregation so long until he knows *them* and they know *him*. I would engage to supply for three months of that time, and then, should the congregation fail or the Church disagree, I would reserve to myself liberty, without breach of engagement, to retire; and you would, on your part, have the right to dismiss me without seeming to treat me ill. Should I see no reason for so doing, and the Church still retain their wish for me, I can remain the other three months, either with or without the formality of a further invitation; but even during that time (the second three) I should not like to regard myself as a fixture, in case of ill success, but should only be a supply—liable to a fortnight's dismissal or resignation.

"Perhaps this is not business-like. I do not know, but this is the course I should prefer, if it would be agreeable to the Church. Enthusiasm and popularity are often the cracking of thorns and soon expire. I do not wish to be a hindrance if I cannot be a help.

"With regard to coming at *once*, I think I must

not. My own deacons just hint that I ought to finish the quarter here, though by *ought*, they mean simply, 'Pray do so if you can.' This would be too long a delay. I wish to help them until they can get supplies, which is only to be done with great difficulty, and as I have given you four Sabbaths, I hope you will allow me to give them four in return. I would give them the first and second Sabbath in February, and two more in a month or six weeks' time. I owe them much for their kindness, although they insist that the debt lies on their side. Some of them hope and almost pray that you may be tired in three months, so that I may be again sent back to them.

"Thus, my dear Sir, I have honestly poured out my heart to you. You are too kind. You will excuse me if I err, for I wish to do right to you, to my people, and to all, as being not mine own, but bought with a price.

"I respect the honesty and boldness of the small minority, and only wonder that the number was not greater. I pray God that if He does not see fit that I should remain with you, the majority may be quite as much the other way at the end of six months, so that I may never divide you into parties.

"Pecuniary matters I am well satisfied with. And now one thing is due to every minister, and I pray you to remind the Church of it, viz., that in private, as well as public, they must all earnestly wrestle in prayer to the God of our Lord Jesus Christ that I may be sustained in the great work.

"I am, with the best wishes for your health, and the greatest respect,

"Yours truly,
"C. H. SPURGEON.

"JAMES LOW, ESQ."

"75, Dover Road, Borough,
"*April* 28*th*, 1854.

" *To the Baptist Church of Christ worshipping in New Park Street, Southwark.*

"Dearly Beloved in Christ Jesus,—I have received your unanimous invitation as contained in a resolution passed by you on the 19th inst., desiring me to accept the pastorate among you.

"No lengthened reply is required; there is but one answer to so loving and cordial an invitation, *I accept it*.

"I have not been perplexed as to what my reply should be, for many things constrain me thus to answer.

"I sought not to come to you, for I was the minister of an obscure but affectionate people; I never solicited advancement. The first note of invitation from your deacons came quite unlooked for, and I trembled at the idea of preaching in London; I could not understand how it had come about, and even now I am filled with astonishment at the wondrous Providence. I would wish to give myself into the hands of our covenant God, whose wisdom directs all things: He shall choose for me, and so far as I can judge this is His choice.

"I feel it to be a high honour to be the pastor of a people who can mention glorious names as my predecessors, and I entreat of you to remember me in prayer that I may realise the responsibility of my trust. Remember my youth and inexperience, pray that these may not hinder my usefulness. I trust also that the remembrance of these will lead you to forgive mistakes I may make, or unguarded words I may utter.

"Blessed be the name of the Most High! if He has called me to this office, He will support me in it, otherwise how should a child a youth, have the presumption thus to attempt a work which filled the heart and hands of Jesus?

"Your kindness to me has been very great, and my heart is knit unto you. I fear not *your* steadfastness, I fear my own. The Gospel, I believe, enables me to venture great things, and by faith I venture this.

"I ask your co operation in every good work; in visiting the sick, in bringing in enquirers, and in mutual edification.

"Oh that I may be no injury to you, but a lasting benefit! I have no more to say saving this, that if I have expressed myself in these few words in a manner unbecoming my youth and inexperience, you will not impute it to arrogance, but forgive my mistake.

"And now, commending you to our covenant God, the Triune Jehovah,

"I am, yours to serve in the Gospel,

"C. H. SPURGEON."

AT MENTONE.

It is very probable that the majority of friends who regularly, or occasionally, attend the services at the Metropolitan Tabernacle are quite unable to appreciate what a holiday means to a man in Mr. Spurgeon's position. To superficial observers the great chapel may seem to be little more than a popular preaching-station, which, indeed, it was represented to be some years ago by a well-known clergyman, now a bishop—a centre of evangelical teaching, of which neighbouring churches scarce knew the existence when the doors were closed and the gas was out. If this were all, the strain on the Pastor would nevertheless still be very heavy; for even a genius in his work cannot preach three sermons a week of a high standard of excellence without being subjected to a wear and tear such as does not enter into the experience of more humble workers. As most persons know, however, the offices in the rear and beneath the Tabernacle are the headquarters of a large number of philanthropic agencies, some of which are of considerable magnitude, while all, in a greater or lesser degree, demand the Pastor's oversight. In the colportage department, in the general secretary's room, and elsewhere on the chapel premises, a goodly number of persons are regularly employed; while at Westwood, two busy assistants, on either side of the large table in the study, have all that they can do to clear up each day's work as it comes. It is thus hardly to be wondered at that commenting and general literary work should appear to go only slowly forward to those who for years patiently waited for the concluding volume of *The Treasury of David*.

In Mr. Spurgeon's case there is supposed to be some connection between excessive suffering from rheumatism and too much work; but if this is so, the invalid is probably paying the penalty exacted by the indiscretions of former days. That the ailment is hereditary we are well aware ; for the Puritan grandfather, who died at Stambourne in 1866, was wont to declare, when verging on ninety years of age, that rheumatism would certainly shorten his days. Still, all the suffering which has afflicted the family since Job Spurgeon lay as a prisoner in Chelmsford gaol for conscience' sake in the time of Charles II. can hardly have amounted to what the Pastor of the Metropolitan Tabernacle has endured in twenty years ; and probably the seeds of a good deal of this pain and weakness were sown when the youthful orator travelled up and down the country preaching a dozen sermons a week ; when, besides the usual inconveniences of the road, such as hasty meals and having to study in express trains, he incurred the more alarming risk of damp beds. It would seem that these well-meant indiscretions of the past are now causing some inconvenience.

As a holiday resort during our English winter and so-called boreal spring, Mentone has many charms ; but perhaps all the encomiums passed upon the picturesque Mediterranean nook have not been verified by the majority who have sought benefit from its sunshine and sea breezes. The climate, enjoyable as it must be when lemon-trees blossom in mid-winter, and flies sport in the sunshine, has not done so much for Mr. Spurgeon as was at first fondly anticipated by those who thought that the rheum might possibly be expelled from the system by genial climatic influences. The fact is, however, that even Mentone is not a perfect sanatorium : " Indeed," says Dr. Benet, " I question whether in the South of Europe, in winter, it is not as difficult to keep free from rheumatic pains as it is in the north." He then goes on to tell how the painful malady exists in all southern climes, including even the Sahara Desert, adding that "the Bedouin Arabs, with the thermometer at 80° or 90° in the daytime, swathe themselves up in woollen garments and woollen cloaks, for rheumatism is their enemy as well as ours." It is plain that, in Mr. Spurgeon's case, a more moderated strain on the mental faculties would effect far more than change of climate.

Social life in a small holiday community like that of Mentone has its sombre aspects, on account of the number of invalids who arrive, never to return to their homes. French consumptives succumb before winter has well begun ; and though they sometimes linger longer, the English who are afflicted in a similar manner surely follow one by one. These losses cast a **shade** over the whole of the foreign settlement, because, as Dr. Benet says, " the departed have endeared themselves to the survivors; they have lived amongst them, they have shared their joys, their sorrows, their exile feeling." The advent of the magnificent southern spring in March may do something towards exhilarating the more ordinary visitors, however; for it is there that the sun asserts a power which no temporary return of winter will challenge, when in the vales, and on the heights alike, wild flowers blossom with a beauty and a profusion which astonish those who look upon the classic shores of the Mediterranean for the first time.

In this favoured region, and on the verge of such a spring as the ancient classic poets praised in their verse, Mr. Spurgeon will secure that rest and quiet which will do more for him than medicine or the physician's art. His own people have sometimes requested that he will remain away for an extended period, and while so doing they also give a guarantee that all will do their best to keep the varied machinery at home in good working order. On some occasions the subscriptions have shown a tendency to fall off when the Pastor has been away, and this has in some measure marred his pleasure, if it has not actually retarded his recovery. If friends near and far away really desire to contribute to

Mr. Spurgeon's holiday, they will ever do so most effectively by keeping the Orphanage, the College, the Colportage, and other agencies well supplied while he is away. The mill is now in all its parts so large an affair, that more grist than ever is needed to keep it going; and when symptoms of falling off betray themselves, none suffer so keenly as the chief overseer himself, on whom the responsibility mainly rests of keeping up the supplies.

On Going to America.

He always set his face against going to America; but during the summer of 1876 the subject was revived by the appearance of a paragraph in *The Boston Globe* to the effect that the much-talked-about visit to the United States was really coming off. On seeing this notice the managers of the Redpath Lyceum Bureau wrote one more application thus:—

"BOSTON, MASS., *June 22nd*, 1876.

"DEAR SIR,—Is the above paragraph true? We have tried so long and so hard for many years to secure you that we thought it impossible, and long since gave up all hope. We are the exclusive agents of all the leading lecturers in America. We will give you 1,000 dollars in gold for every lecture you deliver in America, and pay all your expenses to and from your home, and place you under the most popular auspices in the country. Will you come?"

In Scotland.

To this invitation Mr. Spurgeon returned the following reply:

"CLAPHAM, LONDON, ENGLAND, *July 6th*.

"GENTLEMEN,—I cannot imagine how such a paragraph should appear in your papers, except by deliberate invention of a hard-up editor, for I never had any idea of leaving home for America for some time to come. As I said to you before, if I could come, I am not a lecturer, nor would I receive money for preaching."

"A HOLIDAY (?)."

After the first Sunday in August 1876 he visited Scotland, accompanied by his two sons, for the purpose of enjoying some yachting among the Western Islands or Hebrides. He was for the time being the guest of Mr. Duncan of Benmore. On the Sunday after his arrival he preached at Scone, in the open air, to five thousand persons, seats being provided for the ladies. In consequence of these services the neighbouring sanctuaries were closed. In the morning sermon he spoke of the hatred which separated sects between whom there were but few points of difference, and he warned the Scotch to take care that this was not the case with them. Even a microscope could not discover any material difference between certain of the sects. In the evening he said he would talk in a more familiar strain. He directly addressed those who had heard more sermons than they could count. They had listened to waggon-loads, they were smoked in sermons, and yet were still unconverted. Some people at the Tabernacle, though very few, had heard the Gospel for twenty years and were not caught yet, and it was to be feared they never would be. They were like india-rubber—no matter how often you depressed it, the substance returned to its original form.

On the following Sabbath he preached again at Kilcret to many thousands, who assembled on the hill-side which overlooks the Firth of Clyde. On this occasion the northerners appear to have been surprised at the extraordinary power and clearness of his magnificent voice.

Concerning this so-called "holiday," he sent a brief note to a gentleman at Glasgow, and addressed from Carlisle on his way home:—

"DEAR FRIEND,—I have returned to England. I had eleven clear week-days in Scotland, and was asked to preach more than fifty times. *That* when I came for rest—and in a Christian country, too! 'A merciful man,' etc. God speed you.—Yours truly, C. H. SPURGEON."

IN SCOTLAND IN 1878.

The visit to the North was this year deferred through various causes, and when the trip was

In the Highlands. 141

actually undertaken he was so worried to preach that he did not derive the good from the change he might otherwise have done. A correspondent of *The Baptist* thus wrote respecting this visit:—

"Mr. Spurgeon arrived in the Bay of Rothesay, on Saturday, the 27th July, in Mr. Duncan's fine yacht. The celebrated preacher sailed from Oban to Campbelltown, passing the Mull of Kintyre. Sailing from Campbelltown, he passed round a considerable part of the Island of Arran. The scenery along Arran is most delightful. He passed through the far-famed Kyles of Bute. The Kyles narrow and broaden, and narrow and broaden again. The whole atmosphere is of arcadian seclusion. Tighnabruaich nestles down below the hills, the houses rising a little from the shore only to be half hidden in the surrounding foliage. The very narrowness of the water and the consequent closeness of the land on either side are themselves portions of the fascinations exercised by the place. Here the scenery is of the most charming description. The waterway is so narrow that you can see the land on either side distinctly, and even count the number of the hills. Leaving the Kyles, Rothesay, the charming capital of Bute, is reached, noted for its aquarium. Arrived in Rothesay Bay, Mr. Spurgeon landed for a drive in the island, when, coming down a declivity, the horse in the machine ran away, and great danger was apprehended; but, fortunately, a gentleman caught the frightened animal by the head and held it till the party got safely out. There is a neat Baptist Chapel at Adbeg, Rothesay, ever pleasant and ever popular with visitors. The Baptist Chapel here is usually crowded in summer. Mr. Crabbe, one of Mr. Spurgeon's former students, officiates in the said chapel. With much acceptance Mr. Spurgeon worshipped there in the morning. The chapel was crowded, many failing to get admittance.

"Mr. Spurgeon preached in front of the Rothesay Academy in the evening. He stood upon the top of the porch of the mansion of Provost Orkney, and there preached to the assembled thousands, attracted by the fame of the preacher, from Luke xiii. 10-17. There were present at least fifteen thousand. Behind us, in front of the Academy, there was a great crowd of most attentive listeners. Before us, onwards to the preacher, there was a dense mass of interested hearers. Towards our right hand, the side of the hill, on the summit of which towers the Rothesay Museum, was lined with hundreds on hundreds of hearers. The vast audience being thus seated on a natural amphitheatre, the preacher had full command of his hearers. These had come from all parts of Bute, from Largs, Millpont, and Dunoon, not a few having crossed the firth in yachts and small boats. The weather was delightful. The congregation began to assemble between three and four o'clock p.m., and before six every available seat on the sward was occupied, whilst those who arrived later had to content themselves with standing in the road leading up to the Academy.

"Mr. Spurgeon said: 'Oh that my blessed Master would look around this throng this night and find out those who are bowed down in spirit and almost in despair! He or she who thought himself or herself most likely to be passed by, and so obscure and undeserving of Christ's regard, was most likely to obtain the blessing. Some Christians,' said the preacher, 'seem to think that it is a sin to be joyful. They are always crying out: Oh, this is a waste and howling wilderness! Then, they ought not to howl, but ought to rejoice. Timothy Rogers, who was twenty-six years a prey to melancholy, came, after all, out into the full clear light of Gospel grace. The preacher recollected a young woman who, he believed, was an excellent Christian, who yet thought and said, "I am an awful hypocrite, and I do not love the Saviour at all!" "Will you put your name to that?" said Mr. Spurgeon. The horror upon her face was delightful to see, and she exclaimed, "I will be torn in pieces first." Some ministers,' he said, 'preached in such a way that people were made gloomy and very sad at heart. He wished hearers to follow the practice of the man who got bad milk. "I don't care, now," said the man, "whether there is bad milk or not, because I keep a cow of my own." Thus, when people found that the teaching of the pulpit did not give them comfort, they should take to the reading of their Bibles more than they had ever done before. In that way they could keep a cow of their own, and they would not need to care whether the milk was good or bad. There are some Christians,' he said, ' who always remind us of a person who walks into the class when his face is dirty, instead of washing it with water.' Referring to the Liberator at His work, the preacher said, 'The way of salvation consists of two steps—the first is out of ourselves, and the second is into Christ. None but Jesus— that is the Gospel. Christ,' he said, 'performed this miracle on the poor, bowed-down woman out of common humanity; another motive was that of special property, and a third was a peculiar antagonism to the devil.' Mr. Spurgeon, as is usual with him, preached with great power, and exhibited the glorious Gospel of the blessed Lord with remarkable earnestness and clearness."

The reference to the accident in the above

needs supplementing, the fact being that Mr. Spurgeon, Mr. Duncan, and those who were in the carriage had the narrowest possible escape from a violent death. Their deliverance was entirely providential. It appears, from what I learned of the affair, that it is a custom in the north, with certain drivers, to allow their horses to rush down long steep hills at a headlong pace. While driving Mr. Duncan and his guests, as stated above, the coachman on coming to a declivity allowed the horses to proceed in the customary merry fashion; but not approving of that mode of travelling, Mr. Spurgeon, on their safe arrival at the foot of the hill, expressed a desire that a more English-like manner of driving might be practised. "Oh," said the man, "We always go like that here." He knew more about driving than all the preachers in the world, and was determined to act in accordance with his knowledge. Soon they came to another hill, and to the discomfiture of the travellers, they at once found themselves descending at express speed. Then the harness broke, the man lost all control over the horses, which presented the appearance of frightened runaways. There was a prospect of being knocked to pieces, and Mr. Spurgeon confessed that his thoughts were directed to that subject; and the people at the roadside looked with terror on the spectacle. At the bottom was a zigzag road, protected by a slight fence, and beyond this a precipice; but the party were delivered when the horses, instead of going straight forward to destruction, as nineteen horses out of twenty would have done, turned into another road, which was an incline. Unable to keep on at that rate up the hill, they moderated their speed; and when danger had passed the friend may have come to the rescue, but not before. He said that he never travelled so rapidly in his life, except in an express train.

On the 5th of August, the first Monday evening prayer-meeting, after his return from the north, a crowded congregation assembled at the Tabernacle, doubtless expecting to hear something about their Pastor's adventures in the North. He said he had been lately in many lone places in Scotland, far removed from the haunts of men. He had gone there to seek a restoration of health. He had obtained, in a measure, what he sought, but, owing to the numbers of persons who visited him out of a kindly feeling, even in these remote parts, he had scarcely known what solitude was, and had consequently not derived that amount of benefit, in a bodily sense, which he otherwise would have done. He had been on many fishing excursions, and from them had learned many lessons. In that College—the one attached to the Tabernacle—they were all fishermen, but he could wish that many of the fishermen there had a little more catching bait about them than they seemed to possess. They must get the fish about them by some means or another before they were caught, and to that end a harmless pleasantry was a capital bait. Sometimes he had been blamed for giving vent to witticisms, but in his own mind he had done well by so doing, because people came to hear him, and when they did so many were caught. The fact was, it was a good catching bait. Mr. Spurgeon then proceeded to say that if persons went to fish either for fish or for human souls, they must not be 'fools, for if they were they would be like him when, a few days ago near Rothesay, he threw his lines into the water, and instead of watching them, turned away and allowed the fish to take off the bait without so much as being pricked by the hook. The Sunday-school was a grand place to use catching bait, but they must not allow the young fry to suck off the bait unless they bolted the hook of the Gospel. If the teachers of religion never got a bite, they should not go to sleep, but should bait their hooks afresh, and try different waters. They then might get some to bolt the bait, hook and all, just in the same way as the cod did.

An Adventure in a Crowd. 147

Those were the sort of fellows he liked—the nibblers were scarcely any good. In conclusion he gave a description of the scenery of Scotland, and expressed his thanks for the hospitality he had received.

One or two amusing things happened in connection with his visit to Scotland this year. A correspondent thus referred to these northern services :—

" Mr. Spurgeon preached at Pollokshaws, near Glasgow, on the 1st of August. Long before the hour fixed for the beginning of the service the place of worship was besieged by crowds of people anxious to get admission, and as it was altogether impracticable to allow others than ticket-holders to pass into the place of meeting, thousands who would willingly have paid to get inside were turned away disappointed. An amusing incident is reported as having occurred at the gates, where a policeman or two and several stalwart office-bearers acted in the capacity of sentries and collected the passports. Mr. Spurgeon, having elbowed his way through the crowd as far as the gate, was asked to show and deliver his ticket; but not being a ticket-holder the great preacher was peremptorily told to " cut his stick." Happily some persons who recognised the familiar face, greatly amused at the comical situation, nudged the policeman's elbow, and he immediately gave way. The crowds who had gone in the hope of getting admission without tickets and were excluded were addressed in the Greenbank Public Park by Mr. Spurgeon, jun. Though Mr. Spurgeon's fame as a preacher went before him like the light and radiancy of the bearded comet, his preaching at Rothesay, and we have no doubt at Pollokshaws, has exceeded expectation."

Another incident in connection with this excursion may be mentioned. Such was the pressure of the crowd that the beadle was lost sight of at the time for commencing service, and there was no one to show Mr. Spurgeon to the pulpit in accordance with the Scotch polite usage. A member of Session, however, mounted the pulpit steps, and called out in a stentorian voice that the beadle was "wanted immediately." This incident created some merriment among even a people not remarkable for their witty propensities.

At a field-meeting with his students at Clapham, both before and after dinner, Mr. Spurgeon himself told some further incidents of this journey. Among other things he was privileged to hear a sermon in Gaelic, and rather wearying of listening to what he could not understand, he whispered something to a Highland gentleman, who replied, "If ye pull his coat tail he'll soon have done."

By some means the sermon came to an end somewhat sooner than the preacher intended ; and it then transpired that he had got with the prodigal son into the far country without having had time to get him back again. Mr. Spurgeon particularly noticed the repetition of one word which sounded like *agath*, but on mentioning this he was told that it signified *and*.

After his escape from accident he was especially glad to return to the yacht. After all, he thought the sea the only really safe place. For example, you ran no risk there of being killed by a pantile.

On one of the days while he was in Scotland he dined with a leading family—a gentleman, I believe, who held a distinguished position in connection with the city of Glasgow. At dinner the Pastor, assuming a very grave face, asked this friend, " Mr. ——, are you aware that your office entitles you to go without charge through any toll-gate in England ? " Mr. —— smiled, and though not previously aware of the privilege attached to his office, quite appreciated the honour. Was it really so indeed ? When his curiosity was a little further stimulated Mr. Spurgeon, to prevent any misapprehension, added, " Yes, you are entitled to walk through, but if you take a horse you must pay."

In the field, at the students' meeting, also, he told

this anecdote of Scotland:—When I was in Arran, quite recently, I heard of a minister who preached in a certain church, and at the close of the service was strongly urged to promise for a future supply, the collection after his sermon having been unusually large. "Dear me!" said the minister, with becoming pride, "what might your ordinary collection amount to?" "Last Sunday it was twopence halfpenny." "What is it to-day, then?" asked the other, expecting to hear a large sum. "Eightpence halfpenny," was the reply. "Woe is me!" said the other, "for I gave sixpence of it myself."

UNDER THE LAW OF WORKS.

I was once riding on an omnibus between London and Edmonton, when a very self-righteous methodist began to lament the laxity of the English people in regard to their non-observance of the Sabbath. At last he referred to the conduct of Mr. Spurgeon as especially reprehensible, for Mr. Spurgeon rode to chapel in a brougham.

"Why don't he keep the Sabbath? *I* do," said the man sternly, almost fiercely, and in that self-satisfied tone common to his class. I forget what answer I made; but this objection to the Pastor's riding to chapel was not new. Some busy Pharisee once had the temerity to write to

Clapham on this very question, and received in reply a notification that the horse which ran in the Sunday carriage was in reality so far a Jew that he kept his Sabbath on Saturday. To make sure of this being true, I mentioned the circumstance to Mr. Spurgeon, when I found it was all right; his horse lived under the law of works and not of grace, and hence was not allowed to work on the seventh day. He usually kept two horses, and the fodder for these animals was supplied gratis by Deacon Murrell, "the gatekeeper" at the Tabernacle. "How many horses may I keep, Murrell?"—*i.e.*, "how many will *you* keep for me?"—once asked the Pastor. "Twenty," said the good-natured deacon, and meant what he said.

TABERNACLE DEACONS.

The above will remind some of the readers of this book that Mr. Spurgeon has from the first been peculiarly favoured in his deacons. They have assuredly been a kind-hearted set of men, forward in advancing Christian work, and many of them have been specially adapted for some kind of special service. Those who remember the familiar form of "Father" Olney in the past, will know that he left behind him many fragrant memories; and he was favoured by having sons who followed in his footsteps, while his grandson, the founder of the Haddon Hall Mission, is one of the benefactors of Bermondsey. In regard to serving tables, was there ever one who excelled in that department more than Mr. W. Murrell, who yearly, during Conference week, superintends the daily feeding of hundreds of ministers, besides having to provide the grand supper, at which from six to eight hundred subscribers to the College Funds sit down?

Deacon Murrell volunteered to see after the gates at the Tabernacle, and some other duties associated with that unenviable office. In all weathers his not by any means slender form might be seen, his coat closely buttoned, and his hands hidden deep down in the recesses of his side pockets. It was difficult to prevent some of the ordinary servants from accepting bribes, but woe to the deluded applicant who, in mistake, offered a gratuity to this counterpart of Bunyan's Mr. Greatheart! Once he was severely provoked by an obstinate man who refused to come out of a seat of which he had taken wrongful possession. At last, being unable to control his temper any longer, Mr. Murrell cried out to the offender, "If you go there I'll EAT you!" putting such a terrible emphasis on the threat that the man looked up, startled if not seriously alarmed.

After the service the gentleman complained to the Pastor that a very big man had threatened to eat him in the gallery. "What now, Murrell—have you been threatening to eat a man?" was subsequently asked of his friend and horse-keeper by Mr. Spurgeon. "Well," replied the deacon, "I did say so; he would not get out of the seat, and I did not know what else to say."

A Summer Festival.

Formerly it was Mr. Spurgeon's custom to hold some outdoor services on the farm of Mr. Abraham, at Minster Lovell, in Oxfordshire. In reference to one of these festivals *The Baptist* remarked:—

"The interest which his visits have awakened is not confined to the immediate locality, for his audience is drawn from the country round within a radius of five-and-twenty miles. The narrow lanes which converge to the centre of attraction can only be compared to the roads which lie between London and Epsom on a Derby Day. The bicycle and the barouche, the perambulator and the postchaise, the two-wheeled tumbril and the four-horse coach, indicate the extremes between which the graduated contrivances for locomotion are pressed into the service of bearing their living freights. Hundreds had to avail themselves of the marrow-bone stage. Some who left home in the early morning to be in time scarcely succeeded in completing the return journey on the same day. That such enthusiasm was manifested to hear the Gospel is an evidence that the clergy have not a spiritual monopoly in perhaps the most ritualistic county in the kingdom.

"The services are held under a clump of trees near the spot where the Ringwood Oak stood for many years as a grand relic of the once famous Wychwood Forest. Very little of the forest now remains, most of the land being under cultivation. Mr. Abraham, who farms some 600 acres, makes a capital host, and to him is due the successful arrangements which make the annual visit of Mr. Spurgeon so pleasant to all concerned. His daughters vie with one another in attending upon the guests, who dine in relays at the well-furnished table of the house, while his sons are very busy in making arrangements for stabling the horses. Little groups were to be seen under the grateful shade of the oaks at luncheon, preparatory to the first service, which was held at half-past two o'clock. The scene is one of the most picturesque conceivable. From the house may be seen, in the valley of the Windrush, the ruins of the castellated mansion of the Lovells, made famous by the tragic incident in the song of 'The Mistletoe Bough.' On the slope of the nearest hill rising above the river is the scattered village founded by Feargus O'Connor for a working man's settlement, every house having its garden capable of yielding sufficient to maintain a moderate family in comfort. In the distance the Chilterns form the sky-line, the White Horse at Wantage and the Farringdon Clump being conspicuous objects.

"When Mr. Spurgeon ascended the waggon to commence the afternoon service, there must have been at least 1,500 people present. The singing was hearty if not highly artistic, and during the prayer the Wesleyan brethren betrayed their presence by the responses which they could not restrain. The preacher was at his best, and the subject chosen, 'I will be as the dew unto Israel,' furnished abundant scope for illustration by metaphors which appealed to the bucolic mind. Tea was provided in a large marquee, and, as the various parties were refreshed, they wandered in companies over the pleasure-grounds which surround the house. It required a very slight effort of the imagination to picture the Feast of Tabernacles, when the faithful assembled to tell of the goodness and mercy of God, and to sing praises unto the Most High. Such an opportunity for Christian intercourse is of incalculable value to those Christians who, in out-of-the-way places, receive but slight help in their combat with sin and labour for the Lord, and many must have returned nerved to fresh resolution, or aroused by a new enthusiasm to witness for Christ in their own sphere of life and service!

"As the time for evening service drew on, Mr. Charlesworth and several of the ministers present extemporised a meeting, the speakers being allowed five minutes each. The crowd, swollen now to upwards of 2,000, settled down to the principal service of the day. The evening was calm, and the westering sun threw around the scene a weird charm, as the lengthening shadows of the trees contrasted with the strangely-blended hues which make a July sunset so beautiful. The air seemed to hold a solemn stillness, and there was nothing to break the spell. We never witnessed an open-air service before when everything so conspired to favour the preacher. At times the deep hush of the rapt audience was literally awe-inspiring. It is no exaggeration to say that a wave of spiritual emotion broke over the assembly, few hearts, if any, being insensible to its influence. From the first sentence in the prayer which commenced the service to the last words of the benediction with which it closed, the preacher had the audience in his grip. Never did he enforce his ministry of reconciliation with more earnest appeals, nor move an audience by more tender pleadings. As the assembly broke up we heard more than one minister excla m, 'We shall hear of this service again.'"

SOME SPECIAL OCCASIONS.

"*Still, a minister, wherever he is, is a minister, and should recollect that he is on duty.* A policeman or a soldier may be off duty, but a minister never is. Even in our recreations we should still pursue the great object of our lives ; for we are called to be diligent in season and out of season. There is no position in which we may be placed but the Lord may come with the question, ' What doest thou here, Elijah ? ' and we ought to be able at once to answer, 'I have something to do for Thee even here, and I am trying to do it.' The bow, of course, must be at times unstrung or else it will lose its elasticity ; but there is no need to cut the string. . . . A minister should be like a certain chamber which I saw at Beaulieu, in the New Forest, in which a cobweb is never seen. It is a large lumber-room, and is never swept ; yet no spider ever defiles it with the emblems of neglect. It is roofed with chestnut, and for some reason, I know not what, spiders will not come near that wood by the year together. The same thing was mentioned to me in the corridors of Winchester school : I was told, ' No spiders ever come here.' Our minds should be equally clear of idle habits."—*Lectures to my Students*, i. 181-2.

VI.

SOME SPECIAL OCCASIONS.

A View from the Deacons' Seats.

THERE are several ways of passing into the Metropolitan Tabernacle; and these are tolerably familiar to country visitors, as well as to knowing Londoners. It is also generally acknowledged that London crowds are dangerous, unless carefully managed by suitable regulations. If a crowd be regularly attracted to one building, and each individual be visibly anxious to secure a good place, not hesitating to use hands and elbows in working towards the front, the specified regulations must include locked gates, as well as carefully-guarded side-entrances, which are only available for ticket-holders. The regular attendant at the Metropolitan Tabernacle has necessarily to have his seat reserved, otherwise he would find himself an unequal competitor with the casual hearer, especially if the said casual hearer happened to be an early riser on Sunday morning. Thus there are three ways of going to hear Mr. Spurgeon. We may be one of the favoured few—few, comparatively, when the irregular hearers number so large a proportion of the weekly congregation—who, as seat-holders, walk directly into the building, while the impatient crowd of the court is kept at bay by doors securely bolted and barred. Secondly, should we not rank among pew-holders, and still feel painfully conscious of not possessing strength, either of muscle or of nerve, to hold our own in the column besieging the entrance, we take care to provide ourselves with an early admission ticket, entitling us to the right of waiting in one of the aisles before the doors are opened. In this position a visitor may very profitably exercise the virtue of patience while occupying a standpoint whence he watches the thousands who comfortably sit at ease in the pews, and calculates as to the chances of securing a seat. Should we, however, belong to neither of the classes described, our ingress into the great building will, perforce, become a more interesting, though, possibly, a less pleasant process. We shall take up our position under the portico " early ; " we shall learn that minutes may be long or short according to the circumstances of the situation.

Then comes relief in a sudden, exciting manner.

A Sunday Morning Scene. 161

Bolts shoot backward, and the apparently electrified crowd, as if in response to a preconcerted signal, move forward *en masse;* for, once inside the chapel, all regulations are summed up in one —First come first served.

On a certain Sabbath morning I dispensed with each of the methods above specified of entering that institution of modern London, the Metropolitan Tabernacle. By special favour I occupied a seat on the platform behind the preacher. These seats are twelve in number, forming a double row. They are padded, are lined with crimson velvet, and have arms somewhat after the manner of a first-class railway carriage. Without question they are luxurious in all their appointments; but then they are for the deacons. A deaconship at the Tabernacle is no sinecure, and the occupiers of these seats are known to be worthy of the accommodation they receive.

Suppose it is half-past ten a.m., or thereabouts, when I am politely ushered into my "deacon's seat," and commence to study the extraordinary scene. It is spring-time—the sun is high in the heavens; but within the building the gas is burning, while the view is partially interrupted by a misty atmosphere in sympathy with the slight fog without doors. The immense area, which, to a stranger, might appear to be already nearly filled, must undergo the process of filling till it is packed. The movements of the people can only be compared with the motion of a swarm of insects, not, however, eager and impatient like the crowd outside; for the new arrivals are merely taking up their regularly-appointed places.

Onward move the great hands of the giant clock overhead, until they point to 10.40, when we witness a transformation scene both lively and extensive. Hitherto the "regulars" and "irregulars" had leisurely entered by side-doors, with the comfortable consciousness of being privileged persons; but now all the main front entrances are opened at once, and in pour the broad living streams, to occupy, to the last inch, the standing-room of what appears to be an already overcrowded building. Look this way or that way, or take a general view, and it will be hard to distinguish between aisles and pews. The new comers are manifestly a little excited in their anxiety to find seats; and yet the bustle is not altogether like any other bustle which is witnessed in public buildings. The coughing, talking, and feet-shuffling produce a compound sound peculiar to the Tabernacle; and this is instantly hushed when Mr. Spurgeon appears on the platform.

When the first word of the service is uttered,

the multitude of faces are all turned in one direction—towards the preacher. Those who occupy seats in proximity to Mr. Spurgeon's table may perhaps have observed that the tones of his voice seem to be nicely adapted to the requirements of those who are near, as well as to those who are farther away. To persons sitting near they are never unpleasantly loud; to those in the remotest corner they are loud enough, while they are never indistinct. Not that so vast a concourse can be addressed, even by a man of the greatest lung-power, without a strong effort, though in this instance the strain is barely observed even by those who listen immediately beneath the clock. As seen from the deacon's standpoint, it is also interesting to note how the leviathan congregation allows itself to be managed. It is subject to certain influences as if it were one great being instead of six thousand atoms. It has its recognised coughing times; by way of acknowledging a touch of humour, it smiles like one vast creature which is particularly sensitive. Then it sings "faster" or "slower," according to directions, and is in all respects most admirably managed.

While reading the concluding verse of "Rock of Ages" the Pastor is visibly affected, just as, a few minutes before, he seemed to catch and diffuse the spirit of "that wonderful Gospel chapter," Isaiah lv. Anon, the quiet earnestness of the sermon seems to extend its influence throughout the entire space of the building, until the rapt attention of the crowd, as they listen to exposition and appeal based on the words, "*Without money and without price,*" is found to kindle feelings akin to actual awe. To handle what are called commonplace or hackneyed texts in a manner strikingly original is the *forte* of a great man; the ability to do this with consummate art is characteristic of the genius of Mr. Spurgeon.

It is very common for preachers who stand up before large assemblies to fix their eye on a particular individual; a spectator who views the scene from the deacons' seats at the Metropolitan Tabernacle is extremely liable to find himself doing the same odd kind of thing. There are "characters" enough in the spacious area, if one can only single them out and read their faces. There sits a man in one of the middle aisles of the area; he is middle-aged, full-faced, and altogether in his *tout ensemble* resembles one who makes some pretension to self-culture. Though he uses no pencil and note-book, his brains are, probably, busily at work taking down what he sees. Let us suppose him to be the representative of some slumberless daily newspaper, which will be sure to place the public in possession of ample information should anything special in the morning's proceedings attract his attention. Single out another, and perhaps you will not be far wide of the mark if you set him down to be a 'cute Yankee editor on the look-out for something piquant about the Britishers wherewith to regale his readers in some obscure corner of the American continent. Do you think it possible you may be mistaken? Look again, and ask yourself if the worthy fellow's features and wearing apparel, when put together, do not spell JONATHAN as completely as can ever be done by eight letters? A fair sprinkling of country pastors are sure to be present. Fix your eye on a Baptist, and he will be found in a genial humour; for when so vast an assembly gathers in a Baptist Chapel he thinks, with some show of reason, that his principles are in the ascendant. Select an Independent, and you will judge from his looks that he has not much to complain about; for, after all, this same preacher has wonderfully stimulated the cause of Nonconformity. Besides these, members of the Establishment, of various grades, must be on a level with the rest of the world, and to accomplish this and complete their education they must needs go to " hear Spurgeon." If the Anglican be an Evangelical, he will be abundantly edified ; he will go away regretting that the Pastor is not Archbishop of Canterbury. Should he side with the Ritualists, he will look pitiful and ill at ease —he may even sit with the scowl of contempt playing about his eyes. Should he be of the Broad school, he will be sufficiently charitable to take things as they come. As I view the spacious area from my velvet-lined deacon's pew, I know that the Tabernacle is a common meeting-ground for all the characters mentioned, as well as for many others who might be included in the category.

But it is now time to confess that when we sit in the deacons' seats we occupy a comfortable pew, but, while doing so, sacrifice much that would be cheaply purchased by a hard bench with a deal back. When heard from behind, Mr. Spurgeon is heard to disadvantage. He is not a preacher who should be listened to with a pillar interrupting the view, nor with closed eyes. His features speak as well as his tongue, and this part of the sermon was almost entirely missed while I kept company with the deacons on the platform. As viewed from the ordinary pews, these portly church officers appear to be **so luxuriously accommodated, and to be in** themselves such models of decorum, that dozens of times have they been envied both on account of their state and their station. Let the truth henceforth be known—that, like men of self-denial, they are content to forego much for the sake of their office.

A word may be added relative to the Weekly Offering collection. The boxes used at the morning service were brought into one of the vestries after the crowd had dispersed. How high a figure the total reached nobody knew, for, as Sunday is a day of rest, the money would not be counted until the following morning. Gold, silver, and copper pieces, together with little packets neatly tied with thread, made up the motley heap. One miniature parcel enclosed fifteen shillings from "A Working Man." When the whole mass was placed in a strong black bag, I ventured to raise it for the sake of testing its weight.

"It's pretty heavy," remarked an affable deacon, who appeared to be the Chancellor of the Exchequer of the establishment.

I anticipated that the parcel would not be found to be a bag of feathers. It was certainly the "heaviest" collection I had ever set eyes upon, for it was as much as one could conveniently raise from the table with one arm.

At a Whitsuntide Festival.

"Are you going with Mr. Spurgeon, sir?" politely asked an active carriage attendant on the departure platform of the Great Eastern Railway terminus in London a few minutes before the starting of the midday Cambridge express-train. The man was evidently a shrewd reader of character, or he would not so happily have hit on the truth at first guess, or have drawn so correct an inference from my mien, appearance, and tourist-bag. I gave the honest fellow an answer in the affirmative, secured a comfortable corner-seat, and in a few minutes the train was travelling at a rapid speed through Tottenham marshes, our destination being Willingham, in Cambridgeshire.

On our arrival at Cambridge soon after one, it is clearly manifest that Mr. Spurgeon is expected, and a railway official acquaints us with the fact that large numbers of persons have gone forward by the early trains. After a brief delay we are again in motion, and this time we are on the Wisbeach branch, and at each small station even the porters are on the *qui vive*. At any rate, one of these worthies, who had probably heard a false rumour that the preacher of the day was not coming, shouted in a kind of suppressed tone of triumph, "There he is!" just as our train drew up alongside the platform. We arrive at Long Stanton shortly after two, from whence we drive to Willingham through a rich flat country, the air having been made delightfully cool by the storms of the day before. Throughout the route numbers of country people, dressed in holiday attire, scrutinise the carriage which carries the Pastor with keen curiosity; while in the village proper a considerable crowd has assembled. Of course business in general is suspended; banners enliven the street; householders appear to be keeping open house, though provision for a thousand, more or less, is served in a farmyard and barn hard by. In a word, the village is *en fête*, and that unanswerable authority, "the oldest inhabitant" of Willingham, is well aware that the doings now in progress surpass everything which has come within the range of his experience.

Willingham is situated in the midst of a purely agricultural district, and is some two miles away from the Long Stanton station. The living is a good one; the parish covers an area of five thousand acres; and in Puritan times, under its godly rector, Mr. Bradshaw, the village was remarkable for its piety. In those days, there were "fourscore-and-ten praying families" resident in the parish; and a portion of these, with

Mr. Bradshaw, the ejected rector, appear to have been the founders of the Nonconformist interest which has flourished in Willingham from that time to this. The place has its pleasant memories, and the Willingham of to-day presents us with some of the most favourable aspects of English village life. It acknowledges no great landowner for its sole lord. Small proprietorships are the rule, and the lords of these, comfortably housed in their villa or cottage freeholds, look as though they knew how to enjoy the privileges of freedom. If an Englishman's house is his castle, there are many lords and castles at Willingham. The gardens in the rear of the houses are not the least extraordinary feature of the village, and they completely verify all I have heard in praise of Cambridgeshire horticulture. The gardens are commonly found to be of great length, and they are usually planted with favourite fruit-bearing trees. I was given to understand that in ground attached to the houses of this small place there are not less than fifty acres of gooseberry-bushes in a luxuriant state of cultivation.

The advertisements announced that Mr. Spurgeon would preach the first of his two sermons at three o'clock; and, as that hour drew near, the people who had hitherto thronged the village street adjourned to an adjacent meadow, there to compose a compact multitude. A spacious marquee had been erected; but, ample as its area may have appeared to the contractors, it was ludicrously small when measured against the space required; and hence to speak from a waggon on the greensward seemed to be the only possible arrangement that could be reasonably made. Having, with considerable difficulty, threaded his way through the throng, the preacher ascended the "pulpit," and found himself in the centre of a sea of upturned faces; and, confessing an inability to speak from the back of his head, he notifies in which direction he will chiefly look. The text is taken from 1 Cor. xv. 10: "By the grace of God I am what I am;" and the sermon, with its fervent delineations and soul-stirring appeals, was admirably adapted to produce a lasting effect on the mixed multitude of hearers. The purport of the sermon was—everybody had some ailment; but Christ was "the mighty doctor of grace."

At the conclusion of this service, the people returned to the village to drink tea, which was not difficult to obtain, as everybody still appeared to be keeping open house, and provision for a hungry multitude was made at the farmstead before mentioned. Mr. Spurgeon and a select number of friends drank tea together in one of the long, secluded gardens for which Willingham is or should be renowned.

At the evening service the sermon was preceded by a characteristic address from Mr. William Olney, one of the most active of the deacons at the Tabernacle. When Mr. Spurgeon again stood forward, he was greeted as before by the upturned faces of persons who still drank in his words with unabated eagerness. The text was taken from the dying words of King David to his son Solomon, "If thou seek Him, He shall be found of thee." All that David said was good; but the last words of such a father to such a son as Solomon were especially solemn.

I. They represented our greatest want--they needed their God.

II. David told Solomon how his great need might be supplied—"If thou seek Him."

Lastly, the text had a finger—*Thou*. The preacher went on to show that while the young had a text all to themselves, the old needed not to be discouraged. Some calculations had been made to show that people are seldom converted after forty-five, and as they grow older the chances that they will ever become partakers of saving grace proportionately diminished. In the opinion of Mr. Spurgeon such notions were as ridiculous as they were unscriptural, and statistics were frequently little else than a means of telling lies by figures.

The evening scene was one to be remembered. Parts of the surrounding district had only lately been visited by storms; but during the delivery of the sermon the peace of a summer evening settled over Willingham. A soft breeze carried the sweet scents of the fresh blossoming country on its bosom; birds were merrily singing in the trees and hedges; while the setting sun on one side of the horizon, and the rising moon on the other side, seemed to be looking each other in the face while they supplied the preacher with materials for illustration. The spectacle was very striking as a scene of rural peace and enjoyment. The powerful voice of Mr. Spurgeon rung out loud and clear, reaching to the utmost limit of the crowd. Individuals representative of various classes of sinners were singled out, reasoned with, and appealed to, the text in each instance being driven home to the heart and conscience—" If thou seek Him, He shall be found of thee."

Thus further proof was given, if that were needed, of the hold which Mr. Spurgeon still retains on every class. I inquired of a Cambridgeshire peasant what he thought of the sermon. " Oh ! " replied the poor fellow, " it was lovely; I wish he had kept on all night."

With the Students.

Probably a good many people who once thought otherwise are coming round to the conclusion that "Spurgeon's students" are an institution called into existence by the requirements of the modern Church. While there will be differences of opinion in regard to the young fellows' general fitness for an arduous calling, the majority of judges will concede that they are men of enterprise, who can battle with difficulties and bear hardship. They have many traits which mark their individuality, and they strive to do credit to the common cause, and to be worthy of their schoolmasters. If you will, you may count these young men too daring, too energetic, or too assuming; but while the field is the world, and the world remains what it is, there will be plenty of others who will think that there is room both for the workers and their singularities. It is well known that there are persons, sensitive and not too charitable, who affect to look down on the Tabernacle collegians as innovators or interlopers, or perhaps even as trespassers, who monopolise spheres which common fairness would reserve for better people. To be criticised is a privilege as well as a penalty; for without critics public men would not know their own weaknesses. As regards the "students" in question, we should in justice remember that a very large percentage of those who settle in London make their own spheres. Another large proportion, who remove to the Colonies and to the United States, cease to be in anybody's way—so far as England is concerned.

Mr. Spurgeon never disguises the fact that the College is his best-beloved Institution. He well knows that his system may have its weak points, but that is only saying it is human. In spite of real or imaginary shortcomings, the College is nurtured as a powerful evangelistic agency. It has even been hinted that he expects, or at least hopes to see, a successor to himself come forth from the classes. Such a genius has not yet arisen; to expect his advent may perhaps savour of enthusiasm. The president is a man of faith; there is time enough yet.

Founded and presided over by so shrewd a judge of human nature and of human motives, this College differs from the ordinary run of theological seminaries. The aim of the tutors is very clearly defined. They do not despise learning, but still wish to turn out preachers rather than scholars, and to accomplish their purpose they cannot complain of any want of material. Every candidate is well aware that he will have to pass a searching examination, and that the aim of the examiners will be to discover his aptitude for work—the quality of the human metal—instead of being guided in their decision by what he already knows. The judges put down piety at a higher value than Greek and Latin ; and they believe that love for mankind is better than a mathematical brain. Come what will, the applicant, if he be a man of common sense, is thoroughly assured that he will be judged on his own merits. He needs no friend at court to advance his interests, the recommendation of his pastor being merely a certificate of character. Nothing can be more unprejudiced than this method of election. Even if it were true, which it is not, that it chiefly attracts the plebeian element, even that would be preferable to being spoken of as a pretentious Nonconformist college reserved almost exclusively for those who can help themselves.

Having survived his probation, the "student" feels that he is a unit in a society which exists to promote the conversion of mankind ; and while his interests are not separate from those of his denomination, he will throughout life retain a feeling of clannishness. It is well that it is so, for his difficulties and discouragements are of no common order. Go whither he will, he must resist the opposition of prejudice—a prejudice founded on the poor fellow's supposed lack of good breeding and early advantages. It is surprising how long and correct peoples' memories are when they have to do with things they might gracefully forget. "Spurgeon's student" is often found to be a suffering victim of this persecuting retentiveness. People remember—and if they do not really know they suspect—that he was originally intended for some trade, that he was actually apprenticed, and that he would even now be working at a bench had he not, through some mischance, found his way into college. They do not stop to ask themselves whether similar things might not apply to numbers of other ministers who have passed through other seminaries. Provided only that a college can boast of a certain kind of prestige, the inmates are looked upon as scholars and gentlemen, who have been directed into their proper avocation. Let us not disparage one class at the expense of another, but give both their due, because neither class can afford to throw stones at the other. In common fairness we are bound to judge of men by their works. The cultured man will find his proper sphere, and between him and the more humble, though perhaps not less useful, evangelist, there need be no rivalry. Ministerial successes should be measured by conversions, not by the literary quality of the sermons preached; and so that men are brought in from the bondage of sin into the liberty of Christ, it is hardly worth while to dispute about the polish of the instruments. Who, on looking at an elegant cabinet, asks if the artificer had five fingers on each hand, if he was legally apprenticed, and if the tools used were those of approved makers? The carving is there, and we give the workman his due. If we look at their work from all sides in this spirit, we shall find that "Spurgeon's students" have more than earned their salt. They have established a large number of new churches; they have reclaimed thousands of people who might never have been hauled in from ruin by the kid-gloved hands of a more "regular" agency. They are trained to endure hardship and toil. In a sense, they are undoubtedly innovators; at times, perhaps, they are somewhat too bold and outspoken; but still some of them have become sufficiently distinguished to rank among the chief apostles of Bristol, Rawdon, or even Regent's Park—those classic retreats for well-to-do aspirants and gentlemen's sons.

The ordinary "Spurgeon's student" has many characteristics which bespeak his training and ruling taste. Perhaps he would be a gainer were he to rub off some of his idiosyncrasies; but such as cling naturally to him are best left alone. With rare exceptions, he never affects the fine gentleman; he does not proclaim his profession through the tailor; with his black tie and felt hat he apparently cultivates a *nonchalance* in dress not readily understood in a fashionable age, when ecclesiastical exquisites need not despair of shining as centre attractions in West End drawing-rooms. Thus it happens that the "student's" friends say he has no sham about him; that he wishes to pass simply for what he is—an evangelist; or if settled, a plain pastor. His severer critics say he is an enthusiast, an imitator of the manners and tones of one man, and that his sermons are declamation. In summing up the evidence of these opposite witnesses, remember that man naturally imitates; that it is well-nigh impossible for classes to come into daily contact with one master mind and not contract a few of his mannerisms. To the young men concerned I would say, Strive against a natural propensity which will provoke ridicule and loss of power. To be peculiar is not necessarily to be weak, though if he try to be peculiar it is a sure sign that the man is naturally a weak man.

What has the College done? According to the last returns, 722 have been educated, and there are 547 of these who still labour as pastors, missionaries, or evangelists. There are twenty-one without pastorates ; forty-seven pastors and seven students have died ; nine are permanently invalided ; while seventy-five names have been removed from the roll, not in all cases "from causes which imply any dishonour," as many are working in other denominations. There are 66,835 members attached to the Churches of the Pastors' College Association.

CHRISTMAS DAY AT THE ORPHANAGE.

The Christmas morning to which particular allusion is now made was hailed by the inmates of the Stockwell Orphanage with all the enthusiasm that had characterised former years ; how, indeed, could it be otherwise, when the day dawned with promises of feasting and merry-making quite after the heart of Young England, who has found a home in that well-known Institution? While the weather was cold, foggy, and muddy, the aspect of the dining-room presented a cheerful contrast to the reigning gloom without. The ample area was decorated with flags, evergreens, and mottoes, until it partially resembled a baronial hall of olden times, and numbers of visitors were found passing a holiday hour in inspecting the preparations. Callers and stragglers, who dine late, and who are desirous of seeing all they can before dinner, may find a sight worth looking at on Christmas Day at Stockwell—something to educate the heart as well as feed the mind; and should they leave a donation behind them, the remembrance of what they have done will make music in their souls when they themselves sit down to the feast. So, at any rate, would good George Herbert have said, and George Herbert was right.

Soon after noon a carriage is heard rattling into the grounds, and this, together with the cheers of the boys, is an intimation that Mr. and Mrs. Spurgeon have arrived. Before dinner is laid on the tables a Board-meeting may have to be held; and while more serious business is in progress, fresh loungers are coming in to show their interest in the arrangements. The kitchen appears to possess extraordinary attractions, and well may this be so; for vast as is the quantity of food to be prepared, the admirable apparatus at the command of the cooks sits easily beneath its burden, and even seems to make light of it.

After some further unavoidable delay, the boys and girls are marshalled, shortly before two, to be marched into their places, when dinner is served. Substantial joints of roast beef follow one another from the kitchen, each fresh arrival being handed over to an amateur carver at a side-table. In the meantime, Mr. Spurgeon reminds the boys of the gratitude they owe to God for sending them friends who, in their kindness of heart, have provided so rich an abundance of good fare. The youngsters quite appreciate their President's remarks, and show that they understand their obligations by the hearty cheers which shake the building, a fair proportion of the noise being made in honour of the gentlemen who presented the boxes of plums and the new shillings. Other cheers follow, for standing in the room are certain tried friends of the Institution who merit the boys' affection, and this is especially true of the President, who is hailed with deafening acclamations as the orphans' best earthly friend. At length the noise is succeeded by a calm; grace is sung. "And now, my boys," says Mr. Spurgeon, "I hope you will heartily enjoy yourselves." The beef, which is the best that the London market can supply, is speedily disposed of; and next comes a procession of plum-puddings borne by a regiment of "old boys," who are now out in the world making headway on their own account. After the puddings have shared the fate of the beef, there succeeds a still greater pleasure—each orphan is allowed to retire, and to carry with him to the playground his box of plums, the sweet orange, and the new shilling.

When well enough to do so, and when in England, it has been Mr. Spurgeon's custom to dine with the working staff of the Orphanage on Christmas Day. The last time that he did so was in 1885, when he was accompanied by Mrs. Spurgeon; and he had then not been since 1881. In the last report of the Institution Mr. Spurgeon thus refers to the work in progress :—

"Let those who have aided us in any manner only look in upon the Institution at Stockwell, and the sight will well repay them. What a beautiful square of buildings! What a noble open space in the centre! Then see the boys and girls. Nobody ever said that they looked miserable: it would be too transparent a falsehood. Did you ever see more happy faces in all the world? These bear no brand of pauperdom and wear no trace of being crushed down by hard workhouse discipline. Many a father has felt that if he were suddenly taken away he could desire no better shelter for his children. One minister expressed that sentiment at one of our meetings, and within two years he had fallen asleep, and two of his boys were with us. These dear children, often the descendants of sickly fathers, are, as a rule, in splendid condition; in fact, the average of health is far above that which is common in the best families. While they are with us they receive a good solid education, and are surrounded with gracious influences; and when they go from us, as a rule, they succeed in life, and become useful and honourable members of society. We have received the highest testimony from practical men as to the result produced by the Stockwell Orphanage training. Thus, instead of pining in poverty, and either dying of want or growing up in ignorance, the children are carefully housed and prayerfully trained, and rise into manhood to be an honour to their homes and a benefit to society. Meanwhile, their widowed mothers have been succoured, delivered from hopeless want, and encouraged to bring up the rest of their charge. Friends, we are partners in a very blessed enterprise. Our Lord approves of it, His people delight in it, and even men of the world have nothing to say against it. This work for orphans is one of the best aids to the Gospel: it stops the mouth of adversaries. It is fit that the preacher of free grace should be able to point to his five hundred fatherless ones, and say, 'See the fruit of the doctrines of grace.' Those who are saved by

Home Life of the Orphans. 185

faith alone are yet zealous to maintain good works. To them also, 'pure religion and undefiled before God and the Father is this, to visit the fatherless and the widows in their affliction, and to keep himself unspotted from the world.'

"Our experience confirms us in the practice of THE SEPARATE HOME SYSTEM. We have not huge wards, nor vast barracks, but houses and families after the fashion of ordinary society. The loss of home and parental influence is a calamity to a child, and the wisest course is to minimise the loss as far as possible by keeping up the family form. Covering an area of nearly four acres, in one of the healthiest suburbs of London, the Orphanage is admirably adapted for its purpose. Each home is complete in itself, and each family has its own 'mother.' The boys dine in one common hall according to families; the girls' meals are all prepared in their respective houses; and it is a rule that both boys and girls assist in all the domestic duties of the establishment. Family worship is conducted in each department morning and evening, and the children learn the text for the day from Mr. Spurgeon's Almanack. The terrace on the left-hand side of the quadrangle, with the schools over the centre block, is designed for two hundred and fifty boys, and the terrace on the right for an equal number of girls. The proof of the pudding is in the eating, and in countless ways the excellence of the home system shows itself to those who observe its working.

"Under our system careful supervision of each child is possible, and the best sanitary, moral, and religious conditions are secured. Though we cannot change human nature, nor make even good children perfect, we can do better for them in family groups than if we had them in great masses, and packed them away in grosses, like steel pens. Individual character comes out better in small groups than in large regiments.

"The Institution is UNSECTARIAN : the question of the denominational connection of the parents has no influence with the Committee in considering an application. No child is prejudiced as a candidate by the creed of his parents. Why should he be? In a matter of pure philanthropy, sectarian preferences should have no weight; although the characters of the parents and their usefulness in the Church of God constitute in some cases a plea for a more speedy reception of their little ones; yet if Christian principles were lacking in the father the child should not be punished on that account; on the contrary, there may be all the greater need that the little one should come under religious training.

"The supreme desire of the Committee of Management is that the children shall be instructed in the truths of our common Christianity, renewed in spirit by the Holy Ghost, and brought up in the nurture and admonition of the Lord. We are more concerned that the children should become disciples of Christ than devotees of a sect; and for this we will both pray and labour. . . .

"The Institution is OPEN TO ALL CLASSES OF THE COMMUNITY. No one section of society has the preference. In considering the claims of an orphan, the station in life occupied by the parents has small influence in the counsels of the Committee.

To secure the admission of a destitute fatherless child, NO PATRONAGE IS REQUIRED, AND NO PURCHASE OF VOTES. The most helpless and deserving are *selected* by a Committee, who give the first place to the greatest need.

"The children are NOT DRESSED IN A UNIFORM to mark them as the recipients of charity. We cannot endure this common piece of folly.

"In the arrangements of the Schools our object is to impart *a plain but thorough* ENGLISH *education*, in order to fit the boys for commercial pursuits. In addition to the ordinary subjects, they are taught elementary science, drawing, shorthand, and vocal music. As the boys attain the age for leaving, little or no difficulty is experienced in finding employers who are willing to receive them. Many of the old boys are now occupying good positions in large houses of business, three of them are pastors of churches, and two have resigned first-rate appointments to labour in connection with the Salvation Army. It is a joy to us to know that many others are engaged in works of usefulness, while a far larger number are members of the Christian Church.

"For the girls a plain solid education is attempted in the Schools, and thorough domestic training in the Homes. The Trustees will be glad to give special training where there are special capacities, and as openings occur for female talent they will be glad to have girls able to enter them. The special vocation of the girls must be left to their friends to determine on leaving: our usual plan is to ensure that, as far as possible, they shall be thoroughly fitted for domestic service in good families; but we are anxious to be guided by the providence of God, and the opportunities which offer themselves. No doubt the better the education, if it be of a really practical kind, the better is the child's chance in life."

SUMMARY OF ADMISSIONS.

London	717
Country	358
Wales	17
Scotland	1
Ireland	2
Isle of Wight	4

Total 1,099.

PARENTAGE OF THE CHILDREN:—

Mechanics	261
Shopkeepers and Salesmen	171
Manufacturers and Tradesmen	161
Labourers, Porters, and Carmen	159
Warehousemen and Clerks	117
Mariners and Watermen	38
Ministers and Missionaries	33
Commercial Travellers	21
Farmers and Florists	21
Railway Employés	19
Cab Proprietors and Coachmen	18
Schoolmasters and Teachers	17
Policemen and Custom House Officers	13
Commission Agents	11
Accountants	11
Postmen and Sorters	8
Surgeons and Dentists	6
Journalists	5
Solicitors	4
Soldiers	2
Fireman	1
Architect	1
Gentleman	1

Total 1,099.

RELIGIOUS PROFESSION OF PARENTS.

Church of England	429
Baptist	264
Congregational	121
Wesleyan	101
Presbyterian	22
Roman Catholic	3
Brethren	4
Moravian	1
Bible Christian	2
Society of Friends	1
Not specified	151

Total 1,099.

The head master is the Rev. V. J. Charlesworth, and the working staff have all along, by their efficiency and sympathy, earned the often-expressed gratitude of the President.

THE COLPORTEURS.

The Colportage Association is also an evangelistic agency the influence of which extends into many of the most out-of-the-way corners of the country. When health permitted it has been usual for Mr. Spurgeon to address the men, many of whom visit London in May of each year. The agents are hard-working fellows, and besides selling books, they visit the people in their houses, and even preach the Gospel in places where otherwise the Gospel would hardly be heard.

There are now seventy-six agents employed, and seven book agents; and in the last year these sold pure literature to the amount of £9,525, representing a distribution of 457,527 Bibles and books, besides 320,504 periodicals. Mr. Spurgeon, in common with all who are acquainted with it, are of opinion that this work should be extended, and that Christian people should manifest more interest in the colporteurs' operations. Certainly, its importance is second to no other Christian work, and in proportion as the good done is understood and appreciated, people will extend to such a genuine Home Mission their cordial support.

On the last occasion that he addressed the men in May, 1885, Mr. Spurgeon remarked that while there were old faces present that he was glad to see again, there were also some new hands, to all of whom he wished prosperity. It was hoped that the first would not become weary, and that the younger men would find themselves in happy spheres. Though many had found it otherwise, the past year had been a good time for colporteurs: the sales had not declined, and the higher success achieved had encouraged them all. Though he was not going to preach on the text "Sell the books," that was the first thing a colporteur had to do. They might be good men in other respects, but they did not excel as colporteurs if they did not push the sales. It was just the same with students in the college; they had first of all to be good preachers. Thus the main object of their calling must not be missed. Yankee book-agents had the reputation of being terrible fellows: they would never leave a house without an order, even though it might be an order to get off the premises; and one of the fraternity was said to have so much "cheek," that when struck by lightning in the face—his strongest point—the fluid glanced off to kill an animal some yards away. In a sense, this "cheek" was a good thing, although they would not do much without perseverance. They wanted men to sell books to people who thought that they did not want to buy them. They had no reason to be ashamed of their wares, which were good to sell and good to buy. It was then shown that a colporteur would be judged of in a district by his usefulness. As they loved their Master, therefore, let them abound in all good works to His glory, forasmuch as their labour was not in vain in the Lord.

The Rev. W. Corden Jones, at the Depository, Temple Street, Newington, S.E., supplies all particulars on application.

TWO THOUSAND PRINTED SERMONS.

"Our ministry is a testimony that no new theology is needed to stir the masses and save souls; we defy all the negative theologians in England to give such proof of their ministry as we can. If we must be fools in glorying, we do, we must boast that the old doctrines are victorious, and that the Lord, the Spirit, has most signally honoured them. We do not cite the overwhelming and ever increasing multitudes who listen to us, as a proof in this matter, but, we do and will glory, in the power of the Gospel, in that it has brought so many to the cross of Christ, and raised so many from the dunghill. In every place where the old Gospel has been proclaimed it has had its trophies from the worst of men, and we are no exceptions to the rule. The slain of the Lord have been many. His arrows have found out the hearts of His enemies; many have been overthrown by His Spirit, and have been ultimately brought to find life and healing in the blood of Jesus. The best evidences of the truth of our holy religion, are to be found in the marvellous effects it produces. Drunkards, harlots, swearers, thieves, liars, and such like, when reclaimed and regenerated, are the jewels in the crown of the truth; of such we must say in confidence, 'What hath God wrought?'"—*Preface to Vol. II. of The New Park Street Pulpit.*

VII.

TWO THOUSAND PRINTED SERMONS.

CONCERNING their weekly publication, and concerning individual sermons, many remarkable things are told. Some on special topics have commanded a very extensive sale, the one on Baptismal Regeneration leading the way. When this was first published, it was feared that the circulation would be disastrously affected, but the number of subscribers actually increased.

The history of these sermons would constitute a unique chapter in the annals of the church. Some years ago, an ardent admirer of Mr. Spurgeon gave away, at his own charge, a quarter of a million copies. He had volumes elegantly bound for presentation to the crowned heads of Europe. He also had books, containing a dozen in each, sent to every member of both Houses of Parliament, and to all the students of Oxford and Cambridge. More singular still was their circulation " as advertisements in the Australian papers; one gentleman spending week by week a sum which we scarcely dare to mention, lest it should not be believed." In a sense, Mr. Spurgeon is a preacher to the whole Protestant world ; and if any doubt this remarkable fact, let them note what he himself says about the general diffusion of these pulpit discourses :—

" In America the sale of the edition published there was extremely large, and I believe that it still continues ; but dozens of religious papers appropriate the sermons bodily, and, therefore, it is quite impossible to say where they go, or, rather, where they do not go. Of translations, the Dutch have been most plentiful, making large volumes. An edition of two volumes of selected sermons has been circulated in the colony of the Cape of Good Hope, among the Dutch settlers of that region. In German there are three noble volumes, besides many smaller ones. German publishers, with the exception of Mr. Oncken, of Hamburg, seldom have the courtesy to send the author a copy ; and I have picked up in divers places sermons bearing date from Baden, Basle, Carlsruhe, Ludwigsburg, and so on. How many, therefore, may have been sold in Germany I am unable to compute. In French several neat volumes have appeared ; in Welsh and Italian one volume each. In Sweden a handsome edition in four volumes has been largely circulated, and the translator informed me of the conversion of some of noble and even royal birth through their perusal. Besides these, there are single sermons in Spanish, Gaelic, Danish, Russ, Maori, Telugu, and some other tongues, and permission has been sought and gladly given for the production of a volume in the language of Hungary."

Did literature represent his sole profession, the fruits of Mr. Spurgeon's pen could not be expected to be more abundant than they are, even though the sermons be left out of the category. Authorship is to him a pleasure as well as a duty; and he evidently values literary power as a sacred trust to be accounted for hereafter.

At the present date Mr. Spurgeon has published not far short of two thousand separate sermons in the regular weekly series, besides hundreds of others, so that the position he occupies as a popular preacher is not only extraordinary, but absolutely unique. There are volumes of sermons which have commanded, and still continue to command, a large sale; there is not, however, another instance on record of a pastor's utterances attracting tens of thousands of purchasers through a third of a century. If we examine the quality of the earliest numbers of the series we shall see abundant reason for their instant popularity. By many, whose judgment is worthy of respect, these earliest productions are thought to be quite equal to anything which has followed. The glow of sanctified genius is on every page; and the volumes are pervaded by the warm zeal and freshness of youth which are irresistible. Indeed, I have been told by a gentleman who heard the Pastor of the Tabernacle on the first day of his preaching in London, and who hears him still, that Mr. Spurgeon has never improved, nor has he ever grown in the sense that others grow—he was sent forth complete at first, just as Minerva was never a child, but sprang at once fully armed from the head of Jupiter. Though not prepared to acquiesce in such a judgment without some qualification, I think it is well to record it as a characteristic of a prevalent opinion. The pastor of a Nonconformist church might also be quoted, who considers that the earlier sermons are even superior to those of to-day.

Hence there was every prospect of the undertaking proving a commercial success when Mr. Joseph Passmore, at the close of the year 1854, proposed to the Pastor that a discourse should be issued regularly every week; for long prior to his preaching days the idea had come uninvited into the mind of Mr. Spurgeon himself, that he would

" one day preach sermons which would be printed."
It would appear that some time elapsed before the preacher even thoroughly believed in his own popularity. The sermons had sold in an unparalleled manner as occasional publications; but when a shrewd, far-seeing publisher asked if the publication should be advanced into a weekly institution, the answer in the affirmative was given " with much fear and trembling."

In the preface to the first volume of the published discourses, dated January 1856, the remark occurs : " Little can be said in praise of these sermons, and nothing can be said against them more bitter than has been already spoken." The author also declares that he is " invulnerable either to criticism or abuse." The admission is then conceded that a departure has been ventured on " from the usual mode of preaching." An answer is also given to the question, What is Calvinism ? It is not a slavish adherence to the views of one man ; the word is rather a brief and convenient one to express " that salvation is by grace alone." There are things in the book which may provoke a smile, but what of them ? The preacher " is not quite sure about a smile being a sin, and, at any rate, he thinks it less crime to cause a momentary laughter than a half hour's profound slumber."

A little more than a year after Mr. Spurgeon's settlement at New Park Street a scheme was set on foot for the enlargement of the chapel, which was ultimately carried out at a cost of £2,000. On the last Sabbath of January 1855 a collection was made for this object. The text was, "Thou hast made us unto our God kings and priests." The inferences at the close were, "I am king, I will give as a king giveth unto a king." A priest, if he sacrificed, was not to give a maimed lamb or a blemished bullock. "Excuse my pressing this subject," the preacher continued. "I want to get this chapel enlarged; we are all agreed about it; we are all rowing in one boat. I have set my mind on £50, and I must and will have it to-day if possible. I hope you won't disappoint me." As a result of this appeal the people at once placed £50 in the plates held at the doors, and elevenpence halfpenny over.

On the 8th of July, 1855, while preaching at New Park Street from the words of the Psalmist, "He shall choose our inheritance for us," Mr. Spurgeon referred to the delights of hearing a sermon, which had for so long been denied to himself. He sometimes felt that he should occasionally like to sit down to the feast in God's house, and not always be a serving-man. "I am sure I should be glad to hear a sermon; it is a long time since I heard one; but when I do attend one it always tires me—I want to be improving on it." His sermons were now being published regularly; he was preaching incessantly in the week, so that the opportunities for hearing were necessarily almost *nil*. At this time he had not long completed his twentieth year.

According to his own confession, however, Mr. Spurgeon this year saw and heard something striking at Bristol. After coming away from George Müller's Orphan House, he said, "I never heard such a sermon in my life as I saw there." When asked to address the children, he replied, "I could not speak a word for the life of me." He then received a lesson touching the power of faith which bore abundant fruit; and in connection with this theme we have some first hints respecting the Metropolitan Tabernacle. "I sometimes think we will try the power of faith here," he told his people on the first Sabbath evening in November, "and see if we could not get sufficient funds whereby to erect a place to hold the people that crowd to hear the Word of God. We may have a tabernacle of faith as well as an orphan-house of faith."

The first volume of the sermons was reprinted in America, and at once attained a circulation of twenty thousand copies. This year, 1855, the second of his ministry in London, he called "a year of miracles" in a sermon preached on December 30th; and among other causes for gratitude was the fact that two hundred and ten persons were added to the church, while others were coming in.

On the 6th of January, 1856, at New Park Street, he referred to his conversion, which had taken place exactly six years previously, and at that hour of the day. "Seeking rest and finding none," he said, "I stepped within the house of God, and sat there, afraid to look upward, lest I should be utterly cut off, and lest His fierce wrath should consume me. The minister rose in his pulpit, and as I have done this morning, read this text—'Look unto me, and be ye saved, all the ends of the earth; for I am God, and there is none else.' I looked that moment; the grace of faith was vouchsafed to me in the selfsame instant." *

Shortly after, or on the 10th of February, he preached on behalf of the Baptist Fund, an institution founded in London for the relief of poor ministers in 1717. Some of the illustrations of poverty were as sad as they were striking. Some ministers, when they ascended the pulpit stairs,

---

* As remarked elsewhere, the pulpit in which this sermon was preached is to be seen at the Stockwell Orphanage.

had to be careful lest they tore their worn-out coats. The case of a preacher without means was also mentioned, a man who walked twenty miles and preached two sermons, and received from the deacons a shilling for his services. Another walked eight miles, found no one to give him a dinner, preached three sermons, and was rewarded with half-a-crown. The claims of the Baptist Fund were strongly advocated.

On the first Sabbath of the November following, Mr. Spurgeon preached at New Park Street for the first time after the fatal accident at the Surrey Gardens. He said that he almost regretted having undertaken to preach, scarcely feeling equal to the task. The text was Philippians ii. 9-11: "Wherefore God hath highly exalted him, and given him a name which is above every name, etc.

This text, and the occasion of its being chosen, became more than ever interesting when we are further acquainted with the circumstances of the case. Thus at the Pastors' College Conference, held in April 1879, he mentioned a fact in connection with the accident at the Surrey Gardens Music-Hall which is not generally known. He said that the effect on his mind was such that he was nearly imbecile for a fortnight. The newspapers wrote as though he were responsible for the death of the unfortunate people, and the slanders were almost more than he could bear. Such, too, was the agitation of his mind, joined to the assaults of Satan, that he seemed to lose the desire for prayer and for reading the Scriptures. He went away into the country; and he related how relief came in an instant while walking in the garden of the house where he was staying. The words, "God hath given him a name," etc., flashed into his mind, and he seeing at once that all must be right, whatever the enemy might suggest, his joy was immediately as unspeakably great as his grief had previously been. He even went down on his knees on the gravel to give thanks.

After a storm of trial and persecution, the preface to the volume of sermons for 1857 strikes a more cheerful note. The preacher speaks of the winter being past and the spring-time of renewed vigour and peace having come. "The congregations during the year have been immense and enthusiastic," he says. "Our church meetings have been joyous occasions, for we have heard marvellous stories of profligates reclaimed, drunkards converted, and desponding souls delivered." He now realised that in the hands of God he was far more than the mere pastor of a church; he seems to have felt that he was an evangelist raised up for a special work. Hence "the sermons preached at the music-hall are intended to arrest the attention of the careless, and alarm the consciences of the hardened. The reader will not, therefore, find in them that fulness and depth of doctrine which he may desire." It may be noted that on the 7th of October in this year Mr. Spurgeon preached at the Crystal Palace, Sydenham, to a congregation of twenty-four thousand people, the occasion "being the day appointed by Proclamation for a Solemn Fast, Humiliation, and Prayer before Almighty God : in order to obtain Pardon of our Sins, and for imploring His Blessing and Assistance on our Arms for the Restoration of Tranquillity in India."

The flow of success continued throughout the year 1858. The best results continued to arise from the reading of the sermons. "In lonely places there are churches of Christ whose only ministry is found in these pages, save when a passing evangelist is led to open his mouth among them," we are told. In rooms in the crowded haunts of poverty these are read to hundreds who could scarcely understand any language more refined ; while at races and fairs, and even at pilgrimages of the Romish church, these have been used by earnest brethren as a means of obtaining an audience in the open air." During this year the circulation of the sermons at home and abroad was more than sustained. No less than a hundred and fifty thousand volumes had already been sold in the United States; in Australia more than one edition was printed, while translations appeared in several of the European languages, besides one in Welsh. In the meantime the weekly issue in London was as popular as ever.

Two providential deliverances occurred this year, which many will still remember. On Wednesday, the 7th of April, Mr. Spurgeon preached at Halifax, when, in consequence of a fall of snow and severe wintry weather, he did not anticipate meeting a very extensive congregation. A temporary building was erected, however, and from five to six thousand persons were found assembled. In the afternoon all went well; but in the evening a gallery planned to hold two thousand people suddenly gave way after the service, when two persons were injured. "Now had this happened any earlier, not only must many have been injured," said Mr. Spurgeon to his congregation at the Surrey Gardens, "but there are a thousand chances to one, as we say, that a panic must necessarily have ensued, similar to that which we still remember and deplore as having occurred in this place. Had such a thing occurred, and had I been the unhappy preacher on the occasion, I feel certain that I should never have been able to occupy the pulpit again. Such was the effect of the first calamity that I marvel that I ever survived."

Six months later, or on the morning of October 10th, he appeared at the great music-hall, after having experienced in the week "excruciating pain and continual sickness." After this he was laid aside, and the next published number of the weekly sermon was one preached at Exeter Hall more than two years before. Though so old, the preacher prayed that the utterances might " bud afresh and bring forth fruit, even as old corn, after having been entombed in Egyptian sepulchres for centuries, will often germinate again and yield an abundant crop." For three weeks the issue of old sermons continued, and a letter from the Pastor appears in each. In one he refers to the timbers in his frail barque having been made to creak; in another he speaks of the memorable panic of two years before. On the 7th of November he again occupied the pulpit.

In the course of the year 1859 several sermons were preached which were made wonderfully useful in awakening the careless. They continued to command a very extensive sale in America, and not only in a separate form but in the newspapers. Thus "in the midst of a mass of frivolity and romance the weekly sermon stands like an ambassador in bonds, hopeful, nevertheless, that its free voice may overcome the discordant cries which try to drown its utterance."

On the 13th of March in this year, at the Surrey Gardens, Mr. Spurgeon referred to the opening of his ministry, and again preached from his first text: "It is about eight years since, as a lad of sixteen, I stood up for the first time in my life to preach the Gospel in a cottage to a handful of poor people who had come together for worship. I felt my own inability to preach, but I ventured to take this text, 'Unto you therefore which believe, He is precious.'"

Nos. 268, 269, and 270 of *The New Park Street Pulpit* are filled with an account of "the ceremony of laying the first stone of the new Tabernacle," which ceremony was performed by Sir S. M. Peto on the 16th of August. Many honoured brethren who graced that occasion by their presence have since gone home to heaven. There were two meetings, one on the ground in the afternoon, and one at Rea's Repository in the evening. "In the bottle which is to be placed under the stone we have put no money," remarked the Pastor, "for one good reason—we have none to spare. We have not put newspapers, because, albeit we admire and love the liberty of the press, yet that is not so immediately concerned in this edifice. The articles placed under the stone are simply these: the Bible, the Word of God—we put that as the foundation of the church. Upon this rock doth Christ build the ministration of His truth. We know of nothing else as our standard. Together with this we have put the old Baptist Confession of Faith which was signed in the olden times by Benjamin Keach, whose name is in this book. We put also the *declaration of the deacons*, which you have just heard read, printed on parchment. There is also an edition of Dr. Rippon's Hymn-Book printed just before he died; and then, in the last place, there is a programme of this day's proceedings."

One of the speakers present at the evening meeting was Judge Payne, who, as a matter of course, composed a tailpiece, besides indulging in some sensible wit. "Now what does C. H. S. mean?" he asked, glancing at one of the decorations. "Why, it means, first, Charles Haddon Spurgeon; but *I* do not mean that. C. H. S. means a *Clear Headed Speaker*, who is *Clever* at *Handling Subjects* in a *Cheerful Hearted Style*. He is a *Captain* of the *Hosts* of *Surrey;* he is a *Cold Hating Spirit;* he has *Chapel Heating Skill;* he is a *Catholic Humbug Smasher;* he is a *Care-Hushing Soother;* he is a *Child Helping*

Strengthener; he is a *Christ Honouring Soldier;* and he is *Christ's Honoured Servant."*

At this meeting one of the most interesting speeches of the evening was made by the Pastor's father, the Rev. John Spurgeon, who also gave some reminiscences of his son's youthful days given elsewhere.

In 1860 Mr. Spurgeon felt the pressure of having to sustain a weekly publication. " No man can well conceive what a drain it is upon a preacher to have his sermons constantly printed," he remarked ; "he can scarcely hope to avoid repetition, and will be constantly in danger of running dry." Having preached for the last time at the Surrey Gardens on the 11th of December, 1859, he adds, " This sixth year saw us sorrowfully removing from the Surrey Music-Hall to a far less convenient spot." Individual sermons are mentioned which had been abundantly useful in the conversion of sinners, while the translation of the discourses into Swedish had very greatly increased the circulation.

The morning service was now conducted in Exeter Hall until the 3rd of June, when Mr. Spurgeon departed for the Continent on a brief tour. During his absence several sermons preached at New Park Street on Sabbath evenings appeared in the weekly issue. He appeared again at

Opening of the Tabernacle.

Exeter Hall on the 29th of July; and on Tuesday, the 21st of August, gave an account of his continental tour to a large audience in the unfinished Tabernacle.

The year 1861 saw the presentation made of two hundred thousand copies of the Sermons to the Universities of Oxford and Cambridge. The discourses still continued to be published in numbers of American newspapers, while they were read from village pulpits in our own country. This was the year of the opening of the Tabernacle, and the preliminary services extended through a month. The first prayer-meeting was held at seven o'clock a.m., on Monday, the 18th of March; and on the afternoon of the Monday following Mr. Spurgeon preached his first sermon in the building, the text being Acts v. 42: "And daily in the temple, and in every house, they ceased not to teach and to preach Jesus Christ." In the volume of sermons for this year there are three which are not by Mr. Spurgeon, the preachers having been Messrs. Brock, Stowell Brown, and Octavius Winslow. On the afternoon and in the evening of April 11th, meetings were held for the Exposition of the Doctrines of Grace. After an introductory address by Mr. Spurgeon the following subjects were very ably handled by successive speakers. *Election:* Mr. J. Bloomfield.

Human Depravity: Mr. Evan Probert. *Particular Redemption:* Mr. J. A. Spurgeon. *Effectual Calling:* Mr. James Smith. *The Final Preservation of the Saints:* Mr. W. O'Neill. On the following evening Mr. Henry Vincent gave an oration in the chapel on *Nonconformity*, and this also appears in the volume of sermons.

In 1862 a friend scattered " a large number of sermons in the colleges and towns of Ireland. Working with great discretion, he sowed the seed so rapidly in each place that, before the foul bird, the Popish priest, could hasten to stop him, the work was done."

On the 30th of January Mr. Spurgeon preached on the Hartley Colliery Accident, from the words of Job. xiv. 14, "If a man die, shall he live again?" The evening was wet and cold; but the people nevertheless mustered in force, and the sum of £120 was collected for the relief fund. On the 9th of November he also preached on behalf of the distress in Lancashire.

In consequence of the abolition of the duty on paper, the sermons commenced appearing in large type in the opening of 1862. The last of the small type series has a mourning border, having been preached on the occasion of the death of the good Prince Consort.

During the year 1863 a mention is made of

the friends who send texts for the Pastor to handle. "This we cannot engage to do," he says. " Our habit has been to look to the Lord for our guidance, and when a text comes with power to our soul we preach from it without hesitation; but as we dare not select our own themes, so neither can we receive those suggested to us, unless our Master sends them upon our heart."

The following year was the era of the great Baptismal Regeneration controversy, and the fact is mentioned that at the close of the year the sermons on the question of baptism had reached a circulation of 300,000. The principal discourse was preached on the 5th of June; and the controversy awakened may still be estimated by the scores of pamphlets which were published on both sides. Before this storm had subsided the Pastor dropped " The Reverend " as a ministerial title. It appears for the last time on the sermon number 587, and preached on August 28th. In the following week, and ever since, the name is printed simply, C. H. Spurgeon.

In the preface to the Sermons for 1865 it is said that the " weekly circulation has during the past year been fully maintained," " while proofs of usefulness are as numerous and encouraging as ever." With January of this year commenced *The Sword and the Trowel*, which at once did great service to the cause nearest the Editor's heart. Towards the end of the year there appeared a notice of a bazaar to be held in the Tabernacle, the proceeds to be devoted to the work of chapel building in London. "From the success already achieved," said Mr. Spurgeon, "I am encouraged to attempt yet greater things, and to seek the erection, during the year 1866, of several new buildings." Just at this time a pamphlet, which has long since been forgotten, occasioned the Pastor some annoyance. He was compelled to give notice that he had not written the *brochure*, and that he was shocked at the manner in which a professed minister of the Gospel had employed his name to give weight to prophecies which were ridiculous ravings.

With the close of his twelfth volume in 1866 the preacher rejoiced in the thought that he was still teaching the same Old Gospel with which he had commenced. "Our twelve volumes, like the sons of Jacob, can say, 'we are all one man's sons, we are true men.' In fundamentals we remain like the oak, rooted to the same soil, although in circumstantials here and there a branch spreads itself otherwise than it did ten years ago. Growth there should be, but not wanton change." Now we begin to see the first notice of the Colportage Association. Persons disposed to aid the new scheme were reminded of the " sellers of trinkets," who ages ago on the Continent carried the Bible in their packs as " the best of jewels " ; and of the pedlars who in the seventeenth century carried the best books of the Puritans throughout England. It was at this time also that Mr. Spurgeon appeared for the first time among the Quakers. " Our belief was, and still is," he said, " that it is the bounden duty of the Society of Friends in these perilous times to renew more distinctly their testimony against formalism, ritualism, and unspiritual worship in its many forms, and we hoped that a respectful brotherly admonition might be accepted by them and owned of God." On the 6th of November he addressed a gathering of twelve hundred Friends at their head-quarters in Bishopsgate, feeling at the time much physical pain, and weighed down with a sense of responsibility.

After six years' wear and tear, the Tabernacle was renovated in the spring of 1867, and Mr. Spurgeon preached to vast congregations in the Islington Agricultural Hall, on five consecutive Sabbath mornings. The volume of sermons for 1867 was the last which contained a preface ; and as the succeeding volumes come more within the recollection of readers than those noticed, there is no need to continue these jottings. The circulation is still maintained, and the crowds attracted to the Tabernacle show no signs of diminution. As Mr. Spurgeon is only fifty-two, it may be supposed that, according to the ordinary course of nature, he has much of the best part of life before him. Let friends far and near unite to pray that physical strength may be granted to the preacher who has been chosen of God for the accomplishment of great things, and whose enforced inactivity is a real loss to the church.

*THE PREACHER'S REWARD—ANECDOTES
ABOUT THE SERMONS.*

"What is the crown of a church? Well, some churches have one crown, and some another. I have heard of a church whose crown was its organ—the biggest organ, the finest organ ever played, and the choir the most wonderful choir that ever was. Everybody in the district said, ' Now if you want to go to a place where you will have fine music that is the spot.' Our musical friends may wear that crown if they please. I will never pluck at it or decry it ; I feel no temptation in that direction. I have heard of others whose crown has been the intellect. There are very few people indeed, not as many people by one-tenth as there are sittings, but then they are such a select people, the *élite*, the thoughtful and intelligent! The ministry is such that only one in a hundred can possibly understand what is said, and the one in the hundred who does understand it, is therefore a most remarkable person. That is their crown. Again I say I will not filch it. Whatever there may be that is desirable about it, the brother who wears it, shall wear it all his days for me. I have heard of other crowns ; amongst the rest, that of being 'a most respectable church.' All the people are respectable. The minister of course is respectable. I believe he is ' Reverend,' or, ' Very Reverend,' and everybody and thing about him is to the last degree 'respectable.' Fustian jackets and cotton gowns are warned off by the surpassing dignity of everything in and around the place. As for a working man, such a creature is never seen on the premises, and could not be supposed to be ; and if he were to come he would say, ' The preacher preaches double Dutch or Greek, or something of the sort ; he would not hear language he could understand. This is not a very brilliant crown—this crown of respectability : it certainly never flashed ambition into my soul. But our crown under God has been this,—the poor have the Gospel preached unto them, souls are saved, and Christ is glorified."—*Memorial of Silver Wedding Testimonial*, pp. 23, 24.

VIII.

THE PREACHER'S REWARD—ANECDOTES ABOUT THE SERMONS.

ONE of the peculiarities of the preaching of Whitefield was the large number of persons who would be convicted of sin under one sermon; but in the case of Mr. Spurgeon we have to take into account the world-wide audience which, through the printed sermons, he is always addressing. With his matchless voice, the great preacher of the last century may have been able to deliver his message to some twenty or thirty thousand persons; but that was a small number indeed when compared with the hundreds of thousands in the Old and the New World, and at the antipodes, who, as may be said, make up Mr. Spurgeon's regular congregation. Then, in addition to the English-speaking race, the sermons are also being read in many foreign languages into which they have been translated. The position occupied by the preacher is thus quite unique, nothing like it ever having been known before. During some years past instances of usefulness of the printed sermons, under the head of "Personal Notes," have appeared in *The Sword and the Trowel*, and from these we borrow our illustrations for the present chapter.

We suppose that the examples of enemies tamed have been many; but one striking instance of this kind was that of a gentleman who was greatly prejudiced against Mr. Spurgeon, and dissenters generally, until he visited the Metropolitan Tabernacle, which visit was brought about in a somewhat remarkable manner. "Some time after my conversion I came to London," says the son of this gentleman. "A few weeks later my father was up for a few days, and wishing to see me, I proposed Sunday morning as my only convenient time, and the Metropolitan Tabernacle as a midway meeting-place. I so arranged that we met there just as the crowds were flocking into the building. As I guessed would be the case, seeing such crowds pressing in, my father could not resist the temptation to follow." The result was that he was greatly affected by the sermon—" Deep calleth unto deep," No. 865—and from being an enemy of the preacher the astonished hearer was changed into one of Mr. Spurgeon's most steadfast friends. "I am thankful to testify," added his son, "that what light and peace he had came through the Metropolitan Tabernacle sermons."

On one occasion a thank-offering of £5, which came to the College funds, is connected with the welcome story of the conversion of a prodigal. The father of the young man in question derived some consolation from a sermon by Mr. Spurgeon on the Prodigal Son, and he sent a request that the youth might be prayed for at the ordinary Monday evening prayer-meeting. The prayer was answered, the young man became a changed character; and the joy of the father found vent in the giving of the thank-offering mentioned.

Probably it is a great joy to the Pastor to know that his discourses are frequently a source of great joy to the very poor among his flock. A friend who visits in a certain village of Middlesex tells of an old needlewoman who could not attend public worship regularly. At the best she was not able to earn more than a sorry pittance; but nevertheless, when on a Saturday night she would find herself with no more than threepence to last until Monday, she would still spare a penny for the weekly sermon, after buying what bread and tea she could obtain for twopence. What kind of satisfaction she found in the perusal of the weekly numbers was seen in her confession, to the effect that when she got into the cream of the sermon she would not change places with the Queen herself. She was often so interested that she would even forget to eat her bread; but at the same time her solicitude for others was so great, that when the numbers accumulated she went abroad to distribute them, so that others might share the blessing with herself.

When the Hants Congregational Union met at Bournemouth in 1881, a deacon who was present enlivened the proceedings by narrating the following: "About seven years since a poor woman had saved up a few pounds of money and was going into the town of Christchurch to purchase some things. By some means she lost her purse, which contained a five-pound note, one pound in gold, and some fourteen shillings in silver. She was much distressed at her loss, and had some hand-bills circulated offering a reward for the restoration of her property. A person found the purse and appropriated the whole of its contents, and nothing has been heard of the affair until a fortnight since, when a gentleman went to the printer of the handbill and asked if he could remember the incident. On looking over his file he saw the bill, and the whole of the circumstances came to his mind. The gentleman then said, 'You must ask me no questions, but the purse will be restored.' A few days afterwards the identical purse, with the amount of money lost, and £3 for interest, was sent to the rightful owner. *The cause which brought this about was reading Spurgeon's Sermons."*

There was a youth who died in 1881 who had always been an invalid; and who just before his death settled his little money accounts, apportioning £40 to Mr. Spurgeon's work. " As you will suppose," wrote a relative to the Pastor in September 1881, " he has been for some time taking an interest in your work for Christ, and one of the greatest enjoyments of his life was the hearing you preach one Sunday last spring. He has read your sermons, etc., for a long time, and distributed them among our poor neighbours. His life has been one of much suffering, chiefly from asthma; but now consumption is carrying him off, and he is lying in the most peaceful, tranquil state, waiting the Master's call." The sufferer said he should value a word from Mr. Spurgeon; but although the Pastor wrote by return of post his interesting correspondent died before the letter could reach him.

Among the converts from Ritualism a case occurred of a young man who yielded to the seductions of that Romanising sect after he had been educated as a nonconformist. He became a thorough Anglican, he even went to confession to his vicar; but when disease set in and showed him that he must shortly leave the present world, he found that the specious doctrines of his new friends would not do, and probably he had never very sincerely believed in them. Of course he had heard of Mr. Spurgeon; and having expressed a desire to see some of his works, the wish was very readily complied with, and the invalid then found what he wanted. A Christian friend also conversed with him, until at last the young man showed the possession of a triumphant faith, and so he died.

A friend who happened to be travelling through Nottingham was asked to visit a dying woman at a public-house; but instead of wanting any instruction or consolation, the woman was found to be rejoicing in Christ; and on being asked how she had found such peace, she showed a piece of torn newspaper containing a passage from one of Mr. Spurgeon's Sermons, and which had come with a parcel from Australia. "Talk about the hidden life of the good seed!" remarked the friend referred to. "Think of that sermon preached in London, conveyed to America, an extract reprinted in a newspaper there, that paper sent to Australia, part then torn off (as we should say accidentally), the parcel dispatched to

England, and, after all its wanderings, conveys the message of salvation to the woman's soul. God's Word shall not return to Him void."

An evangelist to whom the sermons were supplied gratuitously by a friend thus shows how the numbers may be widely distributed in a country district: "I know a baker in Norfolk, and to him I send some to distribute among the poor families to whom he delivers his bread, as he goes through the village with his cart. In the same way, by post and other means, to other individuals, as to so many centres, getting them to lend them from house to house amongst their neighbours. I make a few sermons reach a wide circle, chiefly among those who else would never see them. Nor has this been without results, as I have from time to time intimated. Scores have felt in a measure what one woman experienced from reading one; it gave her so much comfort that she told me she had read it a hundred times, and that with undiminished pleasure, and wore it in her bosom until she tore it to tatters."

Of the manner in which the sermons are read by the clergy, and also used by them to good purpose, is shown by Mrs. Spurgeon in her work on the Book Fund; but of course many other examples might be given. Thus, in one instance, a certain evangelical clergyman, who was quite as useful as he was popular, accidentally left his bag at a country railway-station in Kent. The railway authorities looked into the bag, as they are accustomed to do, in order to discover, if possible, some trace of ownership; but on this occasion no revelation was forthcoming beyond what could be given by a number of marked and otherwise well-used copies of Mr. Spurgeon's sermons. In due time a telegram arrived to ask the stationmaster to kindly forward the bag to its reverend owner, who possibly would have continued his useful labours with more difficulty had the bag been irrecoverably lost.

Our friends in the North have ever regarded Mr. Spurgeon as one of their most favourite divines; and thus I will now give some facts illustrative of the work of the sermons in Scotland.

In 1881 a certain fisherman sent to the Pastor a very pleasantly-told account of his conversion: " I remember a colporteur coming to my mother's house, and he asked me if I would buy a book," our northern friend remarks. "'Yes,' says I, 'if you have got any ballads, that is, Scotch songs.' So he says to me, 'If you give me a piece of fish I will give you something that will do you more good than ballads.' I saw he desired my good, so I gave him half a codfish, and he gave me one of your sermons. The text was, 'Look unto

Me and be ye saved, all the ends of the earth ; for I am God and there is none else.' ("Sovereignty and Salvation," No. 60.) While reading that sermon the blessed Spirit of God enlightened my understanding, and I saw Jesus set before me as my Saviour. Blessed hour! Happy day! Jesus washed my sins away."

On one occasion a certain pastor lost himself in one of the Highland glens ; he found the natives to be a kindly race, and although they had little notion of either Lord Beaconsfield or Mr. Gladstone, they were extremely familiar with the name of Spurgeon. "They had a sort of knowledge of that name, for they read your sermons, and fetched a lot out to show me that they did so," remarked the pastor referred to. "I assure you," he adds, "I never saw any man's works with such signs of use upon them. There was no kirk in the glen, so on Sundays they got together and had a service, the scholar of the place reading the sermon." One aged pilgrim declared he would go to Glasgow on his hands and knees to see the preacher ; and though hardly competent to walk as many yards without effort, as it was miles to the commercial metropolis, the light in his eye bespoke his intense earnestness.

On the little island called the Skerries Rock there is a lighthouse, and, including the keepers of this, there were in all sixteen individuals in the place; and having no church they can go to, they are accustomed to conduct a service for themselves on the Lord's Day. "Thus," says *The Free Church Monthly* for December 1882, "the words to which thousands in London listen every week, and which are read in every corner of the world, are feeding and comforting the sixteen inhabitants of a lonely rock, beaten by the fierce waters that surge in the Pentland Firth."

While staying at a certain health-resort, a kind-hearted friend laid a number of the sermons on the table of the coffee-room at the hotel; but while many were pleased to have an opportunity of reading the numbers, there was a certain "stiff aged churchman" who protested against the introduction of "the works of a man who cursed our church." Then a Christian lady came to the help of the Quakeress, telling how both she and her husband prized the sermons highly, and how useful they had been in a district at Aberdeen. In that city there had dwelt a soldier "whose hardened, wretched condition baffled all the Christian labours bestowed upon him, until she lent him 'Only Trust Him' (No. 1635)," when that became instrumental in his conversion. Then "Jesus Only" (No. 924) had proved equally useful in the case of a Romanist, a most miserable being, who till that moment was placing her dependence in confession and penance. The transformation of both of these was described as having been really remarkable. Still more striking, however, was the change which came over the venerable churchman after the lady who had given these instances had departed. He even allowed his Quaker friend to read to him the sermons which had proved so useful, and remarked, " The venom is passing away. I feel it going. I shall buy those sermons and send them to my Broad Church son, and I hope they will do him and his wife good, and that he will preach them in his church." The gentleman went even so far as to confess that the discourses had "softened an old rebel." This is a memorable instance of the power of the Word.

When he was in Scotland in the summer of 1883, Mr. Spurgeon heard of many instances of usefulness through the sermons, especially in lonely Highland districts. " In one far-away village in the north," it is remarked, " the little country shop is opened on Saturdays expressly for the sale of the sermons ; and what the customers want is so clearly understood, that often not a word is spoken by either buyer or seller, but the people walk in, put down the penny, and march off with the sermon that is to be their Sabbath feast. In a Convalescent Home every Sabbath evening during the winter the matron reads one of the sermons to the inmates, who appear to be very grateful for them."

Not very long ago, or in 1884, one of Mr. Spurgeon's evangelists gave a very telling anecdote: "A woman in Scotland who was determined, as far as possible, not to have anything to do with religion, threw her Bible, and all the tracts she could find in her house, into the fire. One of the tracts fell down out of the flames, so she picked it up and thrust it in again. A second time it slipped down, and once more she put it back. Again her evil intention was frustrated, but the next time she was more successful, though even then only half of it was consumed. Taking up the portion that fell out of the fire she exclaimed, ' Surely the devil is in that tract, for it won't burn!' Her curiosity was excited; she began to read it, and it was the means of her conversion. The 'tract' was one of the sermons published in *The Metropolitan Tabernacle Pulpit*. Verily, that sermon, and the woman too, were *saved, yet so as by fire*."

The above instances sufficiently testify to the popularity of the sermons in Scotland; but according to the witness of a certain Methodist minister, who wrote in 1880, the discourses are equally valued in some parts of Ireland. "Many a time these few years I have wondered whether you know that you are preaching in unnumbered pulpits every Lord's Day, in many cases word for word as reported in your volumes," remarks this friend in a letter to Mr. Spurgeon. "You are aware, I suppose, that the weekly sermon is read by two-thirds of the Protestants in Ulster? In some cases ten families join in taking it, and lend it from one to another." After this we need not wonder that the Protestants of Ulster should regard Mr. Spurgeon as their adviser-in-general, even on political matters; and that they should have asked his opinion in regard to Home Rule when they were threatened with Mr. Gladstone's innovations.

We believe it was a Welsh dame who remarked, that if he only wanted one of his eyes Mr. Spurgeon would be worthy to come after Christmas Evans; but be that as it may, the preacher's utterances are as well calculated to be useful in Wales as elsewhere. In one instance, at least, the good which a couple of young men derived from the reading of the sermons did not end with themselves. They were encouraged to begin a Sabbath-school, and having commenced in two cottages with five scholars, they soon wanted more room, and they progressed until at length they were enabled to put up a building in which between two and three hundred children could be taught at once. Beyond this, they took care to circulate more than eighty copies of the sermons every week.

At Bryher, which is one of the Scilly Isles, the hundred and twenty persons who make up the population have a chapel as well as a church for their accommodation; and when service is held in the one place the custom is for the other to be closed. In 1880, when the intelligence was received, it was a usual thing for the sexton and clerk of the church to read one of Mr. Spurgeon's sermons in the chapel, and then to give out Wesley's Hymns for the little congregation to sing, when the Anglican establishment was closed.

The circulation of the sermons in the United States is very large, for not only are separate volumes issued, the newspapers appropriate each weekly issue as their own, so that the general diffusion is more widespread than can very readily be realized. It is quite possible that the readers are even more numerous in the United States than they are in the United Kingdom. It will be remembered by many that some years ago an enterprising American undertook to telegraph each Sunday morning sermon across the Atlantic, in order that the readers in more than one

American city might read on Monday morning what was spoken at the Metropolitan Tabernacle on the day before.

A letter received by Mr. Spurgeon in 1880 shows how his utterances may convey comfort as well as instruction into the most out-of-the-way corners of the American continent. "Several weeks ago I lay ill, far away from London, in the wilds of Florida," remarks the writer. "Weak and faint-hearted, I lay pondering on the strange providence of the Master, when one of your sermons was placed in my hands. The refreshing shower revived me and gave me fresh hope and courage, and I rose from my sick couch to strive still more earnestly to gain access to the hearts of those by whom I am surrounded, and to-day, in a small class that I have formed out here in the wilderness, the Lord made His presence felt, and blessed us with an awakening that I have never seen here before, and tears of repentance were shed by many. I am so full of joy and gratitude to God that I felt, indeed I longed, to let you know that your influence as an instrument had even reached this place."

Thus, the influence seems to reach to the very ends of the earth, and the personal testimony of one friend is frequently outdone by that of another. Thus, in 1881, a pastor in Tennessee made this confession : " Nine years ago I was a wild young man, but I was converted through reading one of Mr. Spurgeon's sermons, and I am now the minister of a large and influential church. The Lord's name be magnified ! "

The tidings which come from the Far West are no less cheering. Writing to Mr. Spurgeon in 1882, a correspondent in Minnesota said :—" You will be pleased to hear that in this Western country, and in this village of six hundred inhabitants, Mr. Spurgeon's books are much valued. I have seen them in several houses here. In the Wesleyan minister's a volume or two of sermons. In another house *Morning By Morning*. In another, that of an old saint, *The Saint and His Saviour*, which he esteems as very precious, saying, with emphatic tone, when he speaks of it, ' This is Mr. Spurgeon's first book, and he has written many since, but never one to surpass this,' though the dear old man has not read a tithe of Mr. Spurgeon's publications."

In 1884, the editor of a paper published in New York, in which Mr. Spurgeon's sermons are regularly issued, sent word to England that he had recently heard of several remarkable cases in which desperately wicked characters had abandoned their ways through reading the Pastor's discourses. Particular reference is made to an exceptionally

Mr. Spurgeon and President Garfield. 235

wicked character: "One aged reprobate, sixty years old, died last week, whose last two years were in startling contrast to all his past life. The transformation was the wonder of the neighbourhood for its completeness. From being a public terror he became a public blessing, as gentle and as kind as a woman. He was delivered from drunkenness, profanity, unchastity, and bloodshedding." On his death-bed this man desired that Mr. Spurgeon might be told of the grateful change which his sermons had been instrumental in effecting.

In 1882 the widow of the murdered President Garfield wrote to Mr. Spurgeon: " It is a choice treasure from my storehouse of beautiful memories that I sat beside General Garfield in the Metropolitan Tabernacle one bright summer Sunday morning (August 4th, 1867), and listened to your voice. I have this morning re-read from his journal the account of that day. A sentence from it may interest you. After describing very fully his impressions of the great audience, of the preacher, and of the sermon, he closes thus:— 'God bless Spurgeon! He is helping to work out the problem of religious and civil freedom for England in a way that he knows not of.'"

In 1880 a young Scotchman, who died of an incurable disease in the General Hospital at

Montreal, gave a fine testimony to the influence of Mr. Spurgeon's sermons; and a Christian friend who visited him in his last illness sent an account of the case to one of the journals of the city :—" The one and only matter of his reading, next to the Bible, was Charles H. Spurgeon's sermons: of these he never tired. Biographies of eminent Scotchmen like Norman Macleod and William Arnot were taken to him, but as he put them aside he would say, ' Spurgeon is always the same, but always satisfying, for he makes you forget himself, as he holds up Him who is fairer than the children of men.'" The preacher's works find ready acceptance in Canada, where the Pastors' College has a separate Association.

To come back to the Continent of Europe, we find that the sermons even have readers among the fishermen of the Mediterranean. A lady tells of an adventure which happened in 1883, and which shows in what sense this is true. While staying at Cette, on the French coast, she went out with a party in a boat on the sea, but in consequence of an adverse gale the craft would have been driven out until their lives would have been endangered had not an Italian fisherman in a sailing-boat gone to the rescue. Subsequently, the fisherman called at the hotel accompanied by his uncle; and the latter explained that, although they were Roman Catholics, he had the New Testament in French and English as well as in his own language—and he was a reader of Mr. Spurgeon's sermons.

Many of the so-called Reformed Churches in Switzerland need a second reformation, and this might well be brought about by a wider diffusion of Mr. Spurgeon's works among the people. In 1881, a young lady who applied for baptism to a Baptist minister in England gave a brief account of her history, and showed that she was a representative example of the wants of the country. Here is her testimony:—" My parents were members of the Protestant Established Church in Switzerland; but though I attended the ordinances, and observed the ceremonies, I always felt that I was a hypocrite, for I never believed in them, but desired something which I could never get in the Church. When I came to England I read a sermon by Mr. Spurgeon which did me good. *John Ploughman's Talk*, though funny, was made a great blessing to me. I then bought his sermons, and read them, and I am now happy to say that I am trusting in Jesus. When I return home I shall distribute these sermons, which have been so blessed to me." Thus the reading of the discourses tends to the multiplication of distributors, so that the good influence never ceases to extend.

Perhaps, on the whole, the Gospel is preached more fully in Denmark than in the once favoured and beautiful land where the Reformation found a refuge; but even in the picturesque and out-of-the-way corners of Northern Europe Mr. Spurgeon's sermons, translated into the vernacular, are doing good service. By way of illustration take this characteristic note which a worthy Dane sent to the preacher in 1880 :—" Through twelve of your sermons, which are translated into Danish, I and my household have this winter been acquainted with your Christian announcement, and we thank you for every clearing and edifying word. We seceded from the Established Church a year ago, because we have so evidently seen the tragical consequences of the connection between the Church and the State, and we could not possibly act contrary to the conviction forced upon us by the New Testament, viz., the incorrectness of the infant baptism." The denomination which Mr. Spurgeon represents has obtained a very respectable footing in Denmark; for although the population is under two millions, who for the most part are Lutherans, the Baptists are able to muster between three and four thousand members.

The vast empire of Russia, needing the

In the Interior of Russia. 239

Scriptures in a great number of languages, is no small world in itself. Early in this century, when the Bible Society began its great mission, the pious Emperor Alexander was a leading patron of the work; and although religion was checked in its progress during the ascendency of Nicolas, there has since been a revival of activity, the circulation of Mr. Spurgeon's sermons being also one of the signs of the times. Writing in 1881 to Mr. Spurgeon, a minister stationed at St. Petersburg says : " By your sermons, etc., you are having a part in the great work of spreading Christ's kingdom both in St. Petersburg and in the interior. You are well known among the priests, who seem to get hold of your translated sermons, and, strange to say, I know cases in which the Censor has readily given consent for your works to be translated when he has been reluctant respecting many." Another friend in the Russian capital made it his business to circulate as many of the translated copies as he could procure, the priests apparently being the most eager recipients.

Another friend in Russia, who wrote in 1880, says : " I came to this country about twenty-four years ago, and have been about in various parts of the interior ever since... I have a wife and eight children. A few weeks ago I explained to them the meaning of the Orphanage, and appealed to their feelings ; the result was that I was authorised to go to their savings-bank and take out three roubles forty kopecks as the children's contribution. We have now made up the sum to fifty-five roubles, which will be forwarded to you from St. Petersburg by a cheque."

In the more remote parts of the Czar's vast empire Mr. Spurgeon's works are not only known, but are promoting the spiritual enlightenment of the people in a way no less striking than gratifying. Writing to the Pastor from Warschaw in 1882, Mr. F. H. Newton, of the German Baptist Mission, thus refers to his adventures : " I have during the last few weeks been visiting a number of our Baptist Churches in Silesia and Russian Poland ; and I think you will be interested to hear of their activity and Christian faith. In almost every town and village one of the first enquiries put to me is, *And how is Brother Spurgeon ?* In many of the outlying stations, where no stated missionary can be sustained, your printed sermons are regularly made use of : and I am sure you will be thankful to our one Master to learn that here in Poland, and elsewhere, many of the Church members attribute their first religious awakening to hearing some of those sermons read. In the meetings which I have conducted in various towns during this tour, I have frequently taken the opportunity of referring to the work of God which you are carrying on in London and elsewhere; and I have thought it only right to tell you of the warm and frequent salutations that are entrusted to me for yourself from our poor and out-of-the-way Baptist brethren in these parts. They especially rejoice to learn that your sons are also preaching the Word, and are particularly interested in the Book Fund established by Frau Spurgeon."

Labrador is an interesting country, not only on account of its brief charming summers and terrible winters. The people are mainly Roman Catholics, one reason being that a mission of that sect is maintained in the country. In 1884 a New York paper contained this piece of intelligence:—" All last winter, in the little mission on the Labrador coast, Mr. Spurgeon's sermons were read in the Mission Church, Sunday by Sunday, by the lady teachers, who were left by themselves for eight months, through the failing health of the devoted missionary who laboured there for many years. These simple services on the Sunday and weekday evenings, when these sermons were the staple of the teaching given, were greatly blessed by God. Many sailors came from the ships anchored off the coast, and, with the resident fishermen, eagerly listened to the Word of Life, and not only were their hearts cheered and comforted, but some were brought to a knowledge of the truth as it is in Christ Jesus."

One distributor of the sermons among the natives of the Falkland Islands found that they were very thankfully received; and in 1880 a somewhat remarkable letter was received from a Red Kaffir, who resided at Port Elizabeth, South Africa. Being full of joy and peace, the man explained how the transformation had been effected: "One day as I was going to my daily work I met a friend of mine in the street. We spoke about the Word of God, and he asked me whether I had ever seen one of Mr. Spurgeon's books. I said, 'What Mr. Spurgeon is that—one of the Independent ministers in London?' and I said, 'No, I never saw such a book in my life.' He said he bought it from the bookseller. I asked the name of the book, and he said it was *The Metropolitan Tabernacle Pulpit*, and I went straight to the shop and bought one. I have read a good bit of it. . . . I am sure I can't tell how to describe the goodness you have done to us, the black people of South Africa. We are not black only outside, even inside; I wouldn't mind to be a black man only in colour. It is a terrible thing to be a black man from the soul to the skin ; but still I am very glad to say your sermons have done something good to me."

Two missionaries labouring in Greece once testified to Mr. Spurgeon : " Your sermons are to us like rain upon a dry land. We have no church to attend, and no friends to associate with." Similar testimony in regard to the great assistance received from the printed sermons comes from South Australia. In 1881 Pastor Thomas Spurgeon, of Auckland, enclosed a piece of *The Melbourne Argus*, which contained the sermon No. 735—" Loving Advice for Anxious Seekers," with this explanation, addressed to his mother : " This scrap of newspaper has been given to me by a town missionary here, who regards it as a very precious relic. It came to him from a man who died in the hospital, and bequeathed it to his visitor as a great treasure. The man found it on the floor of a hut in Australia, and was brought by its perusal to a knowledge of the truth as it is in Jesus. He kept it carefully while he lived (for it was discoloured and torn when he found it), and on his death-bed he gave it to the missionary as the only treasure he had to leave behind him. I thought dear father might like to have it in his book ; if not, send it back to me, that I may return it to its owner, who says he often feels encouraged by glancing at it. It was his desire, however, that I should send it home, that the dear preacher might be encouraged."

There was a certain Christian gentleman who had some of the sermons inserted in the Australian newspapers, himself paying the heavy cost. The above may have been one of these insertions. Another instance was that of a shepherd, who read a sermon in one of the journals while looking after his sheep, and the truth reached his heart. After his conversion he asked a clergyman, who was holding services at a gold-field, to give him Christian work; and after beginning as a Sunday-school teacher, he went on till he became himself a preacher to gold-diggers.

As it is on the mainland, so is it in the islands of the Australasian world. The wife of a pastor in Tasmania once said, in a letter to her father: "If Mr. Spurgeon knew how his sermons are appreciated in our southern forests, where no preachers have been for years until my dear husband went to them, and how many cases of conversion he met with through the reading of them, he would be amazed, and rejoice with unspeakable joy."

The sermons are also read in India, many educated natives, including even some Brahmans, finding great pleasure in the perusal. Having had presented to him No. 1500 of *The Metropolitan Tabernacle Pulpit*, a Brahman B.A. of Madras University wrote this critique on the discourse, and sent it to a friend: " The few minutes I have been reading these sermons daily were spent very agreeably. I always considered Dr. Spurgeon the best orator. I see even the best can improve; as Dr. Spurgeon excels all orators, so his 1500th sermon excels all his other sermons. I doubt very much whether he himself can deliver such another sermon, but that is going too far. I envy those that hear personally Dr. Spurgeon preach."

In another instance a Christian lady lent a volume of the sermons to a Mahometan, and some time after was rewarded by receiving the following note: " Your sermon book has, indeed, converted me to Christianity. I do believe in Christ our Lord, and so long as my belief in Him is firmly rooted, I do not care what I may be called in the outer world. Mr. Spurgeon appears to be an extraordinary man." No one who properly apprehends the situation can doubt that, in proportion as the Gospel extends in our vast Indian empire, the circulation of these sermons will also extend.

The sermons are also found on the sea; and many during a season of enforced leisure find in them the truth that reaches the heart. Not very long ago Mr. A. G. Brown told his people this story of a conversion through reading while on the ocean :—

"There came to me here one day a grand-looking fellow. I had not to ask whether he did business on the water, for the sea-breeze had kissed his brow so often that it had left its mark there. I said, 'Where did you find the Lord?' In a moment he answered, '*Latitude* 25, *Longitude* 54.' I confess that rather puzzled me. I had heard of people finding Jesus Christ in these galleries, and down these aisles, and in all sorts of places, but here was something quite different. 'Latitude 25, Longitude 54! What do you mean?' He said, 'I was sitting on deck, and out of a bundle of papers before me I pulled one of Spurgeon's sermons. I began to read it. As I read it I saw the truth, and I received Jesus in my heart. I jumped off the coil of ropes saved. I thought if I were on shore I would know where I was saved, and why should I not know on the sea? And so I took my latitude and longitude.'"

The sermons thus reach all classes; and not only are they instrumental in the conversion of sinners, large numbers of Christian people are by their perusal built up in the faith. The audience addressed week by week is truly a world-wide one.

At the outset of his career in London, and while preaching at New Park Street Chapel on October 7th, 1855, Mr. Spurgeon himself referred to the extended influence he was even then beginning to exercise on the world through the press, *e.g.* :—

"Oh to think that we may write and print books which shall reach poor sinners' hearts! The other day my soul was gladdened exceedingly by an invitation from a pious woman to go and see her. She told me she had been ten years on her bed, and had not been able to stir from it. 'Nine years,' she said, 'I was dark, and blind, and unthinking; but my husband brought me one of your sermons. I read it, and God blessed it to the opening of my eyes. He converted my soul with it. And now—all glory to Him—I love His name! Each Sabbath morning,' she said, 'I wait for your sermon. I live on it all the week, as marrow and fatness to my spirit.' Ah! thought I, there is something to cheer the printers, and all of us who labour in that good work. One good brother wrote to me this week, 'Brother Spurgeon, keep your courage up. You are known in multitudes of households of England, and you are loved too;

though we cannot hear you, or see your living form, yet throughout our villages your sermons are scattered. And I know of cases of conversion from them, more than I can tell you.' Another friend mentioned to me an instance of a clergyman of the Church of England, a canon of a Cathedral, who frequently preaches the sermons on the Sabbath—whether in the Cathedral or not I cannot say, but I hope he does. Oh! who can tell when these things are printed what hearts they may reach, what good they may effect? Words that I spoke three weeks ago eyes are now perusing, while tears are gushing from them as they read! Glory be to God most high!"

The sermons have become one of the institutions of the church in both the Old and the New World. What should also be universally known is, that the preacher has virtually ministered to his church and congregation for nothing; that is to say, the income received has all been given away in furtherance of the Lord's work in many departments

MR. SPURGEON'S BOOKS.

"It may be added that though the comments were the work of my health, the rest of the volume is the product of my sickness. When protracted illness and weakness laid me aside from daily preaching, I resorted to my pen as an available means of doing good. I would have preached had I been able, but as my Master denied me the privilege of thus serving Him, I gladly availed myself of the other method of bearing testimony for His name."—*The Treasury of David, Preface to Vol. I.*

"I prepared these figures and metaphors that they may serve as *feathers for arrows*, arrows of Gospel truth which I pray may be made sharp in the hearts of the King's enemies."—*Feathers for Arrows.*

"I have somewhat indulged the mirthful vein, but ever with so serious a purpose that I ask no forgiveness. Those who see a virtue in dulness have full permission to condemn, for a sufficient number will approve."—*John Ploughman's Pictures.*

IX.

MR. SPURGEON'S BOOKS.

SOON after he came to London Mr. Spurgeon appeared before the world as an author; and each successive year has so added to his works in this department that, inclusive of the magazine, nearly a hundred volumes have been sent out. If the reader will accept the paradox, Mr. Spurgeon has never written sermons, although during twenty years his sermons have been to him an exercise in writing. In one of those autobiographical articles with which he sometimes enriches the pages of *The Sword and the Trowel*, he says: "The earlier sermons, owing to my constant wanderings abroad, received scarcely any revision, and consequently they abound in colloquialisms and other offences, very venial in extempore discourse, but scarcely tolerable in print; the latter specimens are more carefully corrected, and the work of revision has been a very useful exercise to me, supplying, in great measure, that training in correct language which is obtained by those who write their productions before they deliver them. The labour has been far greater than some suppose, and has usually occupied the best hours of Monday, and involved the burning of no inconsiderable portion of midnight oil. Feeling that I had a constituency well deserving my best efforts, I have never grudged the hours, though often the brain has been wearied, and the pleasure has hardened into a task."

After reading the above explanation we well understand how tongue and pen have worked together to redound to the advantage of both. As a young man Mr. Spurgeon did not entertain very enlarged views concerning the dignity of authorship, and his expectations in regard to the profits of a writer were of a very modest kind. He commenced by committing a mistake for which he paid dear. The copyright of *The Saint and His Saviour* which would have been cheap at £1,000, was sold for a twentieth part of that sum; and the small honorarium was never supplemented by the fortunate publishers. That mistake has not been repeated; and his literary works have, since that day, been sufficiently varied and numerous to represent the fruits of a busy literary life quite apart from the regular issue of the sermons. Hence it appears that a phenomenon is now seen in the printing and publishing world which it would be hard to parallel--extensive printing works in one part of the city, and a publishing house in another quarter, are in the main supplied with grist from the study of one man, and that man a Baptist minister, preaching what many call "narrow theology." Yet they who class the sermons among "narrow" productions will not forget that they are sown over a broader field than is the case with the discourses of any other preacher.

Though Mr. Spurgeon is continually suffering from the effects of over-work, the public is still exacting in its demands; and to judge by the editions issued, readers eagerly welcome each successive offspring of the author's diligent application. Though *John Ploughman* is the Pastor's most popular character, *The Treasury of David* is his *magnum opus*. In the first he writes like one who can do taskwork well; amid the green pastures and quiet waters of the Psalms he explores a congenial land where every advance reveals new beauties, and where labour yields a sweet reward.

The Treasury of David, just completed in seven octavo volumes, has the virtue of being the production of a writer who has been in love with the Psalms from his youth; and, indeed, this enthusiasm for the subject was necessary, for the work has been only completed after more than twenty years of arduous labour. The exposition bespeaks its author throughout ; it abounds in that epigrammatic wisdom which is a sure mark of original genius. Commentaries of olden times —Manton's " long-metre edition of Psalm cxix." being a well-known example—rather alarmed than attracted inquisitive readers ; but after tasting of Mr. Spurgeon's fare, a self-indulgent literary epicure might desire to come again. The book, with its ample store of illustrations, gathered from the entire field of literature, ought to have entertained Dr. Johnson on a journey even better than Cocker's Arithmetic. While it is a rich storehouse for the use of professional men, another, seeking relaxation from the wear and tear of commerce, might make the book a companion on a summer holiday. What is it but the triumph of genius when studies, hitherto supposed to be only suitable for ministers and collegians, are made attractive to general readers ?

Here and there a metrical version of a favourite psalm is inserted to make an agreeable variation. In another place scientific infidels are described as men who " will not touch Him [Christ] with the finger of faith ; but they will pluck at Him with the finger of malice." Sentences which would serve as proverbs might be plentifully gathered.

It is also interesting to take note of the skill with which the illustrations are selected. Take the following on the opening verse of Psalm xcviii. :—

"A clergyman in the county of Tyrone had for some weeks observed a little ragged boy come every Sunday and place himself in the centre of the aisle, directly opposite the pulpit, where he seemed exceedingly attentive to the services. He was desirous of knowing who the child was, and for this purpose hastened out after the sermon several times, but never could see him, as he vanished the moment service was over, and no one knew whence he came or anything about him. At length the boy was missed from his usual situation in the church for some weeks. At this time a man called on the minister, and told him a person very ill was desirous of seeing him ; but added, ' I am really ashamed to ask you to go so far ; but it is a child of mine, and he refuses to have any one but you. He is altogether an extraordinary boy, and talks a great deal about things that I do not understand.' The clergyman promised to go, and went, though the rain poured down in torrents, and he had six miles of rugged mountain country to pass. On arriving where he was directed, he saw a most wretched cabin indeed, and the man he had seen in the morning was waiting at the door. He was shown in, and found the inside of the hovel as miserable as the outside. In a corner, on a little straw, he beheld a person stretched out, whom he recognised as the little boy who had so regularly attended his church. As he approached the wretched bed the child raised himself up, and stretching forth his arms said, ' *His own right hand and His holy arm hath gotten Him the victory,*' and immediately he expired."

The work on the Psalms entailed enormous labour, not merely as a commentary, but on account of the vast array of illustrative passages which have been gathered from the great field of the world's literature; and it must at least be a great consolation to Mr. Spurgeon and his assistants to see how thoroughly their work has been appreciated by the public. At the time of writing, about 107,000 volumes have been sent out, and this is of course a number far beyond the circulation that any commentary on a single book of the Bible has ever before commanded.

To persevere in a task through more than twenty years, when the labour increases in difficulty as it proceeds, is an example of industry not often encountered; but this is what Mr. Spurgeon has done while completing his *Treasury of David*. The ancient classics of Greece and Italy have been read for any dust of gold they might contain; so also have the Christian Fathers, the English classics, and others, to mention the names of which would only tend to the bewilderment of the unlearned reader.

But Mr. Spurgeon is more than a commentator, he is a many-sided genius,—that is, he can work to advantage in various departments, and excel in all. In *The Treasury of David* he is the ripe theologian; in the character of *John Ploughman* he talks philosophy such as the common people like to hear because they can understand; in his *History of the Tabernacle* he is a painstaking historian; in *Lectures to My Students* he is a more lively college professor than any other member of that honourable fraternity with whom I am acquainted. It is worth a substantial entrance fee to listen to one of these Friday afternoon orations; but those who cannot hear should read the book.

In old times, when books were scarce, and good teachers scarcer, a clever University lecturer would attract auditors from foreign climes, who in after life were wont to boast of early privileges. It is really surprising to think how the old schoolmen killed time, and wasted their energies in battling about barren topics, or in establishing their finely-spun theories. The popular mediæval professor, with his host of determined disciples, was hardly a less formidable opponent than we should now find in a confident general who knew that regiments of veterans were ready to give effect to his orders. The shock of controversy often troubled the outside world; but whether the Realists or the Idealists held the field mattered little to the vulgar crowd. Was it ever authoritatively decided whether a thousand angels could, or could not dance upon the point of a finely-sharpened needle? Philosophy was a dead letter, because men worshipped intellect and learning for their own sake, without caring anything about the elevation of the benighted population. Students spent their strength for nought, losing their way in the mazes of casuistry, until nothing short of the mighty awakening of the Reformation sufficed to break their fatal dream.

Had Mr. Spurgeon flourished in mediæval days he would have been renowned as a man of valour, the Achilles of a school, and even now he is scarcely less than this. No college professor ever before gave lectures precisely similar to "Lectures to My Students." The book is weighty and piquant, serious as well as sparkling; many of its philosophical saws gain force from their settings of humour. In every sense it is a popular reading-book; one not too light for grave scholars, nor of

The College Lectures.

that solid dryness which repels those who read for amusement. Every page is racy, the wit is free from ill-nature, and throughout there is a characteristic striving after practical results. Pretty things are never said for their own sake; the smallest apophthegm is aimed at a high mark which is seldom missed. As college homilies these lectures were not delivered with that professional frown which might seem to give weight to their matter and dignity to the lecturer; they were rather spoken with easy grace, and as we read we seem to be looking on a beaming countenance which of itself may teach what is worth even more than a college lesson. "Our reverend tutor, Mr. Rogers, compares my Friday work to the sharpening of the pin," we are told; "the fashioning of the head, the straightening, the laying on of the metal, and the polishing, have been done during the week, and then the process concludes with an effort to give point and sharpness. To succeed in this the lecturer must not be dull himself, nor demand any great effort from his audience. I am as much at home with my young brethren as in the bosom of my family, and, therefore, speak without restraint."

Mr. Spurgeon lets his readers know who the young aspirants are that constitute the Pastors College, and also who they are *not*. To these who assert that he has set up a clerical factory, he replies that he is rather a " parson killer." He is ever doing work similar to "the duty which fell to the lot of Cromwell's Triers." He does not want men who are striving to do the best they can for themselves in this world, and applications are declined which come from those whose " main object is an ambitious desire to shine among men." Self-conceited geniuses are always kindly directed elsewhere. Nor is it believed that the students are generally characterised by "great feebleness of mind," because applicants betraying a mental weakness which is likely to be carried away by any kind of doctrine are counselled to "keep in the rear ranks," in company with other knights of "the kid-gloved order." Another too numerous class, who are not welcomed into the College, are "distinguished by enormous vehemence and zeal, and a conspicuous absence of brains; brethren who would talk for ever and ever upon nothing, who would stamp and thump the Bible, and get nothing out of it at all; earnest, awfully earnest, mountains in labour of the most painful kind; but nothing comes of it all, not even the *ridiculus mus*. There are zealots abroad who are not capable of conceiving or uttering five consecutive thoughts, whose capacity is most narrow, and their conceit most broad ; and these can hammer, and bawl, and rave, and tear, and rage, but the noise all arises from the hollowness of the drum." Of others the name is legion, whose natural defects would render them ludicrous in the eyes of a congregation. One applicant "had a sort of rotary action of the jaw," says Mr. Spurgeon. "I could not have looked at him while preaching without laughter, if all the gold of Tarshish had been my reward." Men who base their "call" on a hedged-up way are not encouraged, because "a man who would succeed as a preacher would probably do right well either as a grocer, or a lawyer, or anything else. A really valuable minister would have excelled at anything." Mr. Self-conceit cannot always see reason when his offer of self-sacrifice is declined. "Do you mean to say that because I have an unusual genius," asked one, in warm indignation, "and have produced in myself a gigantic mind, such as is rarely seen, I am refused admittance into your College?"

Perhaps no volume sold for half-a-crown ever cost an author more trouble than *Commenting and Commentaries*. The student is directed to nearly fifteen hundred works, treating of separate parts of the Bible, or of the whole book. Like Lord Bacon, Mr. Spurgeon must see fruit come of his labour, or he is not satisfied. Such books are not written for money, nor for fame, for the sake of aiding those who have little money to spend in literature; *e.g.* :—

"Here, however, is the difficulty; students do not find it easy to choose which works to buy, and their slender stores are often wasted on books of a comparatively worthless kind. If I can save a poor man from spending his money for that which is not bread, or, by directing a brother to a good book, may enable him to dig deeper into the mines of truth, I shall be well repaid. For this purpose I have toiled, and read much, and passed under review some three or four thousand volumes. From these I have compiled my catalogue, rejecting many, yet making a very varied selection. Though I have carefully used such judgment as I possess, I have, doubtless, made many errors; I shall, certainly, find very few who will agree with me in all my criticisms, and some persons may be angry with my remarks. . . . He who finds fault will do well to execute the work in a better style; only let him remember that he will have my heifer to plough with, and therefore ought, in all reason, to excel me."

It is taken for granted that persons who purchase the book value the assistance of Biblical expositors. "Of course you are not such wiseacres as to think you can expound Scripture without assistance from the works of divines and learned men, who have laboured before you in the field of exposition," the students are told. "If you are of that opinion, pray remain so, for you are not worth the trouble of conversion, and, like a little coterie who think with you, would resent the attempt as an insult to your infallibility." His opinions on the leading commentators are not those of a man who has not taken the trouble to read their works for himself.

"First among the mighty for general usefulness, we are bound to mention the man whose name is a household word, MATTHEW HENRY. He is most pious and pithy, sound and sensible, suggestive and sober, terse and trustworthy. You will find him to be glittering with metaphors, rich in analogies, overflowing with illustrations, superabundant in reflections. . . . It is the poor man's commentary, the old Christian's companion, suitable to everybody, instructive to all. . . . Every minister ought to read Matthew Henry entirely and carefully through once at least. I should recommend you to get through it in the next twelve months after you leave college. Begin at the beginning, and resolve that you will traverse the goodly land from Dan to Beersheba. You will acquire a vast store of sermons if you read with your note-book close at hand; and as for thoughts, they will swarm around you like twittering swallows around an old gable towards the close of autumn."

John Calvin is "a prince among men." Matthew Poole "is a very prudent and judicious commentator." Trapp is recommended "to men of discernment." Gill is a "master cinder-sifter among the Targums, the Talmuds, the Mishna, and the Gemara. . . . I have placed next to Gill in my library Adam Clarke; but as I have no desire to have my rest broken by wars among the authors, I have placed Doddridge between them. If the spirits of the two worthies could descend to the earth in the same mood in which they departed, no house would be able to hold them." He goes on to say that the first money received for services in London was exchanged for Scott's Commentary ; but "for a minister's use Scott is mere milk-and-water."

The *Metropolitan Tabernacle and Its Work* would have been a work of more surpassing interest had the author done what he thinks he could not be expected to do—had he turned his "pages into an autobiography." Mr. Spurgeon will not, however, portray himself. He prefers to see himself as others see him.

John Ploughman's Talk and *Pictures* are Mr. Spurgeon's most popular books, if we judge of popularity by the fact that 450,000 copies of the two volumes have been sold. Then come *Morning by Morning* and *Evening by Evening*, the circulation of the one having reached 100,000, and the other 75,000. *Feathers for Arrows* and *Illustrations and Meditations* are illustrative manuals. *Flashes of Thought*, *Spurgeon's Gems*, and *Gleanings Among the Sheaves* are choice passages selected by other hands from an ample field. *Types and Emblems*, *Trumpet Calls to Christian Energy*, *The Present Truth*, *Storm Signals*, and *Farm Sermons* are supplementary volumes of discourses printed in crown octavo-form. There are several others I have not mentioned which command wide popularity. The shilling series extends to eleven volumes. *All of Grace* shows the plan of salvation; while *The Clue of the Maze* is an antidote to the specious unbelief of the times. Nor ought *The Interpreter; or, Scripture for Family Worship*, with its running comments and hymns, to be overlooked. As a handsome quarto volume, this book is frequently purchased for a wedding present.

The Pastor's printed books, including *The Sword and the Trowel*, thus comprise nearly one hundred volumes; and form in themselves such a comprehensive library as was never before provided by one man.

In the meantime, the work of translating the

Pastor's works into European and even Oriental languages still goes on. Mr. Spurgeon's own portion of *The Treasury of David* is now being rendered into Arabic, while *All of Grace* **is** being rendered into German.

THE BOOK FUND.

"The room is small, and very poorly furnished, a tiny fire burns in the grate, for it is mid-winter; but beyond this, there is an absence of all the suitable surroundings of a minister's study, and you can count the *books* upon your fingers. The pastor sits there with bowed head, and weary body, after a day of heavy work, and, shall I tell it? of very scanty sustenance. A deep sense of responsibility is upon him, and he feels the weight of souls on his heart; but in addition to this, special cares just now press upon him heavily; troubles of church and building matters, questions as to ways and means, fightings without, and fears within, which vex and grieve him sorely. . . . Weary and faint, *he is very, very poor*, and almost overwhelmed by the difficulties of the way, he turns to the fire with his open Bible on his knee and sighs. Oh! such a sigh. Will the angels hear it, I wonder, and come and minister to him, as they used to do to their sorrowful Lord? Perhaps so, but his Heavenly Father has also prepared an earthly solace, and the answer to his cry is even now at the door. The bell rings, and a large parcel is left 'For the Pastor,' and is taken at once to his room. In a moment he knows that relief has come, he knows the superscription, and divines the contents; in his joy he almost caresses the package; then, with trembling fingers, he cuts the string, and spreads the treasures out before the Lord. Yes, literally 'before the Lord,' for now you see him kneeling by the side of the open parcel, thanking and blessing God for such opportune mercy, for such streams in the desert, such blossoming roses in the wilderness."—*Ten Years of my Life in the Service of the Book Fund,* 327-8.

X.

THE BOOK FUND.

AS a benefactor of poor ministers who are unable to buy necessary books, Mrs. Spurgeon has won a wide reputation; and the beneficent work carried on is all the more remarkable because, in past years more especially, it was accomplished in spite of pain and weakness such as would have disabled anyone who could not have exemplified the heroism or endurance which sometimes seems to be peculiar to Christian women. The book distribution, which commenced in 1875, was originally undertaken on a very small scale; and at first no one suspected that the giving away of a hundred copies of Mr. Spurgeon's *Lectures* would lead to the development of a comprehensive enterprise which would extend its influence not only throughout the British Isles, but also to the colonies. In her recently published work, *Ten Years of my Life in the Service of the Book Fund*, Mrs. Spurgeon thus explains how the enterprise originated, which, through the goodness of God, has often proved a solace as well as a labour to the person chiefly concerned :—

"It was in the summer of the year 1875 that my dear husband completed and published the first volume of his *Lectures to My Students*. Reading one of the proof copies, I became so enamoured of the book that when the dear author asked, 'Well, how do you like it?' I answered with a full heart, 'I wish I could place it in the hands of every minister in England.' 'Then why not do so? *how much will you give?*' said my very practical spouse. . . . Then comes the wonderful part: I found the money ready and waiting! Upstairs in a little drawer were some carefully-hoarded crown-pieces, which, owing to some foolish fancy, I had been gathering for years whenever chance threw one in my way; these I now counted out, and found they made a sum *exactly* sufficient to pay for one hundred copies of the work! If a twinge of regret at parting from my cherished but unwieldy favourites passed over me, it was gone in an instant, and then they were given, freely and thankfully, to the Lord, and in that moment, though I knew it not, the Book Fund was inaugurated."

Since that auspicious day the general distribution has not fallen very far short of 90,000 volumes, while the recipients have numbered considerably over 12,000 indigent pastors, who certainly cannot purchase an adequate supply of books if they are not freely supplied to them. Can we estimate the encouragement thus afforded to men who are often wearied and cast down through difficulties and perplexities which are aggravated, if not actually created, by poverty?

Very naturally, perhaps, some persons have supposed that the Book Fund is for Baptists exclusively; but writing in the early part of 1880 in her own pleasant style, Mrs. Spurgeon described the thorough catholicity of her work :—

"A day or two since the good Earl of Shaftesbury paid us a visit, and on leaving he said to me, 'Well, how does the Baptist book-giving prosper?' 'Thank you, my lord,' I replied, 'the Book Fund prospers grandly, all the more that it is *not* a Baptist book-giving, but is free to all the Lord's ministering servants.' If the venerable Earl could have seen my day-book he would have found full confirmation of this assertion, for glancing down the long columns of recipients' names, one cannot but be struck with the constant repetition of the distinguishing titles of Church, Congregational, Presbyterian, Methodist etc., and the comparatively infrequent recurrence of the word Baptist in the list. Thus, in these first four months of the year, I have already on my books the names of nearly four hundred ministers, who during that period have received grants from my Fund, and of this number just *one-fourth* are 'mine own people.' I am delighted to see that the longer record bears the names of fifty Church of England clergymen, and I believe I am justified in anticipating glorious results from the distribution among them of sound and scriptural doctrine. And if in some cases appreciation should lead to appropriation, and from many a stately pulpit in the land the Gospel should sound forth full and free through the sermons first delivered in the Metropolitan Tabernacle, shall aught but joy and thankfulness fill our hearts? 'I confess,' wrote a vicar to me, 'that though I do not preach your husband's sermons *bodily*, I yet so assimiliate them into my own discourses that they are of the utmost value and blessing to me.'"

Of the general need of the work among ministers of all denominations there can hardly be two opinions. I was privileged to assist in the preparation of the first annual Report of the Fund for 1876, and I then described the need of the enterprise in these words:—

"The position of Nonconformist pastors in sparsely inhabited country districts is extremely difficult, and ought to command the sympathy

Pitiful Examples of Poverty. 273

and help of all their brethren. On account of their position appearances have to be studied, and much of their scanty means must thus be expended. Even their rustic audiences would hardly bear to see the pastor in a smock frock and his children barefooted."

The above applies in general terms to the need existing for more books in the studies of our poorer pastors; and that the case is not put too strongly is proved by the fact that the individual examples brought to light by Mrs. Spurgeon more than prove what is said. Thus, for example, in 1880, three representative cases were given of the destitution which exists in the households of three pastors of the Baptist denomination.

"No. I. is a hard-working, painstaking pastor, preaching five times a week, holding large Bible-classes, writing, itinerating, and in every way doing his best for the people of his charge; he is married, has three children, and accepts and manages to exist upon a meagre pittance of sixty-five pounds per annum, supplemented by a new year's gift, which usually comes to about ten or twelve pounds. . . .

"No. II. is in a still sadder plight. For twenty years his salary as a village pastor has never exceeded sixty pounds per annum, and, to use his own words, '*It has often been ten, and sometimes fifteen, pounds below that sum.*' This, with a wife afflicted for thirty years with complicated internal maladies, seeking aid from many physicians, and being nothing bettered but rather the worse, added to other domestic trials, and many deaths in the family, is enough, one would think, to crush all preaching out of a man! 'Few,' he says, 'save our Heavenly Father, know the privations and struggles which we have endured these twenty years.' . . .

" No. III. stands apart upon a pinnacle of special and exceptional sadness. . . . The husband is weak and ill from the lingering effects of a bronchial attack which prostrated him two years since, a young child is in a delicate and critical condition, the wife, though in fast-failing health has just become the mother of their *twelfth* child, all living save one, and *the last five are under five years of age!* Their income from all sources, salary, small business, and gifts from friends included . . . fifty-five pounds a year! Can respectable poverty know a lower depth than this ? "

The cases of poverty in one denomination are quite in keeping with those found in another; and we have to bear in mind that in consequence of agricultural depression and other causes the people are suffering as well as the pastors. Thus,

Mrs. C. H. SPURGEON.

one who has to maintain a wife and children on a little over one hundred pounds a year bears emphatic testimony to what may now be witnessed in the country. " He says he never before witnessed so much poverty and distress in his district; yet, at the same time, he speaks with holy enthusiasm of the trust in God and resignation to His will manifested by the suffering people. 'It is no easy work,' he writes, 'to live in a place like this, where one sees 'trouble' written on every face. I could not go into the houses of my people, and see shoeless feet and empty cupboards, without doing something to help them. Many must have gone to the poor-house, or have died without medical aid, if I had not paid the cost.'" What a commentary is such action as this on the words " Blessed is he that considereth the poor, the Lord will deliver him in the time of trouble." There are no helpers of the poor like those who are poor themselves.

The strongest testimony to the value of the work is seen in the letters of the pastors themselves who receive the books. In a manner that ordinary persons can hardly understand, the parcels of books have carried gladness into many a beclouded home, while they have stimulated many a flagging ministry.

"When I wrote for the fifth volume of Mr.

Spurgeon's *Treasury of David*," wrote a Congregational minister in 1880, " I felt that you would place me under an obligation of lively gratitude by acceding to my request; but when, instead of one volume, I am the fortunate recipient of seven, and all of them of great interest and utility, to congratulate myself and express my thanks to you in a measure proportioned to your bounty, is a task more easily undertaken than adequately performed. . . ."

Another pastor of the same denomination, also writing in 1880, says: " Accept my warmest thanks for the books, and also for the kind thoughtfulness which arranged for their reception on *Saturday*. Having been worried and worked over-much this week, and feeling very far from well, I was in a state of physical exhaustion and mental depression, which by no means augured well for to-morrow, when your parcel arrived. The very sight of it did me good, and when I opened it and discovered its precious contents I cannot tell you how many degrees better I felt at once."

The clergy of the Establishment, including even many of the High Church school, have received gifts; and from the acknowledgments, written in their own characteristic way, we see something of the poverty which abounds in the

Anglican communion on the one hand, while there is superabundant wealth on the other.

A curate in the north wrote: "I felt on the arrival of your parcel as if I must be so un-ministerial as to jump for joy. . . . As the volumes lie before me on my table, my heart is full, and words can but feebly express with what pleasure I subscribe myself," etc.

In 1881 we find that Mrs. Spurgeon had to entertain an exceptionally large number of applications from the pastors of the Established Church; and the cry for books coming from that quarter was responded to with a liberality quite in keeping with the character of the Fund, but which none the less on that account surprised the recipients. "In some cases it may be quite possible that the volumes are sought for the scarcely admitted purpose of wholesale appropriation, but what then?" remarks Mrs. Spurgeon. "Notwithstanding every way, whether in pretence or in truth, Christ is preached, and we therein do rejoice, and will rejoice. How many a young curate, with small ability but gracious spirit, might serve his Master well, and feed the flock of God with more convenient food, were he to cast aside his own manuscript, and preach boldly and bodily a sermon from the Tabernacle Pulpit. I am told this is very often done, and I can but say, May God bless the doing of it." As regards the business of appropriation, we find that one parish "supply" preached Mr. Spurgeon's sermons for nine Sabbaths in the parish church, greatly to the delight and edification of the parishioners. Nor did the good man adopt what some will think to have been his singular procedure without good reason; for he frankly confessed, "Mr. Spurgeon's sermons are the only ones which can be really understood either by myself or the congregation."

At first sight it might seem somewhat anomalous when High Church and Ritualistic clergymen send in their applications for books; but Mrs. Spurgeon, nevertheless, regards the phenomenon with satisfaction, because, as a certain member of the Church declared, the Baptist Pastor's works more accurately represent the doctrines of the Thirty-nine Articles than much of what is preached in many of the churches.

One of the "Advanced" school in the Midlands, who received a grant, had a vicar who had denounced Baptists as "abominable Dissenters"; but the great man was not above writing a recommendation to the Book Fund on behalf of his curate. "Tell Mr. Spurgeon I shall highly value his *Treasury* and *Sermons*, and hope to reap much benefit from his *Lectures to*

Students" remarked the curate. "I never write, without a prayer for God's guidance and blessing, and I shall study these books, looking for the Divine enlightenment. I send you a view of my church—it holds about seven hundred people, and to-morrow I hope to assist in *five services* and preach twice." Another, who also confessed that he was "what is called a Ritualist," said on receiving his books, "I shall point to this present as an instance of kind Christian sympathy underlying considerable difference of religious opinions." He then went on to rejoice that those who really loved their Lord had so much in common notwithstanding outward distinctions.

Among those clergymen who have written about their adventures with Mr. Spurgeon's sermons, however, the writer of the following should perhaps rank first in point of interest :—

"Having heard that you kindly assist poor ministers with books, permit me to state that I am an ordained priest of the Church of England ; and though prevented by age from holding any permanent curacy, I am engaged at a stipend of £30 per annum in two villages, and have to go some distance on Sundays, in different directions, for morning and evening service. On the second Sunday in Lent this year (1881), I was reading a text, when suddenly I remembered the Three

Thens (Isaiah vi. 1-8), by the Rev. C. H. Spurgeon, and gave it as a morning discourse at ———. I was afterwards asked by a district visitor what induced me to select so singular a text, and another hearer said she had never listened to anything like it before, while the majority of the people were so pleased, that during the nine Sundays I was there the church was full every afternoon."

Such are the recipients of the Fund at home; but in some instances the books find their way to the Colonies and to French pastors on the Continent. One of the latter in writing to Mrs. Spurgeon said : " Now, more than ever, Protestant pastors have a great work to do in France. The people are tired of the clergy, while, on the other hand, infidels are trying to make way, and they boast of their science, comparing it with the too well known ignorance of the Romish priests." Since the Reformation won its triumphs, partly through the evangelical books which were vended by the colporteurs, who can help wishing that the second reformation, which alone can save the country from imminent peril, may be advanced by the Book Fund distribution ?

The words of cheer and of appreciation which come from the Colonies are similar to those which are so plentiful at home. " I need not say how the volumes will be prized and valued for their intrinsic merit," says one in Canada on the receipt of a grant, "the inspiration they will supply, the food they will give to mind and heart, and also for the sake of the author, whose dear and beloved form I see outlined before my mind's eye every day, and whose ringing voice I fancy I can hear across the three thousand miles of ocean. God grant that I may be able to catch more and more of that high-souled, consecrated enthusiasm which breathes through his writings like the fresh breeze of morning."

But although the distribution of books is the chief thing to be undertaken by Mrs. Spurgeon, she has extended her supplies to the wives and children of poor Pastors by means of the Pastors' Aid Fund. A small affair when compared with the other and main department of the work, the Aid Fund has still relieved a large number of the most deserving cases of pastors, their wives and children, whose chief cross in life is extreme poverty. Not only money, but clothes are given, so that all the members of a family are found rejoicing together.

Thus, as one recipient writes : " We are all very pleased with the share we have in the contents of the parcel. This is something for wife, children, and myself, and everything is so suitable and helpful. I scarcely know how I shall feel when I get on the nice warm clothes, and my wife says she will look as she once did, in her new dress."

Writing of this friend in 1881 Mrs. Spurgeon herself says: "He has been battling this long time with no small tempest of adversity and sorrow." The preacher himself added, "I feel the load removed which has burdened me so long, I see my precious books saved from dispersion, I see the faces of my wife and children lit up with joy, I seem to hear the congratulations of those comrades in the conflict who have always stood by me."

Scores of cases might be quoted to show the need of the work, and every one is representative of a need which is no less urgent than widespread. Thus one pastor's wife, who is called by Mrs. Spurgeon "One of the bravest little women I know," wrote in 1881: "I have been so very unwell all the winter, that our expenses have been unusually heavy, and I had put nothing by for the little boy's advent, so when he came we had no money in the house, and having to take our salary little by little, times being so bad with the people, we hardly ever seem to possess any."

Quite in keeping with this is the confession

of an Essex pastor, who about the same time wrote: "We never were so straitened as now; my income fell off last year more than twenty-five per cent., and I assure you we have wanted the common necessaries of life, and I have come to my last pair of trousers. When I put the note into my wife's hand, she burst into tears, embraced me, and said, 'What a mercy God has raised up friends to be so kind and good to us!'"

When we ask, Who are they who help this work? we find that they are as cosmopolitan as those who receive the benefit. In the early days of the enterprise the growth of the Fund was supposed to keep pace with a certain lemon-tree in the greenhouse at Clapham. It will be remembered how the Fund was commenced by the surrender of certain crown pieces which had been carefully saved; and this example of self-sacrifice became so contagious that on a spring day in 1881 Mrs. Spurgeon wrote: "Four crown pieces, labelled 'Silver-blossoms for the dear lemon-tree,' were sent to-day by a beloved friend to cheer my heart and help forward my work." Of course the sender had a confession to make—"I have had them a long time lying by; for my dear departed mother used to save them as a little present for me, and I never before could part with them ; but when I read how you began your good work, I felt I must devote them to the Lord in the same way, and they come to you in love and prayer."

On June 16th, 1880, this letter arrived: "Please find enclosed a post-office order for £2 1s. 6d., and a small slip of paper which will explain the use to which the money is to be put. It was directed to be sent to you by a Christian friend of mine, Mrs. D——, of Greenock, and was found in a drawer after her death. I may state that she had a struggle to support herself by her needle, and selling small furnishings, and was long in poor health, but her heart was in her Master's work, and she now receives her reward." The slip of paper contained a note in the widow's own handwriting, to the effect that all threepenny-pieces taken in the way of business were to be " dedicated to the Lord's work under the hand of Mrs. Spurgeon."

Thus, while some give of their abundance, there are others who still give even though poverty might well excuse their doing anything in the way of contributing to the wants of others. Some give money, but good books are of course as acceptable as cash, the only drawback to presents in kind being, that on some occasions certain donors, with more benevolence than sense, or with a nicer perception of their own convenience than of the character of Mrs. Spurgeon's needs, have sent mere lumber instead of serviceable works. Take the following episode by way of illustration :—

"Would that my record of 'presents' ended with those which call forth my gratitude and admiration. Alas! I have to renew my yearly complaint that people in mistaken kindness *will* send me the rubbish they know not how else to get rid of. I remember saying ... that I had received nearly every sort of inappropriate and unsuitable volume except a 'Cookery Book,' and I congratulated myself that such an indignity had not yet befallen my Fund. But I have now been brought to that 'lowest depth;' for in one of the unwelcome parcels forwarded to me lately there are two musty old tomes which bear the title of '*The Complete Housewife, and Accomplished Gentlewoman's Companion*, being a Collection of upwards of seven hundred of the most approved receipts for Cookery, and above three hundred receipts of Medicine. London 1766.' After this, I thought I might have borne anything; but to-day has brought me a still sharper experience, and I feel constrained to exclaim against the cruel kindness of people who thus so thoughtlessly trouble and burden me. I had received an anonymous note bidding me expect the arrival of a case of books for my 'Clerical Library,' carriage paid as far as possible. With much anxiety I awaited the advent of the case, and when it made its appearance its size was so imposing that I did not grudge the *nine shillings I had to pay for its transit*, confidently hoping to find many choice treasures in its contents. Judge, then, my annoyance and my indignation on seeing when it was opened that, with the exception of a few well-bound books, of thirdrate worth, the case was chiefly filled with old hymn-books, works by Unitarians, and books against believers' Baptism ! Does it not seem cruel to mock my dear work thus, and give me a 'stone' for my poor ministers who are asking for 'bread' at my hands? How to get rid of the rubbish was now the question. 'Put the old lumber in the furnace,' said an excited helper in the unpacking. 'No,' said another, whose manifest annoyance somewhat solaced me; 'no, it would only choke up the flues—it is not fit even for that use.'"

Such is the work of the Book Fund. Mrs. Spurgeon has conferred benefit on the Church both far-reaching and lasting; and the pastors of all denominations have become her debtors.

REVIEWS IN "THE SWORD AND THE TROWEL."

"Our Magazine . . . will address itself to those faithful friends scattered everywhere; who are our well-wishers and supporters in our work of faith and labour of love. . . . Our friends are so numerous as to be able to maintain a Magazine, and so earnest as to require one. Our monthly message will be a supplement to our weekly sermon, and will enable us to say many things which would be out of place in a discourse. It will inform the general Christian public of our movements, and show our sympathy with all that is good throughout the entire Church of God. . . . We do not pretend to be unsectarian, if by this be meant the absence of all distinctive principles, and a desire to please parties of all shades of opinion. We believe and therefore speak. We speak in love, but not in soft words and trimming sentences. We shall not court controversy, but we shall not shun it when the cause of God demands it. . . . We would sound the trumpet, and lead our comrades to the fight. We would ply the trowel with untiring hand for the building up of Jerusalem's dilapidated walls, and wield the sword with vigour and valour against the enemies of the truth."—*The Sword and the Trowel, January,* 1865.

XI.

REVIEWS IN "THE SWORD AND THE TROWEL."

AFTER he had laboured in London rather more than ten years, Mr. Spurgeon established a monthly organ of his own, the title of which may at first have seemed quaint or eccentric, but which has since become thoroughly familiar to lovers of good things throughout the British Isles. Not that this threepenny magazine has ever really enjoyed a popularity commensurate with its merits, although the circulation has always been large for a denominational magazine. From the first, one of its leading and most attractive features consisted in the Expositions of the Psalms, which commence in the first number, and which have since taken a more permanent form in *The Treasury of David*. The magazine also showed that from the first it would become an authority on books; for the quality of the notices given proved that those who examined the works for the purpose of giving judgment really took the trouble to read what they criticised. Of course all the notices were not written by Mr. Spurgeon, and the editor early protested against the habit of some publishers affixing his name to advertised extracts. At the same time, when anything unusually smart or witty was said, it did not require any very acute judge to say who was the author. In quoting a few extracts let us begin with the poets.

"How briskly the fire burns in the grate! Yes, the editor has received a fresh lot of poetry." Thus suggestively opens a notice of "A Poem," *alias* "Bones and Fiddles." "We wish the author had let verse alone, for we do not believe that he would be half so prosy in prose as he is in rhyme."

The following appeared in 1882 :—

"*Verse and Verse. Rhymes for Dinner Times. Poem on a Boot Jack. Ode to a Poll Parrot. Meditations and Agitations*, etc. Tirem, Borem, and Co.

"The above titles are given in lieu of many others which have come before us. Our table groans with Cowpers and Tennysons in an embryonic condition. A San Francisco paper having been driven desperate by voluntary poetical contributions, sounds this note of warning :—' We don't know exactly how newspapers were conducted at that distant period, but during some recent excavations in Assyria a poem on *The*

Impatient Poets. 291

Silver Moon was dug up. It was engraved on a tile, and close beside it were lying a large battered club and part of a human skull. You may draw your own conclusions.' We are led to quote this as a warning to the many small poets who send books of verses for review. Happily in our case no club is kept on the premises, and we are most gentle in temper; but really, we are tried up to the boiling point by the poetic coals which are heaped upon us. Still, Job is our patron saint, and we are resolved to endure unto the end. If any verse-maker does not find his poem, or her poem, mentioned in these notices, it is because we do not like to cause pain by saying what we think about the precious compositions. Please do not write to say that your poetry must have been overlooked; for the fact is, we have looked it over, and think it the wisest course to be silent. Perhaps the work is too sublime, too elevated in thought, too superb in diction, for our grovelling taste. Pray think so, or think anything else, so long as you are happy. For the most part these minor poets are our affliction, and if they would be so good as to take offence, and never send us another specimen of their wares, we would bless them in our heart of hearts."

More recently, a certain "Romaunt" called forth this response: "No; we cannot. If we were condemned to a week's imprisonment, or to read this poem through, we should be weak enough to choose the latter; but as we are not driven to that alternative, we will neither go to prison nor read this blank verse." On another occasion we come across the question, "Is there any rule for writing poetry? Yes. *Don't.* So has a wise editor settled the matter, and in ninety-nine cases out of a hundred the decision is not to be questioned." Again, "A cynical old editor, who overheard an enthusiast remark that nature is full of poetry, snarled out, 'So is my waste-basket.'" Another editor commends to his contributors the example of Tennyson, who composes very slowly, and adds, "Never send in a poem to-day that can be sent in to-morrow. Perhaps there will be a fire before to-morrow." On another occasion amateur poets received this general advice from one who keenly felt that their work represented "one of the miseries of the editorial chair." "We recommend all poets, good or bad, to write carefully, correct seventy-two times, keep the manuscript ninety-nine years, and give orders for it to be buried in their coffins with them. We only except our personal friends, and any others who read this magazine regularly: they have our plenary indulgence to write as much as ever they please and send it on to us, enclosing a guinea with each line."

In one case, wherein a second copy had been sent, the author fearing that the first had been overlooked, the unhappy editor remarked, "The volume is altogether beyond our reach. If we receive a dozen copies of it we are afraid we shall still gaze upon the work with wondering awe, but shall never be able to see wherein it is superior to Milton."

At the end of 1874 this timely manifesto appeared : " Poetry again ! This grunt rose as naturally to our lips as the words ' Cold mutton again!' to the hungry husband who had looked for better fare. The cross and burden of our reviewing lies in the poetical department ; we can never please the authors, and the authors do not often please us. Why do they print ? It cannot be for profit, their minds are far above so base a consideration. It must be from the notion that they bestow pleasure, and we can assure them that they are greatly mistaken. . . . It is the books, the big books *to be reviewed*, that we are sore about, books of which we have two, three, four copies sent because we have forgotten to review them ; books we wish we could forget, and which one never means to say anything about for fear our memory should be cruel enough to remind us of them."

One of the minor brotherhood who had the

temerity to send in his production "Just after Christmas too!" was asked, "What does he want with Philetos and Zön, with two dots over the 'o'? What is the whole business about? Why did not the author put it in prose, and then we should have known all about it in a reasonable space of time? It seems that he sat on a bough and 'rocked his musings into drowsy rest,' and then dedicated them to Tennyson, 'the sweetest songbird of our native land.'"

Of course there is occasionally something to commend even in the work of minor poets, and when real merit is discovered it is cordially recognised. Many examples might be quoted were it needful to do so.

Mr. Spurgeon has never disguised the fact that he does not greatly care for tales; he seldom reads these himself, but at the same time he has given novelists plenty of wholesome advice. In the case of one historical novel, written by one who was supposed to rank as a popular author, it was remarked: "Here are power, beauty, pathos, philosophy, theology, and history all strangely mixed together, and the result, while flattering to the author's powers, is severely puzzling to the reader. Half the ability here displayed, if only the style could be made clear and transparent, would be far more effectual than it is now,

How we wish writers would not be too clever! It would make them doubly interesting and doubly popular if they could be understood by ordinary folk."

Of another historical story about Gutenberg, the inventor of printing, it is said, "The worst of it is, one does not know how much is true and how much is a mere tale; and this is one of the mischiefs of this sort of literature, that it diminishes the distinction between fact and fancy, and is too apt to make young people think little of sober truth."

Sometimes the reviewer's patience is about as sorely tried with the smaller fry in the realm of fiction as with the persecutions of the minor poets. We find it said of one, for example, "The woodcuts are so hideous that no story could survive them, and certainly not so weak an affair as this. With a new story and new pictures, like the boy's knife with a new handle and a new blade, the book might then be worth having." But we suppose that even this was outdone by a certain "grey-covered shilling'sworth of pietistic nonsense about Christianity in general, and Methodism in particular;" of which it is added, "If Wesleyanism could be killed by fulsome flattery and idiotic goodyism this would be its death-blow. But there—no one could read the tale all through, and our wonder is that the compositors could set it up; but they are a long-suffering race." Again, of another we have this definite verdict, " This is the silliest book we have ever read. Perhaps this will induce some silly person to buy it."

The teetotal movement is frequently advocated by writers of fiction; and one of these is depicted as " an accumulation of horrors, enough to make one lay awake by nights and shiver with fright; and yet no one of the horrors is in itself overdrawn or improbable. We should not like to be a drink-maker or a drink-seller and have this tale within ten miles of us. It has a mysterious hand like that in Belshazzar's dream, and writes awful things on the wall of the conscience."

Story-tellers are also taught that mere eccentricity is not a legitimate road to success, such for example as writing in a provincial dialect. " It is the thought a man cares for; and to get that one can put up with Cornish, or Scotch, or Zummerzet; but when the vein of gold no longer appears in the quartz, we cease to be enamoured of the rock. You may write in double-Dutch if you like, when you have something to say; but when your matter is commonplace, you will never make it go by writing it in your country jargon."

The wearisome books from the reviewer's standpoint are legion, such, for example, as " A wordy book about words, the value of which may be summed up in few words." Of another of this class we learn that "the title is the most striking part of the book, but we warn our readers that the only reference to it is found on the title-page." Then it is added, "What a pity it is that good people should be silly enough to waste time and paper and ink in writing what could scarcely benefit any human being."

The reviewer's office is thus no sinecure, and it is especially trying when a dry and empty theological book calls for notice. "A very thoughtful book, no doubt, but who will ever read it?" we find it asked of one of these. "Some conscientious reviewer may perhaps complete the task; we with equal conscientiousness decline it. Sitting one day at the foot of a mountain at our ease, we advised all our friends to climb it, and awarded all sorts of praise to those who achieved the feat: so now, we say, 'Here is a grand book for you, my lads; never mind its being dry; just tackle it, and show your stamina.' 'Oh,' you say, 'read it yourself.' Not if we know it. We have other fish to fry." But perhaps even this was to be preferred to another—"Rubbish in rhyme, without any reason." Then hardly more reassuring is an elaborate work on misunderstood texts by one who gives sufficient evidence that she also misunderstands them. In one instance a General is found writing an exposition of the last book of the New Testament, but harder to be understood than the Revelation itself.

There are some authors who succeed only up to a certain point; and the following timely caution addressed to a certain writer can be well accepted by many others: "The style is clear, crisp, and attractive up to a certain point, and will be sure to be read; but we are half-afraid it is too 'preachy.' Souls are wondrously shy things, and must be very wisely dealt with: the old-fashioned tract style of writing is scarcely likely to do much to-day."

Books which attempt to tell things beyond such as are revealed are always a mistake, and are not at all in accordance with Mr. Spurgeon's taste. Of one of the best known of these we read: "Time spent in examining this rubbish we greatly grudge. Dreamy, foolish nonsense, with a touch of something worse. Messrs. —— have brought out many curiosities; this is certainly one of the oddest of them, and, we think, the most worthless."

The following relates to the Welsh and their preachers:—"Our brethren of the Principality are as good sermon-hearers as any people under heaven, and their ministers, encouraged by their enthusiastic appreciation, are urged on to excel in pulpit eloquence. Moreover, as their language is, according to their own judgment—and they ought to know—so heavenly, so divine, it is no great marvel that those who use it are able to produce extraordinary results. As we see it in print, we feel that our friends are right; it is an unearthly language and to us unutterable. Ll and a w, double l again, and a y, and then the rest of the alphabet shot down like a load of coals— what can this muddle mean? The man who can pronounce these jumbles of consonants must be a born orator."

The writers on prophecy are a somewhat numerous tribe, and are a source of annoyance to old-fashioned students of the Bible like Mr. Spurgeon. " The subject has been dragged in the mire so long that thoughtful men are slow to write on it." When some " Short Papers" appeared some years ago it was said, " The best thing about these ' Short Papers ' is that they are *short*."

Of a well-known magazine, mainly devoted to speculations in this department, and the editor of which was personally much respected, it was said : " Its present light is not equal to the production of a lunar rainbow, such as lovers of the old, fashioned gospel of covenant grace delight to look upon; in its prophetic moonshine, and short-punishment theorisings we see no rainbow, unless it be a lunar one."

Again, it is remarked on this subject : " That good paper and ink should be wasted in maunderings over vials and trumpets is bad enough, but that Christian men should be led to draw vain imaginings as to coming events from the grand Apocalyptic vision is grievous to the last degree. The imposture of those who foretold the end of the papacy in 1866 ought to have covered them with shame sufficient to have deterred all aspiring prophetlings, but it seems to have called forth another band of vaticinators, who set the date a little later, or, more wisely still, postpone it to the year 2000, by which time they expect to have spent their profits, and to have retired from the scene." One writer of mature age made out that the geological periods of creation had corresponding periods in redemption. Says the reviewer, however : " The only analogy we could see was between the book itself and the earth when it was without form and void, and darkness was upon the face of the deep." Twenty years ago the " wonders " that were to appear before the end of 1875 were terribly striking to lovers of the sensational in theology ; but when a well-known cleric narrated some of these in a separate publication his work was characterised as " Probably the wildest of all the wild things which the present prophetic mania has produced. This volume of nonsense is adorned with pictures such as would suit the outside of a travelling show, and its matter will have great weight with the sort of audience which gathered to see Katterfelto and his black cats, Katterfelto with his hair on end at his own wonders, wondering for his bread."

From all this it is pleasant to turn to what is said about Puritans, with whom Mr. Spurgeon is probably as familiar as any preacher in the kingdom.

Nearly twenty years ago it was proposed to reprint Caryl's two vast folios on the Book of Job, the reading of which has for generations been regarded as the best possible discipline in the virtue for which the patriarch was famous. Mr. Spurgeon does not think with the crowd on Caryl, however. " Caryl is not tediously prolix, as some imagine," we are assured ; " he is deep but interesting. Truly he is a mountain, but the sheep feed even to the summit."

Then what about Bunyan, imitations of whose allegories still continue to appear ? " If you eat honey you cannot taste the sugar in your tea ; if you read John Bunyan you cannot enjoy any other allegory. There is only one sun, and when you look upon it you never think of mentioning candles in the same hour." Some years ago the Vicar of Elstow published a capital book with the object of getting a stained-glass window put up in the parish church. Mr. Spurgeon confessed that he could not see "the congruity of the thing." It was asked, "Why not repair a Catholic chapel as a memorial of Martin Luther? or the Baptist chapel at Elstow as a memorial of Charles II.? ... If John Bunyan's ghost walks the earth it will haunt the church until the stained-glass window is removed, if, indeed, it is ever placed."

The writings of Gurnal are said to be "peerless and priceless; every line is full of wisdom; every sentence is suggestive." Of "The Christian in Complete Armour" it is added: "The whole book has been preached over scores of times, and it is, in our judgment, the best thought-breeder in all our library." Again, Gurnal "is one of the greatest of the giants of the Puritan age. Many of our modern theological treatises are so devoid of real substance, that we are reminded of the chicken-broth which the sick husband returned to his wife, with the urgent request that she would coax the chicken to wade through it once more; but when we turn to Gurnal, the old English roast beef loads the board."

"Rare John Trapp," the seventeenth century commentator, is called "our favourite author."

His work on the New Testament " is worth its weight in gold at the least, and sooner than not possess it we would throw in a diamond ring or two, if we possessed such things."

Many leading divines of the second half of the nineteenth century are noticed. More than twenty years ago the prophetical doctor, *alias* *The Times* Bee-Master, diversified his pulpit vagaries by publishing a book on Bee-keeping, in which he expressed a wish "that somebody would send Mr. Spurgeon a super of good honey" to sweeten his temper. " Why he should need to drag *us* in among his bees, we cannot tell, unless it be that our faithful rebukes of Anglican abominations have reminded him of his own unworthy silence on such matters, and he therefore attempts to drown the voice of his own conscience by finding fault with us." It is then added : " In spiritual things we greatly prefer salt to honey ; remembering that it is written, 'In all thine offerings, thou shalt offer salt ;' and again, 'Ye shall burn no leaven, nor any honey, in any offering of the Lord made by fire.' Salt, though sharp and penetrating, is the deadly foe of all corruption ; and honey, on the other hand, though sweet, is corruptible, soon ferments and turns sour. Fire speedily spoils the sweetest honey. We advise the doctor to use more salt in his public ministry."

The opinion given on Mr. H. W. Beecher's Sermons, published in 1865, would, we believe, hold good to-day : " He professedly deviates from the old American standard of orthodoxy, and in the same proportion, as we think, departs from the truth. As an improvement upon the theology of the Puritan fathers, his teaching will be rejected by the best of men in this and in every subsequent age. . . . Lessons of moral wisdom, of social endearment, and of practical piety, may be gathered from these sermons ; but for sound doctrine we must look elsewhere. It is a lawful book if a man use it lawfully."

Speaking of the late Thomas Binney in 1868 *The Sword and the Trowel* said : " He has ways of his own of putting things which some in years gone by have been frightened at, but we greatly question whether any man after all was sounder at heart towards the old-fashioned Gospel. In this delightful volume—" From Seventeen to Thirty "—he proves himself to be the greatest business man in the ministry. He talks as if he had been bound apprentice to Mr. Samuel Morley, had worked his way into the warehouse, had become a partner, and was now appointed by the court of aldermen to see to the morals of the city apprentices. He ought to be an archbishop over this nation of shopkeepers. . . . Set him among a very spiritual audience of half-pay officers and wealthy spinsters, and he would be like a lion on a hearth-rug, but for where he is and for what he is, where is his equal?"

The editor has no sympathy with those who devote too much attention to objectors while the multitude need the pure Gospel. When a work appeared, "Ingersoll Answered," Mr. Spurgeon said, "We neither care for Ingersoll nor the answer to him. There is enough to do in England with cutting up our own brambles; nine out of ten of our people know nothing of this American briar, and there is no need they should." He said also to another author on a certain occasion: "Why need 'Essays and Reviews' and Dr. Colenso be put up just to show how elegantly they can be knocked down? Orthodox divines too often do the advertising for heretics, and turn bill-stickers to the devil. Why should they? We are getting tired of ghost-hunting."

Thomas Cooper, the ex-Chartist, and ex-Secularist lecturer, but who since his conversion has done good service as a preacher, etc., has long been a favourite with Mr. Spurgeon. "It is no disgrace to Cooper, or to any other man, to have been a Chartist," it is said in the magazine for August 1878. "The Chartists only lived a little before their time, all the points of their terrible

Charter having at length been granted, in effect, if not in letter; and there was nothing unrighteous or revolutionary in their demands. It was a far grander thing to have our mechanics caring for politics than to see them fighting for a double allowance of beer and a short spell of work. The modern agitator is a poor being compared with his predecessor of forty years ago. By so much as thinking is better than boozing, the discontented artizan of Thomas Cooper's early days was superior to the man on strike of the present period."

Some years ago certain books by Francis Jacox were popular. " Mr. Jacox appears to have read through the Bodleian and all other collections of books; he does not talk like a book, but like the British Museum library. . . . We do not know any books in modern times at all like Mr. Jacox's; they are unique; in fact, they are curiosities of literature. . . . The man must be a cyclopædia; we expect to come across him one day, and to find him bound in cloth, lettered. He ought to be in several volumes, but we suppose they are bound up in one thick royal octavo, and contain more matter than a hundred volumes of Dr. Going or Dr. Septimus Losequick."

In 1883 the Rev J. De Kewer Williams

published his lecture on "The City Mottoes, and Other Wise Saws." This was said to be "a clever talk by a witty man, who is withal as wise as he is facetious. We spent a very pleasant hour in listening to a reading of this telling lecture: it was under the palmtrees at Cannes, but we forgot our surroundings, and thought we were in the dear old city of Gog and Magog and Fog, with Mr. De Kewer Williams for our pedagogue."

In 1880 reference occurs to a once popular "History of the Jews":—" Milman's is an elaborate work, but it seems to us to cut down the glorious Old Testament narrative to the dimensions of an Eastern romance. There is not much real breadth in these Broad Church writers: they can hardly tolerate a miracle."

When "Julius Cæsar" appeared in 1865, *The Sword and the Trowel* contained a characteristic notice, *e.g.*:—" This great work is beyond doubt a most valuable contribution to history, and an honour to the pen of its imperial author. It will not disappoint the high expectations which its announcement excited. It is written with one object, and works towards its intended end most cleverly. Napoleon III. is the preacher, Cæsar is the text to be spiritualized; the excellences of imperialism are the subjects of the homily, and glory be unto my immortal uncle is the conclusion."

Children's books have always demanded a large share of attention; and by his notices of these Mr. Spurgeon has shown how greatly he is in sympathy with the little ones. Sometimes he seems to be so enchanted with what is provided for juvenile readers that he wishes he were once more in a jacket himself, so that he could more legitimately enjoy the literary dainties peculiar to the present age. Then take this example of the reviews—a notice of a work on geography which appeared in 1880:—" Happy young England to be taught thus pleasantly ! One while the tree of knowledge bore thorns and crabs, but now it is a dainty tree, beflowered as with golden lilies of pleasure, and befruited with rosiest apples of delight. *Geography*—have we really been taking in a whole jar of that verjuice? Yes, and we thought we were out a-gipsying, roaming from town to town, o'er hill and dale. Ah me! This is not the geography which made our little head ache, and caused school to be a torture both to the teacher and the taught."

We will close this chapter with a few miscellaneous references illustrative of the wit and wisdom on other every-day topics which is continually enriching the pages of *The Sword and the Trowel* in the review department.

When many church-members are apparently

asking themselves how far they can go in conformity to the world, the following notice of Anna Warner's "Tired Christians," which appeared in 1882, will show what kind of sentiments Mr. Spurgeon holds on this subject :—"Just our mind with regard to dancing, theatre-going, and the like. Well does our authoress confess her difficulty in writing about amusements for Christians, since no such word as amusement, recreation, game, or pastime can be found in the Scriptures. No : in the sacred book we read that time is short, and we are bidden to redeem it, but never taught how to waste it. . . . Tired Christians will find frivolous amusement a poor means of rest ; we fear that many are more wearied by their play than by their work, and are more likely to be jaded by dissipation than by devotion."

What is the relationship between work and genius ? The answer occurs in a notice of Mr. H. Curwen's "Plodding On," published in 1879 : "By the way, it would be a gross error if men imagined that men of genius do not work. To our mind, genius generally means that a man has a tendency and an aptitude for double to in a certain direction, and hence he prospers in it. A genius for hard work is the only genius we believe in. We once knew a fellow who was called a *genius*, and boasted that he could make his fortune in a year: the last time we heard of him he could not make a personal call to borrow five shillings because his uncle detained his coat and waistcoat. We shall not advertise for him if we never hear of him again."

What is Spiritualism? The question was answered in Mr. Pridham's "Spirits Tried," published in 1874. In a notice of that work we read :—"We had aforetime considered Spiritualism to be a mere humbug, to be best assailed by ridicule, and such we still believe it to be in most cases; but Mr. Pridham's work puts a more serious face upon the business, and certainly makes us think that the devil has a good deal more to do with it than we imagined. We gave him credit for more sense; he is certainly a greater fool than we took him to be. We always had the lowest possible opinion of him morally, but we thought he could not come down so low as to be in league with idiotic spiritualists. He is certainly a deal meaner than when Milton wrote about him."

Writers who are too florid are not generally admired, especially in *The Sword and the Trowel;* so that in order to catch the editor's attention, and to command his approbation, it is not well to be "one of those who would go into raptures over a broomstick, and praise the picturesque beauty of a dust-heap." Nor in general does plagiarism meet with anything short of the severest condemnation. I will close these extracts with a description of the treatment accorded to a book whose author was detected in stealing other people's wares. The work in question was published some years ago, and related to the pulpit, its occupants, its literature, etc. "*Notes on reading this volume :*—Received it with great pleasure, liking the subject and respecting the publisher, and also the author. . . . Reached page 12, and smelt a strong smell of Roman candles while reading remarks on baptismal regeneration, fonts, and altars. Passed on, and began to sniff again, for there was a remarkable odour of abounding plagiarism. Remembered to have heard Mr. Paxton Hood's lectures to our young men, now published as 'Lamps, Pitchers, and Trumpets'; marked the same extracts, often beginning and ending with the same word, and with the same headings. Pitched the book to the other end of the room, and despite a few interesting novelties could not bring our soul to do other than cry out, 'Dead robbery!' Picked up the book with its back broken, and muttered, 'Served it right.'"

Every month the pages of Mr. Spurgeon's

magazine devoted to reviews thus contain a great fund of instruction as well as of entertainment. In a word, Mr. Spurgeon, who is the most celebrated preacher of this age, has also made his mark as a reviewer of new books. If we desire to see how he can deal with old ones we have only to consult his *Commenting and Commentaries.*

CONCLUDING THOUGHTS AND REMINISCENCES.

Let us turn our earnest attention to the subject of OUR POSITION TOWARD OUR LORD. . . . As he stood in our stead, *we also stand in his stead.* To our hearers we can truly say, "We pray you, in Christ's stead, be ye reconciled to God." Our Lord Jesus Christ lays his pierced hands upon our shoulders, and he says, "As the Father hath sent me into the world, even so send I you." We are commissioned to plead for Christ, even as he is commissioned to plead for us. For him we climb those stairs to point that sick and ignorant woman to the blood of reconciliation. For him we stand in the pulpit, and speak of sin, and righteousness, and judgment to come. In his place we cry "Behold the Lamb of God, which taketh away the sin of the world!"—"THE MINISTER IN THESE TIMES," *A Conference Address at the Pastor's College, April* 22, 1890.

XII.

CONCLUDING THOUGHTS AND REMINISCENCES.

SPURGEON was first of all, and most of all, a preacher.

Into the preacher's work he stepped at sixteen, and from that moment all who heard him—and at length all the world—recognized his right to be there. All else of the vast work he has done has been founded upon and centred around the pulpit work of preaching. He devised his Pastor's College to train other men to preach—and to preach to the people—as the universities were not training them to do. His commentaries look out into the pulpit rather than back into the study; the homiletic element in them overshadows the scholarly. His printed sermons were to preach to all the English-speaking race, and, beyond that, in all the languages of men. Through them he had the gift of tongues. For this he maintained that wonderful series, numbering now more than 2,000, never allowing him to repeat himself or to sleep on his laurels for well-nigh forty years.

Even his Orphan Asylums, his Home for Aged Ministers, his Old Ladies' Home, and other charities were the outgrowth of a pastor's warm heart. His "Sword and Trowel" was a kind of week-day preaching, and his "John Ploughman's Talks" are homilies on everyday religion—simply an uninspired Book of Proverbs.

Personal Memories.
By Rev. J. C. Fernald.

On the first Sunday evening, after reaching London, more than twenty years ago, the writer sought out Spurgeon's Tabernacle. How to find it? That was very easy. Any Londoner could tell. It is "just opposite 'The Elephant and Castle.'" Now "The Helephant and Castle," as the Londoners most appropriately call it, is a great gin-palace. You go down through streets which it is not always safe for men to traverse, even in the early evening, till you come where the lights of the gin-shop gleam, and the green doors swing, swing, to the constant traffic in drink, and poor, sodden, or emaciated creatures stand or sit hopelessly around the entrance. That is your landmark, and you know that by just turning your back on that scene of desolation and sin, you will face Spurgeon's Tabernacle.

It is a dull, rainy evening, and you flatter yourself it will be a good chance to hear the great preacher, because there will be no crowd. But when you reach the great gray stone portico, its rows of columns enclosing a space large enough for a fair-sized church, lo, the crowd is there already. The space is half full of people, standing closely packed, right up to the great doors. People quickly crowd in behind you, till you are wedged fast. You turn to your neighbor, a plain, honest-appearing man, and ask if there is anything special to take place here this evening. He seems rather surprised, and answers "Nothing but Mr. Spurgeon's regular service," as one who would say "What more would you have?"

The rain pours down, and the people pour in, till the great vestibule is full. The hour arrives, the doors are opened, and with a rush—quiet but determined—the crowd surges in. People have been admitted by ticket at a side-door for an hour past, and the pews are perhaps half filled. They are filled to the doors in an instant now; for the law of the Tabernacle is that every seat is free from the moment the main doors are opened. You are quickly shoved into a seat, and fastened in tight by those who follow, and still the crowd presses on and on, like a bayonet charge, till every seat is full, and a solid phalanx packs every aisle, two-thirds of the way to the pulpit; standing there, silent, attentive, expectant. While waiting for the preacher, you glance at your neighbors. In the pews are many who are evidently thoughtful, Christian people; there are scholarly and clerical men—some of distinguished appearance—scattered through the crowd, yet the first feeling of a well-bred New Englander is a certain disgust. These blear-eyed men, these loudly-dressed, coarse-faced women, these poverty-stricken, unwashed street denizens thronging around you—some in your very pew whom you would not care to be seen with on the street! Your involuntary feeling is, that you are in disreputable society. You are not accustomed to go to church with such people, and you want to get out. Suddenly it occurs to you that Jesus used to draw a crowd which the proper people of His day did not approve of. You remember the question " Why eateth your Master with publicans and sinners?" and you begin to wonder if the Scribes and Pharisees did not feel just about as you do; or, to put the case another way, whether you do not feel pretty much as the Scribes and Pharisees did. You remember that they did not get much encouragement for that state of mind. You recall the words of the Lord: " They that are whole need not a physician, but they that are sick. I came not to call the righteous, but sinners to repentance. The Son of Man is come to seek and to save that which is lost." Well, here they are, the "sick," the "sinners," the "lost" beyond peradventure. You settle back into your seat, glad that any way they can be won into the house of God. But will they get any good from such a service, or are they drawn only by curiosity, a crowd, and a shelter? There is a subdued hum and rustle, and, attended by a little company of friends, deacons, and honored guests, the great preacher comes in. Hardly a moment elapses before he comes forward, offers up a brief prayer, and gives out a hymn. You forget the crowd, and everything else but the man, and the worship of Almighty God, to which he has called you.

Mr. Spurgeon does not exactly "line off" the hymn, but he remembers that many of those people have no books, and that many of them cannot read. So he reads one verse of a hymn, and waits for it to be sung—then reads another—and so on; he standing there as leader through all. A clear-voiced chorister takes up the hymn, and thousands of voices join, "like the noise of many waters." Ah, it is grand, thrilling! The Scripture is read as by a man who believes it; every word clear, with here and there a comment, to "give the sense, and cause the people to understand the meaning."

Mr. Spurgeon has no pulpit. When the opening services are ended, he steps forward to the front, and resting one hand easily on the railing that encloses the platform, he begins to preach, with clear, terse, strong sentences. There are no dubious explanations, nothing faltering or cloudy. "I believe, and therefore have I spoken" is behind every word. Soon there is a felt hush through the vast throng, as the preacher mightily "reasons of righteousness, temperance, and judgment to come." Then, as he tells of the tender mercy of our God, "not willing that any should perish, but that ALL should come to repentance," tears steal down the faces of these rough men and women with whom you at first hardly thought fit to worship in the same sanctuary. Oh, how reverently they depart when the sermon is ended! Who shall say what results to follow in new hearts and lives? You go away with wondering exaltation, the New Testament somehow translated anew. Spurgeon has his Master's credentials. "The common people hear him gladly. The poor have the Gospel preached to them."

Again and again you go, and the experience is the same—the crowd never less—the preacher's power never faltering—the speaker never repeating himself—the one great theme of salvation always his message, yet new as the changing days. He is one with his audience. He worships with them. He prays for them. You feel instinctively when he prays, that here is a man strong enough and good enough to bear up on his anointed hands toward heaven the prayers of a host—the grandest idea that ever entered into the thought of a priesthood between God and men.

But his preaching is at the furthest remove from any priestly idea. It is that of a plain man to plain men; but of a man who has got farther than you on the way to God—is glad that he has, and eager to tell you of it, that you may "go there too." He is at home with his audience. One Sunday morning, when he had given out the first verse of a grand old hymn, the people had somehow not caught the spirit of it. The moment the last sounds of the song died away, Mr. Spurgeon closed his hymn-book, with finger still between the leaves, and resting the book on the railing before him, raised the other hand, in his familiar gesture, and exclaimed, "That is not to the praise and glory of God. You would not sing those words like that if you thought what they meant." Then, opening the book, in a few ringing sentences he gave the thought of the hymn, adding, "Now let us try that verse again." He read it once more, and it was sung with thrilling, heart-moving power. This well illustrates one characteristic of Mr. Spurgeon. He utters no killing criticisms or anathemas. He never exposes or denounces fault or sin for the sake of exposing or denouncing it. Sometimes he seems to lay bare the hearer's very soul before the moral law and the Majesty in the heavens. But just when the heart is most oppressed and humiliated with the consciousness of unworthiness, he says in effect, "Let us try again ; let us return unto the Lord," and sweetly rings out the Gospel of hope.

Spurgeon's power as a preacher is not according to accepted rhetorical standards. He has not the stately figure and fine presence which are said to be essential. He is not above medium height, and too stout for what is called grace of motion, except the grace of massive solidity, consistent with itself. He has not the *spirituelle* cast of countenance, the lofty brow, and delicately cut features, nor the soul-piercing eye. The expression of eye and face is not that of one who has come to search you, but to tell you something he is greatly in earnest to tell, and glad to tell, and expects you to be interested in.

But his voice takes you captive from the moment it strikes your ear. Full, deep, mellow, clear, penetrating, it rolls forth and fills all the space with rich waves of sound. Yet, at first, you do not think of the voice, but of what the voice is saying. The preacher seems to be speaking directly to you, and for you, and there is nothing so natural as to listen to what he has to say. It is only when you have come again and again, and listened from every point in the vast building, when you find that right under the platform you are not stunned, and do not seem to be shouted at, and that standing just inside the door of the farthest gallery you hear with perfect ease and without the slighest strain on your attention, just as if someone were to come up and make a remark at your side—only then do you realize what a marvellous organ is the great preacher's voice. Then, the charm of it is, that he makes no perceptible effort. He seems to speak as easily as if you were seated in his parlor, and he were just entering into conversation on some pleasant theme.

Again and again—sometimes through long stretches of the sermon—each hearer, whatever his place, rank, or character, feels as if he were personally addressed. Mr. Spurgeon has come to speak to you, and a few thousand heads more or less between you and him make no sort of difference. "He that hath ears" cannot choose but hear.

He can be closely personal in his preaching. One Sunday night he preached on the little text, "And He shall be great"—and how great that text became! The burden of the sermon was that Christ is made great by victories of salvation; and the salvation he spoke of was that of individual sinners. In the peroration, he applied this redemption as a personal possibility to the host, class by class, and almost man by man. At one moment, he swept his hand and glance across the high gallery at his left, and exclaimed, "If Christ would come to that drunkard, and *wash his mouth out*, wouldn't that make Jesus Christ great?" There is no describing the intonation which the speaker put upon those homely words "wash his mouth out." As he uttered them, they seemed to carry the entire physical and moral renovation of the man, till you could see him cleansed from his pollution, " at the feet of Jesus, clothed and in his right mind." Then, the ringing triumph with which the closing words were uttered "*wouldn't that make Jesus Christ great?*" was like an echo of angels' songs of "joy over one sinner that repenteth." It was a word to give to the forlorn wretch the thought that even *his* redemption would be a glorious triumph for the crucified Redeemer, over which all the good in heaven and earth would rejoice.

As we came away, one minister of our party said, "Well, he preached to the publicans and sinners, the drunkards and the harlots, and *he had them all there.*"

The writer went one Sunday afternoon into the Young Men's Class, in one of the large basement rooms of the Tabernacle. It was a strange service viewed from the American standpoint. There were something more than a hundred young men, and the exercises were largely of a conference-meeting character. One of these young men would arise, read a verse of a hymn, speak of his own religious experience or work, and sit down; then another and another would follow. Often it was hard, stumbling work to read through the four lines of some simple stanza. Such an exercise would not, at first thought, seem likely to be very profitable. But here is one young man who has to be helped through his reading, who tells his story about as follows:

"I was sent with Brother B. down to —— Street; and found our mission in a room over a shop. It was a good, large room for that quarter; and Mrs. —— made it very interesting, but there were only a few people there. I said to Brother B. 'It's a shame to have that nice, big room, and such a good leader, and the room not half full; and people so thick about here.' He agreed with me, and we prayed over it, and the next Sunday morning we started out early, and went to the top of one alley, and began to sing. Pretty soon a crowd came round us, and then we told 'em what a good thing 'twas to love Jesus, and all the good it had done us, and told 'em about our room down on —— Street, and that we'd have service there at half-after-ten, and they'd all be welcome. Then we went to the next alley, and did the same; and when the time for service came, that room was full.

"Next Sunday we went again. We sung and went down through the alleys and gave tracts to everybody that would take 'em, and told 'em about the meeting, and the room wouldn't hold the people; and Mr. Spurgeon got us a bigger room, and he sent Mr. L. from the pastor's college to preach; and now there's a revival and Mr. Spurgeon says we shall have a chapel down there, and he has part of the money for it."

So they went on with stories, not always so striking as this, but all of work done, and the Lord's blessing received, in answer to prayer, labor, and sacrifice. There was not much talk of their own feelings, but of *something done* for Christ ; and that a something which was level to their power and opportunities, and brought a sure result of good. It occurred to us that the Lord God Omnipotent could dispense with reading and spelling ; that devout hearts and simple, direct work for souls could accomplish much good with little learning. We thought, too, that it would be quite possible to educate these men too much — away from "the common people" of whom they were now a part, and with whom they were in such hearty sympathy. Assuredly we err, if we hold that the world must wait for conversion till every preacher can have ten years of school and university training.

Spurgeon's Pastor's College is built on a solid basis of lay preachers, from whom there is a constant coming up, by natural growth in the work, into the regular ministry; while many remain for life in the useful ranks of unordained workers for souls. The Pastor's College expressly aims not to give a kind of learning that would educate men away from this homely and wholesome service, but only what will prepare them better for it.

Sickness and Suffering.

One remarkable thing about Mr. Spurgeon's work is, that it has been done for many years in the midst of ill health, involving often great weakness and intense pain. He has been obliged almost every winter to visit Mentone in the South of France for some temporary relief from his persistent enemy, rheumatic gout. But, through all these years, even his sick-room life has been fruitful. Exquisitely beautiful discourses, spoken to his fellow invalids, have gone forth to the sick-rooms of the nations, and with a message to troubled hearts everywhere.

In one of these "talks," as he calls them, he gives a bit of personal experience which throws an interesting light on his methods of work. He says: "It has been my habit for years to make everything yield me an illustration. The other day it rained, and I could not leave my room. My window looked out on a little square, in which the only thing to notice was a pump. What illustration could there be in that? Well, I watched the people who came to draw water, and at length I saw one man who came over and over again. I asked myself why he came so often, and I said, 'It cannot be for himself. He must be drawing water for others. Then surely, I, who have so many to pray for, ought to go oftener than other men to the throne of grace.'"

Yet his ill-health has scarcely been allowed to check his great work. Through all, he has been the same toiling, achieving man. Macaulay said of the old Puritan, "In his retirement he prayed with convulsions and groans and tears. But when he took his seat in the council, or girt on his sword for war, these tempestuous workings of the soul had left no visible trace behind them." So when, after illness and pain, Spurgeon has stood in the Tabernacle pulpit again, it has not been as an invalid or martyr; not as an object of pity, but as one indeed able to draw water from the wells of salvation for all the throng—a commander, a helper, a deliverer. It may be that he has been stronger for the very weakness and pain he has conquered. Somehow his diligent studies have gone on. *The Sword and The Trowel* has regularly appeared. His great work, *The Treasury of David*, has been finished. He has kept his hand on his Pastor's College, and its students have felt his inspiration and sympathy. The number of his printed sermons has been steadily augmented, and every little while, as it has seemed, he has uttered somewhere in England one of those *Conference Addresses* in which he indulged himself in the play of a light and genial humor which does not appear in his sermons, but which sets truth before the mind with a freshness and vividness that cannot be excelled, and is not easily forgotten. One of the very best of these was his latest, *The Greatest Fight in the World*, in which he defended with all the vigor and power of his earlier years the doctrine of the Inspiration of the Scriptures which he so devoutly cherished.

THE BIBLE, THE CRITICS, AND THE CHURCH.

In this latest published address, speaking of the arrogant claims of certain scientists and critics, Mr. Spurgeon exclaims:

"But where shall infallibility be found? The depth saith, 'It is not in me'; yet those who have no depth at all would have us imagine that it is in them; or else by perpetual change they hope to hit upon it. Are we to believe that infallibility is with learned men? Now, Farmer Smith, when you have read your Bible, and have enjoyed its precious promises, you will have, to-morrow morning, to go down the street to ask the scholarly man at the parsonage whether this portion of the Scripture belongs to the inspired part of the Word, or whether it is of dubious authority. It will be well for you to know whether it was written by *the* Isaiah, or whether it was by the second of the 'two Obadiahs.'"

Or again:

"We travel now at so rapid a rate that we rush by sets of scientific hypotheses as quickly as we pass telegraph posts when riding in an express train. All that we are certain of to-day is this, that what the learned were sure of a few years ago is now thrown into the limbo of discarded errors. I believe in science, but not in what is called 'science.' No proven fact in nature is opposed to revelation. The pretty speculations of the pretentious we cannot reconcile with the Bible, and would not if we could."

Here is an exceedingly apt hit at certain preachers of doubts and negations:

"Don't puzzle your people with doubtful speeches. 'Well,' said one 'I had a new idea the other day. I did not enlarge upon it; but I just threw it out.' That is a very good thing to do with most of your new ideas. Throw them out, by all means; but mind where you are when you do it; for if you throw them out from the pulpit they may strike somebody, and inflict a wound upon faith. Throw out your fancies, but first go alone in a boat a mile out to sea. When you have once thrown out your unconsidered trifles, leave them to the fishes."

Of some "explanations" of Scripture, he says:

" If you smash up an explanation you must not imagine that you have damaged the scriptural truth which seemed to require the explanation; you have only burned the wooden palisades with which well-meaning men thought to protect an impregnable fort which needed no such defence. For the most part, we had better leave the difficulty where it is, rather than make another difficulty by our theory.

Here is his view of the mission of the church:

" We are rowing like lifeboat men upon a stormy sea, and we are hurrying to yonder wreck, where men are perishing. If we may not draw that old wreck to shore, we will at least, by the power of God, rescue the perishing, save life, and bear the redeemed to the shores of salvation. Our mission, like our Lord's, is to gather out the chosen of God from among men, that they may live to the glory of God. Every saved man should be, under God, a saviour; and the church is not in a right state until she has reached that conception of herself. The elect church is saved that she may save, cleansed that she may cleanse, blessed that she may bless. All the world is the field, and all the members of the church should work therein for the great Husbandman."

With such an ideal in the heart of their pastor, no wonder the young men of his church go out to sing in the alleys, and to gather, in some "large upper room," congregations of London's poor!

Reminiscences.

BY PROFESSOR W. C. WILKINSON, D.D.*

"YOU are an American!" These were the very first words ever addressed by Mr. Spurgeon to me. It was thirty-two years ago. How well I remember the occasion! The words were uttered half as affirmative, half as interrogative. I wore a tell-tale hat, different from the English fashion.

Fresh graduate from my seminary studies, and pastor-elect of a church in New Haven, I had crossed the Atlantic for a little vacation tour before beginning work. I carried a letter of introduction to Mr. Spurgeon from his American publishers. Having heard him preach one Sunday morning in Surrey Gardens Music Hall, I sought him after the services were over, and met him walking with Mrs. Spurgeon on his arm through a corridor of the building on his way out into the street. As I approached him, he frankly and cordially put out his hand to welcome me, with recognition of my quality, as at once a stranger and a kinsman, expressed in the words, "You are an American!" That same Sunday, in the late afternoon, at a prayer-meeting, attended by perhaps a thousand persons, Mr. Spurgeon as leader recognized the

---

* To urgent, repeated requests from the American publishers that he would contribute to this volume something in the way of reminiscences of his own personal observation of Mr. Spurgeon, Professor Wilkinson at length responded by writing the sketch here introduced.

young American in the throng and called on him to offer prayer. This illustrates the alertness of attention and of thought that characterized this many-sidedly remarkable man.

A far better illustration of the same quality is furnished in an incident of two or three years later, in which I was concerned. Health broken, I was again in England. Our civil war had been some ten months waging. A missionary meeting, presided over by Mr. Marshman, son of the celebrated missionary of that name, was held in the Metropolitan Tabernacle, then new. A crowded audience was present. Mr. Marshman, in his opening address, referred to the "fratricidal" war going on in the United States, as a reason for diminished gifts from American Baptists to the cause of missions, and, therefore, a reason for increased gifts from English Baptists. My patriotism was sensitive, and I did not like the speaker's adjective, "fratricidal"; and, besides, I knew a fact that made the implication of his language seem false. If I had not been a sick man, there would undoubtedly have been a short speech on that occasion not set down in the programme. As it was, I sent my card to Mr. Spurgeon on the platform, briefly stating that, in point of fact, the receipts of the American Baptist Missionary Union were *not* diminished from those of the year before, and asking that this correction of the chairman's implication be publicly made. I presently felt the flutter of a responsive oral message undulating toward me from the platform. Mr. Spurgeon wished to speak with me. I obeyed the summons. The chairman was still speaking, when Mr. Spurgeon said to me: "You are quite sure of what you here say?" "I have it recent and direct from a responsible American source," I said. "The Missionary Union's receipts are as large this year of the war, as they were the year before?" Mr. Spurgeon asked. "The unquestionable fact," I firmly responded, venturing to press the claim for a public correction. Mr. Spurgeon reflected a moment, and then asked: "But, in anticipation of the war, amid the financial troubles of the hour, may not the *previous* year's receipts have fallen below the average standard?" What a bright, vigilant, sagacious question! I was not able to assure him that his conjecture of the probable was wrong—for I did not know how the case stood. Mr. Spurgeon was fairly quit of the necessity of making an awkward public correction, and I had to content myself with being introduced to Mr. Marshman, and giving him my London address for further communication on the subject.

Mr. Spurgeon's own speech that evening was the only example from him of oratory, not preaching, that I ever heard. It was so consummately good that I remember thinking what a master of men that man would be in the arena of popular politics. For my own part, I have no doubt that Spurgeon—with his infallible instinct of the average popular mind, his unsurpassed gift of popular address, his knack of wide popularity, and, then, besides these things, his statesman-like capacity of applying common sense to the administration of affairs, joined to his thoroughly, typically, English cast of intellect and of character—would have run a full even career of rivalry with Mr. Gladstone himself for leadership in British imperial politics.

Three years ago, I heard Mr. Spurgeon again after a long interval. At the close of a Sunday morning service, I went, conducted by a deacon of the church, to present myself to the pastor. The reception-room was thronged with people, many of them Americans paying their respects to a famous man, known to be glad to give countrymen of ours the grasp of his hand. To illustrate the bluff, kind, large heartiness of his manner, I may report that I heard him say to one of the number present on this occasion, whom, on introduction, he recognized as author of some books that he liked : " Those are magnificent books. You have the educational bump. You know just what to say and just what *not* to say. I have done by those books what I do not do by many; I have *read* them *through."* The books referred to were not religious books, and one observation which Mr. Spurgeon added about them was peculiarly significant coming from *him.* The author remarked that he had tried to make his books, while not expressly religious, still loyal to Jesus Christ. " Yes, yes, I noted that," said Mr. Spurgeon. " Every time you got a fair chance, you put in a true word for Him. *And such books do more good than religious books."* There was so much common sense expressed in this last saying, and so much freedom from narrowness, so much open-eyed capacity to see things without the mere preacher's spectacles interposed, and it was said so emphatically, that I represent the spirit and effect of the remark by printing it in italics. It exhibits a trait in Mr. Spurgeon's mental and moral character that those who have learned him only through his sermons would not, perhaps, have suspected in him.

The following day I met him for a private interview at an hour appointed. "You are the first American I ever knew to keep an appointment punctually," he said briskly, with pleasure expressed at the exception, rather than disapproval of the rule, as I presented myself, fortunately, on the stroke of the clock. If, indeed, my respected fellow-countrymen have, as Mr. Spurgeon so strongly implied, been habitually tardy and derelict keepers of London appointments, I can easily attribute it to the uncalculated great distances that have to be traversed in London in going from one quarter of the metropolis to another. To tell the truth, I had earned my own praise for punctuality from him, by presenting myself *impransus*, and actually faint with fasting. I had mistakingly calculated that I might reach the place with time enough to spare for taking a hasty meal somewhere in the neighborhood before the interview.

We talked a pleasant hour—that is, Mr. Spurgeon did, I only now and then for an instant changing my part from that of listener to that of speaker. I mentioned very briefly the case of a young man who told me, many years ago, that Mr. Spurgeon, not long before, had singled him out from the congregation and made him a target for the general gaze by describing his appearance and the manner in which he was dressed. The young fellow felt seriously aggrieved, and I could in no wise persuade him that he had mistaken a mere coincidence for intention on the preacher's part. Afterward, and this I told Mr. Spurgeon, I met at a dinner-party in Paris an American gentleman who, when I recited the young man's story, confirmed it, by saying that he was present on the occasion, sat near the young man, heard Mr. Spurgeon describe him to the life, saw people looking at him ; there could be no mistake, he thought. So much for a very curious coincidence. For pure coincidence, Mr. Spurgeon assured me, it was. He never, he said, did such a thing in his life as to single out one of his hearers in that way. "Many singular coincidences," he said, "have come to my knowledge. Once for example, drawing the bow at a venture, I said, ' There is a man now here, sitting on the left-hand side of the house, who came in with a bottle of gin in his pocket. I proceeded to say what I hoped might do such a man good. A little while after, a man came to me, and said: ' How did you know I came into the church that day with a gin-bottle in my pocket? So I did, but how did you find it out ? You got me on the wrong side, though. I was on the right-hand side of the house, instead of the left.' I smiled and told him that depended upon how he reckoned. Right-hand to him would be left-hand to me. Strange to say, on that very occasion, there was a second man in the audience with a bottle of gin in his pocket. This one sat on the opposite side from the other, but he reckoned differently, and so he too was assured in a similar way, when he said I had placed him wrong. Both men were converted," Mr. Spurgeon added. He narrated several other cases of curious coincidence that had been made known to him, occurring in the long course of his preaching weekly to those immense congregations of his.

The stress of the " Down-grade " controversy was on at the time of this interview, and that naturally was one of the main things talked about. Two points chiefly impressed me ; one was the unalterable magnanimous sweetness of Mr. Spurgeon's temper toward those whom he thought radically wrong, and the other was the unshakableness of his conviction that he was himself right, not only in his doctrine, but in his way of asserting his doctrine through secession from the Baptist Union. At the same time, I was sure I could see signs in him of sincere suffering at heart from the sundering of old ties. But he suffered and was strong.

During my last visit to London, ending early in May of the past year (1891), I twice heard Mr. Spurgeon preach ; but I personally met him only once, and that for no more than a greeting and a hand-shake. " We shall see each other again, I hope, friend Wilkinson," were the kindly words with which he then let me go. The good old-fashioned accosting style of " Friend " Wilkinson was a way he had of expressing the sentiment of comradeship. The state of his health, manifestly feeble, forbade my again seeing him in private. Two or three brief notes from his own hand faithfully answering questions with which I had reluctantly brought myself to trouble him, revealed the sense of overburdening labor and care under which he daily staggered. He was almost foundering with the very weight of his lading.

It happened to me, during the months of my stay in London, to be brought more into contact with those who differed theologically from Mr. Spurgeon than with those that thought as he did. The testimony, in fact, unconsciously borne, of these opponents and critics of Mr. Spurgeon's course, to the overtopping greatness of his character and of his influence, was to me most impressive. I acquired from it a quite new, an immensely augmented, estimate and measure of the solitary preëminence of the man. There was no minister like him, for commanding influence in all the three kingdoms—there probably never has been. Mr. Spurgeon was the one dissenting minister of Great Britain—and there was no instance comparable afforded by the clergy of the Church of England—whose movements, whose state of health, whose utterances, formed a staple topic of news and of comment for the daily newspapers of the metropolis of the world. It was the staunch character, standing four-square to all the winds that blew, almost more than it was the eloquence and the genius of the man, that explained his unique position, his unparalleled power. What other personal breakwater could stem, as he stemmed, the tremendous current now sweeping theological thought in Great Britain, no one knows whither, in the direction of liberalism. Were he right, or were he wrong, it was nothing less than sublime to see him stand, and let their surging charges, breaking upon him, foam themselves away.

Something of the pathos of evidently waning physical strength added itself to the effect of Mr. Spurgeon's later eloquence. His hair and beard had grown visibly gray, and he stayed his steps with a staff, as he slowly descended to his standing-place on the platform where he preached. Only his voice seemed almost to have renewed itself from the fountain of perpetual youth. Of course, it was not quite what it had been in its prime, but it was wonderful, incomparable, yet. It has left the world lonely now that it has ceased to be heard ; but its last accents, how Apostolic they were, how full of the old gospel which, during forty years of an unparalleled ministry, it had successfully commended to so many !

THE " DOWN GRADE CONTROVERSY."

The famous "Down Grade Controversy," to which Dr. Wilkinson refers in the above, took place in 1887, when Mr. Spurgeon withdrew from the Baptist Union, because of what he believed to be a defection from some of the cardinal doctrines of evangelical religion on the part of a number of his brethren, and the toleration of such laxity by the Union. His reasons for the step, as given in *The Sword and The Trowel* for August, 1887, were that, among those connected with what he terms " The Broad School of Dissent,"

" The Atonement is scouted, the Inspiration of Scripture is derided, the Holy Spirit is degraded into an influence, the punishment of sin is turned into a fiction, and the resurrection into a myth.

" At the back of doctrinal falsehood comes a decline of spiritual life, evidenced by a taste for questionable amusements and a weariness of devotional meetings. At a certain meeting of ministers and church officers, one after another doubted the value of prayer meetings; all confessed that they had a very small attendance, and several acknowledged without the slightest compunction that they had given them up.

* * * *

"As for questionable amusements—time was when a Nonconformist minister who was known to attend the playhouse would soon have found himself without a church. And justly so; for no man can long possess the confidence, even of the most worldly, who is known to be a haunter of theatres. Yet, at the present time, it is matter of notoriety that preachers of no mean repute defend the playhouse, and do so because they have been seen there."

While not claiming that his brethren of the Baptist Union were generally open to charges such as these, he felt that since some against whom they could be made were members of the

Union, his only effectual protest was to withdraw. In his own words:

"Christian love has its claims, and divisions are to be shunned as grievous evils, but how far are we justified in being in confederacy with those who are departing from the truth? It is a difficult question to answer so as to keep the balance of the duties. . . .

"A chasm is opening between the men who believe their Bibles and the men who are prepared for an advance upon Scripture. Inspiration and speculation cannot long abide in peace. Compromise there can be none. We cannot hold the inspiration of the word, and yet reject it; we cannot believe in the Atonement and deny it; we cannot hold the doctrine of the fall, and yet talk of the evolution of spiritual life from human nature; we cannot recognize the punishment of the impenitent, and yet indulge the 'larger hope.' One way or the other we must go. Decision is the virtue of the hour.

"Neither when we have chosen our way can we keep company with those who go the other way. There must come with decision for truth a corresponding protest against error. Let those who will keep the narrow way, keep it, and suffer for their choice; but to hope to follow the broad road at the same time is an absurdity. What communion hath Christ with Belial?"

The frank, Christian manliness of these utterances no one can question. Good men have differed greatly regarding this step: whether so great laxity did exist to any wide extent, and, even if so, whether Mr. Spurgeon took the wisest way to meet it. But there has been no difference of opinion as to the nobility, unselfishness, and perfect candor of the great preacher.

THE ALARMING ILLNESS.

On Feb. 8, 1891, Mr. Spurgeon, after three months' absence, preached in the Tabernacle pulpit, with great power, and universal rejoicing—the vast congregation singing the doxology, " Praise God from whom all blessings flow." They sung it, we are told, " with thunderous effect." He presided at the annual church meeting, on February 17th, when the following statistics were given of the work centering around the Metropolitan Tabernacle :

Present Membership of the Church.................... 5,328
23 Mission Stations, with seating capacity for.......... 3,740
27 Sunday-Schools, containing Teachers................ 592
"   "   "   "   Scholars 8,001

With occasional slight indispositions, Mr. Spurgeon continued steadily for the next three months at his great work. On Monday evening, May 4th, he presided at the prayer meeting " after having spent the morning in preparing his weekly sermon for the press, and the afternoon in seeing inquirers. He asked special prayer for the spiritual services in which he was to be occupied during the week." These services were : preaching before the Sunday-School Union the Annual Sermon to Sunday-School Teachers, on Tuesday evening, May 5th, Bloomsbury Chapel, where the service was held, being crowded to the doors, and "large numbers unable to obtain admission"; on Thursday evening, May 7th, a sermon at the Tabernacle in aid of the British and Foreign Sailors' Society; then, on Friday afternoon, May 8th, a gathering at Hendon with the President and students of the College, where "Mr. Spurgeon read and expounded Gen. xxiv., as illustrative of the Lord's servants who are sent to seek out the bride of Christ"; after "a tea," in the evening, a public meeting for testimony was held, the subject being "The Church of Christ, its headship, its membership, and its position in the world"; as two out of three announced speakers were laid aside by influenza, Mr. Spurgeon bore the chief burden of this service, also. Of all this he says, in *The Sword and The Trowel* for June:

"A drive of two hours there (to Hendon) and two hours back made the engagement a heavy draught upon time. Friends will note that *all the above meetings were held in one week*, which also included two Sabbath services and the great communion at the Tabernacle, besides all the regular home work, correspondence, etc. In addition, the Lord's day morning sermon had to be revised, and published the following Thursday; and the sermons to Sunday-school teachers and sailors were received for revision and duly attended to. Is it any wonder that the worker gets weary, and has to beg friends not to impose further burdens on one who is already terribly overladen?"

Following this we read:

"On Friday evening, May 15th, Mr. Spurgeon spoke at the Presbyterian Missionary meeting at Exeter Hall. It was a time of peculiar bodily weakness, and of special spiritual strength. God bless our friends who so kindly received the message aud the messenger!"

The next intelligence is that:

"On Sunday evening May 17th, Mr. Spurgeon could not preach, and the doctor found him laid aside with congestion of the lungs and other matters, which forbid his quitting his chamber for some little time to come. 'My times are in thy hand.' We would be always preaching; howbeit, the Lord thinketh not so."

From this attack, which proved to be of the dreaded influenza, or *la grippe*, Mr. Spurgeon rallied, though but momentarily. In the July number of *The Sword and The Trowel*, we read:

"On June 7th, A. M., though still weak, he preached at the Tabernacle. The following day, he went into the country for rest and change, but unhappily took a chill, which was followed by gout. At the time of making up these notes, he is still confined to his bed, and suffering greatly."

Then followed a season of severe and perilous illness, attended with delirium, during which, at times, his death was momentarily expected. Of this, the best account is that found in *The Sword and The Trowel* for August, which gives particulars down to July 23d, evidently at first-hand, with the suggestion and approval of his family and immediate friends:

"At the beginning of July, there appeared to be good ground for believing that the disease was being subdued, although our poor patient's pains were very acute; but on the evening of Saturday July 4th, the delirium which had passed away for some days returned, and it was evident that a most serious state of affairs had been reached. From that time,

Dr. Miller has slept at "Westwood" every night, and Dr. Kidd has been in consultation with him every morning. At intervals, a few bright rays of hope have shot through the dense darkness which has surrounded the sick chamber; but these have been followed by periods of most painful suspense, in which the precious life has seemed to reach the very verge of the unseen world. All that medical skill, patient watching, and careful nursing could do, appeared, for a while to be of no avail.

"It ought to be stated, however, to the honor of God, that even when almost the last hope of recovery had to be given up, those who were most deeply concerned in the issue of the terrible trial had one source of consolation left. Among the letters that poured in daily, from all quarters, there were many from godly men and women who wrote, not merely to say that they were praying for Mr. Spurgeon's recovery, but that it had been impressed upon them most powerfully that this sickness was 'not unto death,' and that the Lord would raise up his servant even from the very gates of the grave. This assurance was a great comfort to the weary watchers, and enabled them, like Abraham with Isaac, to give up the loved one without reserve to the divine will, 'by faith . . . accounting that God was able to raise him up even from the dead.'

"In such a struggle between life and death, hope and fear alternate with sorrowful frequency. Sometimes the morning has brought manifest improvement which has not been maintained during the day. On other occasions, the night has closed in with the most gloomy forebodings (not for Mr. Spurgeon: for him to depart and to be with Christ would be far better, yet many feel that it is needful for them that he should for a while abide in the flesh). When the morning has come all has been changed, and gladness has taken the place of sadness. It was so on July 16th and 17th. On the Thursday afternoon and evening, the bulletins had been truly alarming; but on the Friday morning a slight improvement was reported: this was confirmed in the afternoon and again on the following day, and also on the Sabbath ; but alas! even the sacred hours of the Lord's day were invaded by the dreaded delirium, and day after day, the most trying suspense continued. At the time of writing these "Notes," there appear to be some signs of slight improvement: but the dear sufferer's condition remains exceedingly critical."

A World's Sorrow and Prayer.

The copy of the magazine quoted above contains an added note, concluding with a few touching words dictated by Mrs. Spurgeon:

"A whole mumber of *The Sword and The Trowel* would scarcely suffice for an adequate acknowledgment of the *telegrams, letters,* and *messages,* and *resolutions of sympathy* that have been received by Mrs. Spurgeon from all parts of the world. . . . Mrs. Spurgeon cannot express the deep gratitude that she feels to all who have shown their sympathy with her in this season of indescribable trial. In her weak state, the labor of opening and reading so many extra letters has been a heavy burden; but it has been also a great blessing. She has found it to be quite a means of grace to be brought into communication with so large a number of the Lord's praying and believing children."

The following correspondence between England's foremost statesman and foremost preacher, when the one was sorrowing for the death of his son and the other seemed passing into the shadow of death, is of deep and tender interest.

Mrs. Spurgeon received the following letter from Mr. Gladstone:

"CORTON, LOWESTOFT,
"*July* 16.

"MY DEAR MADAM—In my own home, darkened at the present time, I have read with sad interest daily accounts of Mr. Spurgeon's illness, and I cannot help conveying to you the earnest assurance of my sympathy with you and with him, and of my cordial admiration, not only of his splendid powers, but still more of his devoted and unfailing character. May I humbly commend you and him, in all contingencies, to the infinite stores of the Divine love and mercy, and subscribe myself, my dear Madam, faithfully yours,
"W. E. GLADSTONE."

Mrs. Spurgeon sent the following reply, the postscript being in her husband's handwriting:

"WESTWOOD, UPPER NORWOOD,
"*July* 18, 1891.

"DEAR MR. GLADSTONE—Your words of sympathy have a special significance and tenderness coming from one who has just passed through the deep waters which seem now to threaten me. I thank you warmly for your expression of regard for my beloved husband, and with all my heart I pray that the consolations of God may abound towards you, even as they do to me. Although we cannot yet consider the dear patient out of danger, the doctors have to-day issued a somewhat more hopeful bulletin. I feel it is an honor to be allowed to say that I shall ever be your grateful friend,
(Signed)   " S. SPURGEON."

"P. S.—Yours is a word of love such as those only write who have been into the King's country, and have seen much of His face. My heart's love to you.—C. H. SPURGEON."

Of these letters, *The National Baptist* of July 23, 1891, fitly says:

"This loving correspondence between two such noble and great Christian men has few parallels; it is all the more noticeable since, a few years ago, when Mr. Gladstone announced his policy as to Home Rule, Mr. Spurgeon declared himself distinctly against it, though (as he said to the writer) 'it was hard to oppose one who had been a dear personal friend.' The world is rich in goodness so long as it has two such men as Gladstone and Spurgeon."

The Speaker (London) a very able political weekly, strongly Gladstonian in its spirit, on July 18th, at a time when little or no hope was entertained for the recovery of Mr. Spurgeon, said:

"Mr. Spurgeon still lives; but his life seems to be hanging by a thread, and even before these words appear in print, the thread may have been snapped. How many people, we wonder, are fully conscious of the loss which the breaking of the golden cord will inflict upon London and the world? The time has long since passed when it was fashionable to deride this master of the English language in its noblest form, this preacher whose tenets were of a former day, whose creed, as fervid as it was narrow, seemed little likely to lay hold of the sympathies of a generation like the present. There was a time when Mr. Spurgeon was, on the whole, the best-abused person in England; when orthodox church circles regarded him with horror as the representative of everything that was odious to the members of an Established Church; when men of light and leading sneered at him as the typical Philistine, and when great essayists, in weekly reviews, regarded him as a butt provided for the special purpose of enabling them to sharpen their small wits on him. Long ago, Mr. Spurgeon lived down all the bigotry, the folly, and the flippancy of which he was for so many years the mark. People came at last to see that even if they could not share his creed, they could admire the fervor of his zeal, the purity of his life, and the large-hearted charity which he showed in every matter that did not appertain to dogma.

"And even our men of light and leading, after years of scoffing at his pulpit style, awoke to a perception of the fact that, in Mr. Spurgeon, England had one of those born orators of whom this generation has seen only two, to wit, himself and Mr. Bright. Gifted with splendid common sense, with a genuine humor, with a large-hearted love for his fellow-creatures, which no narrowness of creed could stifle or distort, and with those unequalled powers as a preacher, which enabled him for nearly forty years to sway the largest congregation in the world, Mr. Spurgeon has undoubtedly been a figure of real importance, as well as real interest, in the community in which he dwelt. . . . Well tried by time, which tries all things, Mr. Spurgeon's life and character have been shown to be of that pure gold against which the sharp edge of ridicule and satire must ever be turned in vain. In parting from him, we part from one who was both great and good; and whatever differences on points of theology may separate us from him, there are few among us who do not feel that when he dies, the world will be poorer for his loss."

The *Spectator* of London, about the some time, published a most interesting letter, showing the esteem in which Mr. Spurgeon is held among many in the Church of England, and ending with a characteristic incident:

" May I conclude by giving the following anecdote which was related to me by an enthusiastic young Liberal? After one of Mr. Spurgeon's sermons, this young man went into the vestry to thank the preacher for his faithful discourse, and, wandering away a little from the matter in hand, referred to the ritualistic party in the Church of England, ending

A Catholic Spirit. 349

a somewhat severe denunciation of their views by saying, 'Surely you must have a feeling of strong indignation against such teachers, and see with fear the harm they are doing,' Mr. Spurgeon answered: 'No, not entirely so; they have stirred up much earnest work, and we all may take a lesson from their self-sacrificing and devoted lives.' This answer is, I think, proof of a truly catholic spirit.

"I am, sir, etc.

"A. G. T."

This is surely beautiful, as showing how one so uncompromising in doctrine, and ready so earnestly to "contend," on occasion, for "the faith once delivered to the saints" can maintain through and under all, a spirit of deep and tender Christian kindness. This spirit has drawn to him the love of those wholly outside the Christian fold, as shown by the following remarkable and touching letter addressed to Mrs. Spurgeon:

"OFFICE OF THE CHIEF RABBI,
16 FINSBURY SQUARE, LONDON,
E. C.,

"*July 21.*

"MY DEAR MADAME—Pray be assured that, although owing to my absorbing official duties I have not called to inquire personally, I have been following the bulletins touching the health of your dear husband with deepest interest, and with earnest prayer to our common Father that his precious life may be spared for yet many years. I was delighted when the reports on Saturday were more reassuring, and I am deeply grieved to learn this morning that this improvement has not been maintained. May the Father of all flesh sustain the patient sufferer on his bed of languishing; may it please him to restore him to health and strength; may he sustain you and yours during the period of trial. With every good wish for Mr. Spurgeon, yours sincerely,

"N. ADLER, Chief Rabbi."

Indeed, the world was waiting around the sick-bed of the great, good man in his long approach to death. Probably never before did such a volume of prayer encircle a single sufferer, and plead for one man's life. Rev. N. W. Miner writes from London to the Chicago *Standard* under date of July 23, 1891:

"Meetings for prayer have been held daily in the great Tabernacle; sometimes as many as three thousand are in attendance; and all over the country earnest and united prayers are offered up, that God would spare the life of His honored servant. Bulletins in regard to his condition are issued twice a day, which are read the first thing in the papers. Letters of sympathy and telegrams come to Mr. Spurgeon from all parts of the country. The Prince of Wales has requested that he might be informed daily of Mr. Spurgeon's condition. The most distinguished persons in London visit Mrs. Spurgeon to inquire after her husband, or send messages of sympathy. Among those who have called are the Bishop of London, and several bishops from different parts of Great Britain, members of Parliament, and other high officials.

"The sickness of Mr. Spurgeon has awakened more interest, and has called forth a wider and more pervading sympathy than could have been awakened by any other individual in England. I believe he is better known and more dearly beloved than any other living man."

Then came the surprising and delightful news of the great preacher's partial recovery. The acute symptoms yielded, and he came out from the immediate shadow of death. Early in September he was able to be taken out of doors in a carriage. It was mentioned that "When he went out for his first drive, he was taken to Westminster. During the afternoon, he was seen to alight from his carriage, and, after tottering along between two supporters, he leaned upon the parapet of Westminster Bridge, and watched with evident interest the new mission steamer for the Congo, the 'Good will,' then on the river. A few minutes later, he was again led to his carriage, and driven back to his residence." Even at such a time, "in weariness and painfulness," just risen from what was almost the bed of death, his recreation was to view something destined to help extend the kingdom of Christ in a far, dark land.

Then, about October 1st, a welcome letter from his own hand appeared in *The Sword and The Trowel*, in which he said : *

"I am unable to send a personal letter of thanks to the thousands of friends of all ranks and religions who wrote sympathetic letters to Mrs. Spurgeon and to myself during the dark days of my illness; but I beg in the best manner possible to me to return my hearty thanks to them all. To my dear sorrowing wife, the kind words from all quarters were, by God's blessing, an unutterable consolation. I was too ill to know much about the matter; but, now I am recovering, the reading of these generous expressions fills my eyes with tears, my mind with astonishment, and my heart with gratitude.

---

* With the exception of the words *to me*, the italics are the editor's. In a few later instances, the same liberty has been taken of giving emphasis to passages now especially significant.

"Surely there is a unity deep down in the church of God and on fit occasions it shows itself; that I should furnish such an occasion overwhelms me. *Some of these affectionate expressions from persons ecclesiastically divided from me, are as fervent as if we agreed on every point, and are vastly more true and precious than if that were the case.* Brethren and sisters in Christ, the Lord recompense upon each of you a hundredfold your tender consideration of one who had no hold upon you but his great affliction!

"*To those who are not of the Christian faith, I cannot but feel a singular tenderness* when I read not only their respectful enquiries, but their generous sentiments towards me. It is astonishing to me that I should have so warm a place in their esteem, and I trust I may do nothing which will prove me unworthy of it.

"I have also the happy task of thanking the countless friends who did not write *to me*, but lifted up their hearts in prayer on my behalf. *I have been saved from death by prayer.* In very many instances, there has been an assured faith with the prayer, and this has been the certain token of prevalence with God. To hear that friends unknown to me spent whole nights in supplication for me, and that multitudes of churches presented special intercession, made me very happy, and caused me to say at the very worst, 'I shall not die, but live, and declare the works of the Lord.'

"*That every one of those who thought of me so lovingly may thus be remembered by the Great Father in any future hour of sorrow, is my fervent prayer.*" C. H. S.

At the same time, there was much to check extravagant hopes of final recovery. The Rev. J. A. Spurgeon, of Croydon stated that his brother was not only suffering severely from the old disease, the root of which still remained, but that, in addition, he suffered very much from his heart. Anxiety was felt for some days of warm, sunny weather during which he might repair to the seaside and there remain until a favorable opportunity should present itself for a passage across the channel *en route* to Mentone.

A little later, in reply to words of friendliness expressed towards him by the Sussex School Union Conference, Mr. Spurgeon wrote as follows:

"QUEEN'S HOTEL,"
"*October* 8, 1891.

" DEAR SIR—I was much cheered by the kindly expression of the meeting over which you presided last night. It is so sweet to live in the hearts of workers among the young, that even a sickness that gives me the assurance that I do so, has a bright side to it. Go on with your holy service, and may our Lord give you many tokens of His approval. My secretary has gone back to attend to home work, and I regret that I was too near my bed last night to sit down and answer your note there and then. The invalid cannot do what he would. Two remarkable men have just passed away through a chill, but dear fellow-Christians seem resolved by the warmth of their love to allow me no risk of a chilled heart. I thank you and every individual in the meeting. God bless all your Sunday-schools. I beg a continued interest in your prayers for a wasting disease upon me. I have not half escaped from its grasp.

" Yours very heartily,
" C. H. SPURGEON."

DR. PIERSON AT THE TABERNACLE.

Among the memorable leadings of Providence which have attended Mr. Spurgeon's career, is that which permitted him, just in this emergency, to secure as preacher at the Metropolitan Tabernacle, Rev. A. T. Pierson, D. D., of Philadelphia, the able editor of the *Missionary Review of the World*. Mr. Spurgeon's own account of the matter is substantially as follows:

"Early in August, the Pastor remembered that the good doctor had kindly offered to come to London at any time when his services might be required, so he directed his secretary to make inquiries as to his address, probable engagements, etc. *The very next morning* a loving letter arrived, and among other hopeful words were the following: 'If by coming across the sea I could now serve you, I would cheerfully do all in my power.' To this a reply was at once sent, and after conference and special prayer on both sides of the sea, the cable brought to Mr. Spurgeon the message: 'Acts xvi, 9, 10.' The passage reads: 'And a vision appeared to Paul in the night: There stood a man of Macedonia, and prayed him, saying, Come over into Macedonia, and help us. And after he had seen the vision, immediately we endeavored to go into Macedonia, assuredly gathering that the Lord had called us for to preach the gospel unto them.' October 25th was fixed as the date of Dr. Pierson's first services at the Tabernacle."

The spirit of true Christian unity which called a Presbyterian preacher to a Baptist pulpit, an American to the heart of London, has been honored by Dr. Pierson's success in that difficult field, the church and congregation being held, and the great Tabernacle filled, at his services, Sunday after Sunday.

The longed-for opportunity for travel came. "Baron Rothchild's private saloon-carriage was placed at Mr. Spurgeon's service to travel in

The Journey to Mentone. 355

throughout France to Mentone." He enjoyed the sea-voyage from Dover to Calais on Monday, Oct. 26th, and travelled on Oct. 27th from Calais to Marseilles, proceeding from thence to Mentone. He was accompanied by Mrs. Spurgeon, his brother Rev. James Spurgeon, and Mrs. James Spurgeon, his private secretary (Rev. J. Harrald), and by some of the Metropolitan Tabernacle deacons. The " Doxology " was sung by those assembled, as he left Hearne Hill Station, London.

November 7th, still apparently improving in health, he wrote from Mentone :

"I am far away in body, but not in spirit. I am a sick man physically, but in heart I am strong in the Lord. A great waste of life-force still weakens me; but it is not so great as it was. It is a great trial to be unable to preach in the pulpit, but it is no small comfort to be able to preach through the press. By the aid of friends, the discourses which I have delivered in former times have been piloted through the press in a masterly manner, and would be forthcoming for several years even if I were taken home to God; for hundreds of manuscripts are in my publishers' stores, and so I shall live and speak long after I am dead. Will each kind reader do me the great service of increasing my congregation by increasing the circulation of these sermons? The loan of a copy, or a kindly word, may win me another reader, to whom the message may be life, or light, or liberty. I earnestly desire a still wider audience. If I could not myself preach, I think that the next best thing would be to spread the sermons of one whose words were useful to my own heart. Please do not *merely think of* fulfilling my desire; but DO IT."

Again he writes on November 21st:

"This morning I read in *The Times* that 'Mr. Spurgeon is *rapidly* recovering.' These words exactly describe what I am *not* doing. The symptoms are the same as when I was at home. I am tossed up and down upon the waves of my disease and what is thought progress to-day is gone to-morrow. I have seasons of utter prostration. Always weak, it seems at times that I have no strength whatever, and must altogether collapse. The result of the doctor's recent examination has been disappointing. He did not feel pleased about a certain 'murmur,' which was by no means less than when I was at home. I had hoped that this was reduced to the imperceptible, but it was not so. By another test it was soon apparent that the *disease* itself was not changed from what it was in Norwood, or, if any change was manifest, it was for the worse. The leakage of life-power was not stopped. I shall *recover*, for this is the tenor of the prayers which our God has so far answered; but there are no traces or signs of anything *rapid* about my condition. *Emphatically*, any advance I make is of *the slowest of all slow things*. I write this at once, to prevent disappointment of sanguine friends. I know not why I should be the object of so much tender sympathy, but as I am thus privileged I would have a sensitive regard for the feelings of such benefactors and warn them against statements for which there is no basis in truth. Their friend remains feeble, and has no hasty recovery to expect. Please continue fervent prayers on my behalf. Have great patience. Relieve me of anxiety as to the institutions; and praise God for what He has already done."

The December number of *The Sword and The Trowel* contains a preface by Mr. Spurgeon, in which he thus states some of the lessons which he himself read in the long trial:

"We may not always expect to see the why and wherefore of the Lord's dealings; but, in this case, certain points are clear enough.

"*The work which centres at the Metropolitan Tabernacle has been tested.* It has been assumed by many that the death of the pastor would be fatal to the work which he has inaugurated. This has been shown to be a mere assumption. Like Isaac, he was 'as good as dead,' but the institutions were maintained, and the preaching of the Word was sustained by divers men of God, till at last the man (Rev. Dr. A. T. Pierson) came who has filled the great house, and moved the heart of the crowd by his noble witness for the truth. The members have not forsaken the church, and the workers have not stayed their hand. Such an experience is reassuring, and is a practical rehearsal of what may be done on another day, when he, who has again and again been drawn out of the waters of death, shall in very deed go up the mount, and fall asleep, and no more lead the flock through the wilderness.

"*Equally memorable has been the latent Christian love which has been made manifest.* . . .

Had the sufferer been an Episcopalian, the clergy could not have been more solicitous; had he been a Presbyterian, Wesleyan, or Independent, members of those bodies could not have been more loving. All sorts of Baptists have been more than brotherly. . . . Twenty years ago, one who had prophesied that a dissenting minister would have been lovingly mentioned in St. Paul's Cathedral, and in numerous Episcopal churches would have been reckoned among madmen; yet the fact is sure. *Surely there is a real and growing unity among those who are spiritual, when even towards one who has been very outspoken concerning religious differences* such brotherly kindness has been shown. May it be an omen of a time wherein the true union of all who are in Christ Jesus will make similar outbursts of sympathy to be of ordinary occurrence!"

On December 5th, he writes:

" The last month of the year is upon us, and mercy, like a river, continues to flow side by side with the pathway of our lives. I hope I am climbing the hill of returning strength. As yet I have hardly crept upward enough to be quite sure that I am, on the whole, a little above where I was when I left home. My publishers wished to begin the year with a portrait, and I submitted to be photographed, but the result is too painful. I do not think that any of my friends would wish to see the picture twice. To those who meet me I do not appear much the worse for wear; but when I sit down before the camera, the unflattering sun puts down details of countenance which it would not be pleasing to remember. I mention this that I may ask the continuance of the prayers of the sermon-readers. I am anxious to be soon in my pulpit, or at least to be making progress towards fitness for it. Meanwhile, may our Lord use these sermons for the good of His Church and cause."

Again, on December 12th, appeared another letter, still full of thought for others :

" Beloved readers of my sermons will greatly oblige me if they will place their copies in the way of persons for whose salvation they are pleading with God. It may be that the Lord will use the discourses to the end they so much desire. My silent Sabbaths breed in me a great hunger for the salvation of those to whom I can only speak through the press. Oh, that my Lord would honor me by making me fruitful in this winter of my weakness! I have a word for this season, which I must not forget. Christmas is near. Our orphan children must have their festival, though I cannot have the joy of presiding at it. Will my kind friends remember my family of five hundred children and keep up the general funds and add some little treat for the boys and girls ? I am sending a Christmas present to all the subscribers whose

The Last Christmas.

names we have on our list, but as we may miss some, let them not feel that they are left out. I invite their thoughtful consideration to the matter. Direct to the secretary, Stockwell Orphanage, Clapham Road, London, and thus gratify your old friend, C. H. SPURGEON."

As Christmas drew near, December 24th, he wrote to his flock at the Tabernacle:

"Though I cannot be present to wish you the blessings of the season, I would say from my heart, 'I wish you a most happy Christmas!' Upon your family gatherings may the best of blessings rest! May all your children be the Lord's children, and thus may your union in the bonds of the flesh be made eternal by the bonds of the Spirit! Joy be with you, yet let it be the joy in the Lord. I think I can fairly say I am better. Whether or no the disease is disappearing I cannot say, though I fear there is not much difference, but in general health I must be improved, or else my feelings are sheer delusions. At any rate, I am very hopeful and praiseful, and I wish I could stand up and give out Ps. ciii."

In the *Metropolitan Pulpit* of Dec. 31, 1891, Mr. Spurgeon published a New Year's sermon, "Intended for Reading, on Lord's Day, Jan. 3, 1892," on the text found in Psalm cxviii., 17, 18: "I shall not die, but live, and declare the works of the Lord. The Lord hath chastened me sore; but he hath not given me over unto death." The sermon is entitled, "Gratitude for Deliverance from the Grave," and an introductory note states that it was preached at the Metropolitan Tabernacle, "in connection with the dedication of the Jubilee House, which commemorated the fiftieth year of a life often threatened by grievous sickness." Mr. Spurgeon adds a note at the close of the sermon, which reads like an Old Testament Psalm, yet, with the firm, clear tone of a Pauline epistle, and which may now be termed his dying Declaration of Faith. He says:

"This sermon begins a new volume; in fact, it commences Vol. XXXVIII of *The Metropolitan Tabernacle Pulpit*. I have, myself, selected it, and prepared it for the press, because it is most suitable as my own personal testimony at the present moment. The subject is even more my own this day than it was seven and a half years ago; for I have been in deeper waters, and nearer to the mouth of the grave. With my whole soul I praise delivering grace. To the Lord God, the God of Israel, I consecrate myself anew. For the covenant of grace, for the revelation of infallible truth in the Bible, for the atonement by blood, and the immutable love of the ever-blessed Three-in-One, I am a witness; and more and more would I abide faithful to the Gospel of the grace of God. I see each day more reasons for faith, and fewer excuses for doubt. Those who will, may ship their anchors, and be drifted about by the current of the age; but I would sing, 'My heart is fixed, O God, my heart is fixed; I will sing, and give praise.'

"The whole passage, Ps. cxviii, 13–18, is inscribed upon a marble slab on the Jubilee House at the back of the Tabernacle, and I am told that many went to read it while I lay in the greatest peril through sore sickness, and were comforted thereby. When the Lord permits me to return, I must raise yet another memorial to his praise."

Early in the New Year, in regard to one of these carefully "piloted" sermons, "Is God In The Camp?" Mr. Spurgeon wrote the following, full of the ringing heartiness of his old-time pulpit utterances:

"BELOVED FRIENDS—The one want of the Church in

these times is indicated by the title of this sermon. The presence of God in saving power in the church will put an end to the present plague of infidelity. Men will not doubt His Word when they feel His Spirit. It will be the only security for the success of missionary effort. If God be with His people, they will soon see crowds converted and added to the church. For a thousand reasons, we need that Jehovah should come into the camp, as aforetime he visited and delivered His people from bondage in Egypt. Could we not all unite in prayer for this as fervently as all united in prayer for my life? It is a far greater and more necessary subject for intercession and the Lord will not be slow to hear us. Come to Thy church, O Lord, in fullness of power to save! If the Great Advent is not yet, indulge us with outpourings of grace in times of refreshing! Oh, that all Christendom would take up this pleading and continue it until the answer came!

"Receive, dear readers, my hearty salutations. Personally, I scarcely make progress during this broken weather; but the doctor says I hold my own, and that is more than he could have expected. Whether I live or die, I would say, in the words of Israel to Joseph, 'God shall be with you.'

"Yours ever heartily,
"C. H. SPURGEON."

"MENTONE, *January* 9, 1892."

The Metropolitan Tabernacle of January 21, 1892, published the following letter from the great preacher, dated only two weeks before his death. It is touching to see the play of his genial humor at such a time, and impressive to observe how his thoughts go out from himself, to take in nations, and to sympathize with all other sufferers. He writes:

"MY DEAR READERS—Your weekly preacher is still

weakly; but, though his progress towards strength is slow, it has been steadily maintained during the late trying weather. When we consider how many have died, your chaplain is very grateful to be alive, to be able to send forth his usual discourse from the press, and to be, as he hopes, half an inch nearer to his pulpit. Happy will he count himself when he is able to preach with the living voice.

"Would it not be well for all the churches to hold special meetings for prayer concerning the deadly scourge of influenza? The suggestion has, no doubt, been made by others; but I venture to press it upon Christians of all denominations that they may, in turn, urge all their pastors to summon such meetings. Our nation is fast learning to forget God. In too many instances, ministers of religion have propagated doubt, and the result is a general hardening of the popular feeling, and a greatly increased neglect of public worship. It is written 'When thy judgments are in the earth, the inhabitants of the world will learn righteousness.' Let us, who believe in inspired Scripture, unite our prayer that it may be even so. With a court and a nation in deepest mourning, it is a time to cry mightily unto the Lord.

"I have been able again to revise a sermon without assistance. It is upon Psalm cv. 37; and, if the Lord will, it will be published next week.

"Yours, in deep sympathy with all the sick and the bereaved

"C. H. SPURGEON."

"MENTONE, *January* 17, 1892."

But the hopes of final recovery were not to be fulfilled, and, in the closing hour of January's last Sabbath, he whose every Sabbath for forty years had been a day of impassioned pleading with man, and of triumphant worship of God, entered on the eternal Sabbath of Heaven.

As regards the seemingly unanswered prayers

for his final recovery, none would say more submissively and decidedly than he himself, that every true prayer has for its proviso " if it be possible— nevertheless, not my will, but thine be done." He did not look upon it as a calamity to die. In his sermon, near the close of the year 1890, on " The Man Who Shall Never See Death," he speaks as fellows :

"Now we turn to the delightful part of our subject, namely, THE GLORIOUS DELIVERANCE, which our Lord here promises: ' He shall never see death.' Our Lord did not mean that he shall never die, for he died himself; and his followers, in long procession, have descended to the grave. Some brethren are cheered by the belief that they shall live until the Lord comes; and, therefore, they shall not sleep but shall only be changed. The hope of our Lord's appearing is a very blessed one, come when He may; but I do not conceive that to be alive at His coming is any great object of desire. Is there any great preference in being changed beyond that of dying? Do we not read that,'We which are alive and remain unto the coming of the Lord shall not prevent them which are asleep?' This is a great truth. *Throughout eternity, if I die, I shall be able to say, I had actual fellowship with Christ in the article of death, and in descent into the grave*, which those happy saints who will survive can never know. It is no matter of doctrine, but yet, if one might have a choice in the matter, it might be gain to die."

Beside this thought of the blessedness of dying, we may well place the great preacher's view of the preacher's work in the immortal life:[*]

" A long life will only suffice us to skirt the shores of this

---

[*] "The Greatest Fight in the World," p. 21.

great continent of light. In the forty years of my own ministry I have only touched the hem of the garment of divine truth; but what virtue has flowed out of it! The word is like its Author, infinite, immeasurable, without end. If you were ordained to be a preacher throughout eternity, you would have before you a theme equal to everlasting demands. Brothers, shall we each have a pulpit somewhere amidst the spheres? Shall we have a parish of millions of leagues? Shall we have voices so strengthened as to reach attentive constellations? Shall we be witnesses for the Lord of grace to myriads of worlds which will be wonder-struck when they hear of the incarnate God? Shall we be surrounded by pure intelligences, enquiring and searching into the mystery of God manifest in the flesh? Will the unfallen worlds desire to be instructed in the glorious Gospel of the blessed God? and will each one of us have his own tale to tell of our experience of infinite love? I think so, since the Lord has saved us 'to the intent that now unto the principalities and powers in heavenly places might be known by the church the manifold wisdom of God.' If such be the case, our Bible will suffice for ages to come for new themes every morning, and for fresh songs and discourses world without end."

Spurgeon dead! How grand a life is ended, of a man who could afford to die! Out from his life of pain, from the pulpit which he has filled with more than kingly power, as ambassador for the King of kings, from his heart-touching, heart-filling charities, surrounded by the tearful intercessions of the host he has blessed in every land, leaving monuments more enduring than marble or bronze, he ascends to his Father and our Father, to his God and our God.

LAST SCENES AND LAST SERMONS.

"I have fought a good fight, I have finished my course, I have kept the faith.

"Henceforth there is laid up for me a crown of righteousness, which the Lord, the righteous judge, shall give me at that day: and not to me only, but unto all them also that love his appearing."— 2 Tim., iv., 7, 8.

XIII.

LAST SCENES AND LAST SERMONS.

THE funeral pageant was one of the most remarkable that London ever saw. There was no royal pomp, no military display—nothing to appeal to idle curiosity or traditional reverence for rank and title. Yet for four miles mourning crowds lined the way, in addition to the vast numbers that moved in the procession.

All along the way, all shops and warehouses were closed, all flags at half-mast. More than sixty religious bodies were represented in the procession. Those of the most diverse creed and rank joined in the common sorrow. The Prince and Princess of Wales sent despatches of sympathy, the dwellers in humble homes closed their blinds in token of grief, and followed on foot in the sorrowing throng ; delegates of the Salvation Army occupied a carriage in the procession, and the Bishop of Rochester, of the Church of England, pronounced the benediction at the grave.

In life and in death, this one man seems to have touched alike the high and the lowly, awakening anew the sense of our common humanity, our common dependence upon the one God, the universal need of the sympathy and help of the one Redeemer for whom he so mightily pleaded. The fuller accounts of the closing scenes, carry us back to the last week in January, when unfavorable news began to come from Mentone, and it was learned that Mr. Spurgeon's sickness had assumed very much the form which it had in the sad days of the last summer.

As the tidings through the week continued more unfavorable, those who loved him were drawn to the Tabernacle even on week-days, and in the early morning. A touching account of some of these services is given in the *London Daily Chronicle* of February 1st, which says:

"Friday's news was anything but reassuring, and hence it was that a small body of worshippers, some on their way to daily toil, proceeded to the Lecture Hall at the rear of the Tabernacle so early as half-past seven on Saturday morning, almost before the day had fairly dawned. They were met by Mr. Dunn, one of the deacons, who had no further information beyond that contained in the morning papers. Heartfelt prayer was then offered up, first by one and then by another, that God in His mercy would raise the stricken pastor from his bed of pain, and allow him to continue the work in which his soul delighted. It was a pathetic little meeting in the grey light of the early morning, but those who were present were earnest and sincere—a remark which will not apply to many gatherings of a more pretentious character.

"It was half-past eight when the meeting dispersed; and three hours and a half later a similar gathering was held, Mr. Dunn again presiding. It commenced with the singing of the hymn, 'Great is the Lord our God.' Only two verses, however, for the chief business was to pray. And pray they did—not perhaps in the ornate and rounded periods of the ecclesiastic, but in sound and fervid language, coming straight from the heart. Then Mr. Dunn said that up to that time they had no means of knowing their pastor's present condition, but they expected news every moment. Their pastor (continued Mr. Dunn) would be the last man in the world to claim any credit to himself. He thought he could hear him saying, 'Speak not of C. H. S. but of I. H. S.—Jesu Hominum Salvator'—but they could not be unmindful of the many who had need to cry for his restoration to health. What a friend the poor would lose if Mr. Spurgeon were called away! In the last letter he (Mr. Dunn) received from him, Mr. Spurgeon said, 'Do what you can for my poor people. Do not let them want anything. Let them be well attended. Speak to the deacons about it, and do all you can to help those in need.' Then came more prayers until one o'clock had sounded.

"Three in the afternoon saw another gathering, at which the same deep and earnest supplications ascended; and then, when the shades of evening had fallen, came the largest meeting of the day, the usual Saturday evening gathering for prayer. But there was little news—only the morning bulletin, which said that the pastor had passed a restless night, and that there was no improvement in his condition. Mr. Graham and other Church officers were present, and the time was spent in prayer—prayer for the pastor, prayer for those who are suffering by reason of the dreadful scourge which is now upon the land, and which had taken away the high and mighty ones of the earth as well as the humble and lowly."

The last Sabbath of January began with the praying assembly in the early morning, and at the usual hour a great congregation thronged the Tabernacle for the morning service, all hearts reaching across sea and land to the bedside of their pastor, even then dying far away. No certain intelligence could then be given, but a letter from Mr. Harrald, Mr. Spurgeon's secretary, was read to the assmbly, in which was included a message from Mrs. Spurgeon expressing her gratitude to the church and congregation "for their affectionate remembrance and tokens of Christian love."

"Then the Rev. Dr. Pierson, who has himself been suffering, spoke a few words, saying in conclusion, ' Let us leave our loving pastor in the tender arms of One who loves him more than we can do, and every drop of whose blood is precious in His sight. Each of you has thought about your pastor in his own mind, and before we engage in public prayer let us spend a few moments in silent prayer.' Then, in a stillness that could almost be felt, the large congregation bowed its head in silent supplication, broken only by the voice of the minister putting into words the general wish of all. The service was then proceeded with, but over all there seemed a sense of apprehension, a feeling that at any moment the worse news might arrive. Just before the morning service came to an end, the bulletin from Mentone was read to the congregation.

"In accordance with the rule which obtains at the Metropolitan Tabernacle, the principal doors are not opened until five minutes prior to the commencement of the service. Long before half-past six last evening a large crowd of intending worshippers had assembled at the entrance, and very soon after the doors were thrown open the immense building was filled in every part. The Rev. Dr. Pierson again officiated, but beyond a reference in his general prayer no allusion was made to the subject which was uppermost in every one's heart until a later period of the evening, when the afternoon message from Mentone was read, deepening the gloom which had been noticeable throughout the day, and the service was curtailed in order that a special prayer-meeting of the whole congregation might be held. This was of an impressive character, and brought the day's proceedings to a close, still under the shadow of impending calamity."

Meanwhile, at Mentone, after a very restless night, Mr. Spurgeon began the day in exceeding weakness, still able to take a slight quantity of nourishment, but, as the day wore on, even that became impossible, and his strength gradually waned, until, at half past three in the afternoon, he had become unable to recognize his watching friends or even the wife he so tenderly loved. From that time, in quiet unconsciousness, with no pain, but with increasing weakness, he steadily sank, until, at five minutes past eleven o'clock at night of January 31st, in the presence of his wife, his secretary, and two or three friends, he "fell asleep in Jesus."

As the telegraph flashed the news to London, on the Monday morning, the people were profoundly moved. The *London Standard*, of February 2d, gives a touching record of the scenes at and around the Tabernacle:

"Sympathetic crowds assembled yesterday in front of the Metropolitan Tabernacle to read and comment upon the printed copy of the telegram received from Mentone, posted upon the railings. It was as follows: 'Mentone, 11.50. Our beloved pastor entered heaven, 11.5, Sunday night.—Harrald.' The people, especially of the Newington district, in which Mr. Spurgeon was so well known, spoke regretfully of the death of the pastor of the Metropolitan Tabernacle. Signs of respect were not wanting in the immediate neighborhood. In the streets radiating from the Elephant and Castle shutters were placed upon most of the shop windows, and in the windows of the upper parts of the houses the blinds were drawn. This was also the case in the business portions of Stockwell; and in the Clapham Road, near Mr. Spurgeon's Orphanage, there was not a private house in which the blinds were not drawn. Upon the Orphanage itself the Union Jack was at half-mast; and it was stated, upon inquiry, that every person in the institution, from the master and matron to the humblest orphan, was grief-stricken at the news which conveyed the death of the founder of the Orphanage, who took the greatest pride in its success, and who was ever solicitous for the welfare of the orphans. Irrespective of creed, the people of South London intimated, in one form or other, their regret for Mr. Spurgeon's death.

"Special devotional meetings were held yesterday morning, afternoon, and evening, at the Tabernacle. At the evening meeting, at which Dr. Pierson presided, there was a very large assemblage, mostly in tears; and a large crowd gathered outside."

Dr. Pierson made a brief, but most impressive, address, which was in substance as follows:

"My mind has turned to the fourth chapter of St. Paul's second epistle to Timothy, the first portion of which I have read. It might have been spoken by your pastor, if he were with you to-night. His dying message might have been these words: 'For now I am ready to be offered, and the time of my departure is at hand. I have fought the good fight, I have finished my course, I have kept the faith. Henceforth there is laid up for me a crown of righteousness which the Lord shall give me at that day: and not to me only, but to all them also who love His appearing.' After all, our grief is a selfish thing. We look around and see the vacant places in every direction which Mr. Spurgeon once filled, but how little do we think of that glory of which he is now the sharer—that ineffable, unspeakable glory, which, if a man experienced it and came back, it would not be possible for him to describe. Almost twenty-four hours have passed since Charles Haddon Spurgeon met his Lord and Master face to face, and just think of the people who have been waiting for him to come. I marvel whether since St. Paul departed this life there has been any one of God's saints who has entered into heaven and found so many people there who have been led to Christ through his ministry. I wonder whether any saint has had such a welcome to glory as Mr. Spurgeon had. There is no man or woman in this house who feels this sorrow more than I, but I cannot think of my grief altogether. I am bound to think of your pastor's joy. Just think what a crown of glory he now has! He was so humble, and loved his Lord so much, that he would not wear the crown for a moment, but would cast it at His feet and say, 'It does not belong to me.' But there are thousands, tens of thousands, hundreds of thousands of jewels in that crown, and every jewel represents a ransomed soul won by his preaching or his writings. So let us not be selfish in our grief, but mingle with our prayers and supplications praise to Almighty God that your beloved pastor has been taken from the midst of suffering, and entered into glory."

Flowers and Palms.

At the conclusion of this address, Dr. Pierson invited the congregation to join him in singing "All hail the power of Jesus' name."

A dispatch from Mentone of February 1st, says:

"Mentone, February 1.—The remains of the Rev. Charles H. Spurgeon, the noted English divine, who died here last night, are lying on the bed on which he died. The bed around the body is almost hidden from sight by the number of floral wreaths which have been sent by relatives, friends, and admirers of the deceased. The features of the dead man show not the slightest evidence of death agony. *He looks as though he had simply fallen asleep, and his face bears the placid expression of one at rest from toil.* The body will be removed to-morrow to the mortuary chapel in the cemetery. Mrs. Spurgeon is bearing up well under the great sorrow that has come to her."

On the same date, it is added:

"The telegraph traffic is completely blocked with messages of condolence arriving from all parts of the world."

The body was embalmed and sealed up in a leaden case which was enclosed in a beautiful coffin of olive-wood, on which was inscribed the last quotation from the Scriptures uttered by Mr. Spurgeon to his secretary, Mr. Harrald, before his death, the strikingly appropriate words of the Apostle Paul, recorded in 2 Tim. iv, 7.

"I HAVE FOUGHT A GOOD FIGHT, I HAVE FINISHED MY COURSE, I HAVE KEPT THE FAITH."

Mrs. Spurgeon requested that, instead of flowers, palm-branches might be brought to the funeral service. Before the departure from Mentone, on Thursday, February 4th, a service was held at the Scottish Church, to which the body had been previously conveyed.

"Every seat in the sacred edifice was occupied, and a large number of persons who were unable to obtain admittance remained standing outside. The decorations inside the church were of a very simple character. In compliance with Mrs. Spurgeon's request, there were few floral wreaths, but palm branches were abundantly displayed.

"The service lasted exactly an hour, and was of a very impressive character."

On Monday, February 8th, when the remains arrived at Newhaven, over fifteen hundred people, in spite of the cold, damp morning, were assembled. Prayers were offered by ministers of various denominations, and the whole assembly joined in singing the hymn, "Forever with the Lord." On arriving in London :

"At the railroad station an immense crowd of people had assembled, and saw the placing of the coffin in a plain hearse, which was driven to the Tabernacle. So dense was the crowd at that place that it was found necessary to take the coffin to an adjacent park, Kennington Common, where the masses defiled before it and impromptu services were held, and many addresses were made by various pastors and college officials."

Through all of Tuesday, the body was practically lying in state at the Tabernacle, in order that friends might have ample opportunity of viewing the remains, as they could not do during the progress of a service. The request had been publicly made, by Rev. J. A Spurgeon and the deacons, and urged by Rev. Dr. Pierson, that there should be no flowers, but that those who had contemplated bringing floral offerings, costing in many cases large sums of money, would, instead, contribute the money these would cost, to the Stockwell Orphanage, which the deceased pastor so tenderly cherished, and for which he pleaded in some of the very last letters he ever wrote. Such an expression of regard, they felt assured, was most in accord with what would be Mr. Spurgeon's wish.

Almost all of Wednesday, January 10th, was occupied with memorial services, as follows: At 11 A. M., a service for members of the Tabernacle church, and of organizations connected with it; at 3 P. M., for ministers of the gospel and college students only, a special invitation being sent out to pastors who had been students at the Pastors' College, and special place reserved for them; at 7 P. M., and again at 10.30, services for the general public. The last service, which was in the nature of a watch meeting, and under the conduct of the well-known evangelists, Fullerton and Smith, is mentioned as especially solemn and impressive, the Tabernacle being crowded, and the exercises continued till after midnight.

At 11 A. M. of Thursday, February 11th, occurred the great funeral service at the Tabernacle. which, it is almost needless to say, was crowded to its utmost limit. The shops all around the Tabernacle and on the route to the cemetery were for the most part closed, and nearly all the buildings bore mourning emblems. Within the Tabernacle, the preacher's platform, which had so long been Mr. Spurgeon's place of power. was heavily draped with black. Below lay all that was mortal of the great preacher in its olive-wood coffin, which, in spite of all requests to the contrary, was fairly covered with flowers. Noticeable among the floral offerings was a wreath of roses sent by the French Baptists. Upon the flowers lay an open Bible, the same from which Mr. Spurgeon had so faithfully preached the Word. Those of Mr. Spurgeon's family who were able to be at the time in London, members of the House of Commons, the Mayor of Croydon, the Baroness Burdette Coutts, and deputations from sixty religious bodies were among those assembled. The boys of Stockwell Orphanage sang at the opening of the service the last hymn Mr. Spurgeon had announced before he was taken sick :

> " The sands of time are sinking,
>   The dawn of heaven breaks,
> The summer morn I've sighed for,
>   The fair sweet morn awakes ;
> Dark, dark hath been the midnight,
>   But day-spring is at hand,
> And glory, glory dwelleth
>   In Immanuel's land.
>
> " Oh, Christ, he is the fountain,
>   The deep, sweet well of love ;
> The streams of earth I've tasted,
>   More deep I'll drink above.
> There to an ocean fullness
>   His mercy doth expand
> And glory, glory dwelleth
>   In Immanuel's land.
>
> " The bride eyes not her garment,
>   But her dear bridegroom's face ;
> I will not gaze at glory
>   But on my King of Grace—

> Not at the crown he giveth
> But on his pierced hand;—
> The Lamb is all the glory
> Of Immanuel's land."

Rev. Dr. Angus delivered an impressive address, recalling the history of the Metropolitan Tabernacle, and the wonderful work for good done through and by it, with a hearty eulogy of the departed pastor. Rev. Dr. Pierson then read a letter from Mrs. Spurgeon, praying that the people's faith might not fail in this hour of trial, and saying of her departed husband, "He is not here, but is risen," and that not for one moment would she wish him back, though dearer to her than tongue could tell. Dr. Pierson delivered a most eloquent memorial address, dwelling upon Mr. Spurgeon's wide and powerful influence, and drawing a striking parallel between his work and that of John Wesley. As the coffin was taken from the catafalque and borne down the aisle, the entire congregation arose, and joined in singing the hymn, "There is no night in Homeland." The sides of the hearse in which the coffin was placed bore the same triumphant inscription, "I have fought a good fight, I have finished my course, I have kept the faith." Forty mourning coaches and a vast number of private carriages followed the hearse. So, through four miles of streets where blinds and shutters were closed, flags at half-mast and mourning emblems everywhere displayed, amid the solemn tolling of church-bells, past the Stockwell Orphanage, where a raised platform, erected especially for the occasion and heavily draped in black, enabled the five hundred boys and girls to witness the last honors paid to their benefactor, and, most touching of all, between miles of human beings lining the sidewalks on either side, almost all wearing some token of mourning and watching in reverent, tearful silence, the body of Charles H. Spurgeon was borne to its rest. Norwood Cemetery, though none had been admitted but by ticket, was already thronged. Here, the Rev. Archibald G. Brown, pastor of the East London Tabernacle, delivered a funeral oration, Rev. Dr. Pierson offered a prayer of heart-touching tenderness and power, and the Right Rev. Randall Thomas Davidson, Bishop of Rochester, pronounced the benediction. After the services, the people present formed in line, and slowly filed before the open vault, and took their last look upon the casket enclosing the remains of the beloved and honored preacher of righteousness, now at rest from his earthly work.

THE STATUTE OF DAVID FOR THE SHARING OF THE SPOIL.—1 Samuel xxx: 21-25.

A SERMON DELIVERED ON LORD'S-DAY MORNING, JUNE 7TH, 1891, BY C. H. SPURGEON, AT THE METROPOLITAN TABERNACLE, NEWINGTON.*

THOSE who associate themselves with a leader must share his fortunes. Six hundred men had quitted their abodes in Judæa; unable to endure the tyranny of Saul, they had linked themselves with David, and made him to be a captain over them. They were, some of them, the best of men, and some of them were the worst: in this, resembling our congregations. Some of them were choice spirits, whom David would have sought, but others were undesirable persons, from whom he might gladly have been free. However, be they who they may, they must rise or fall with their leader and commander. If he had the city Ziklag given to him, they had a house and a home in it; and if Ziklag was burned with fire, their houses did not escape. When David stood amid the smoking ruins, a penniless and a wifeless man, they stood in the same condition. This rule holds good with all of us who have joined ourselves to Christ and His cause; we must be partakers with

---

* We find a sermon on the text, " Out of weakness were made strong," extensively quoted as Mr. Spurgeon's last. That sermon, however, was " Intended for Reading, June 21st," while the one here given is that which Mr. Spurgeon actually delivered on the morning of June 7th, just after his recovery from the influenza; it was on the very next day that he took the chill which was the beginning of his protracted and at length fatal illness (see p. 343). A touching reference to his recent sickness appears in the opening paragraph of division II. (p. 386.) In this connection, the editor desires to express his grateful acknowledgments to *The Independent*, *The Examiner*, and *The Christian Inquirer* for valued courtesies; and especially for favors received from the *Christian Herald*, which has published Mr. Spurgeon's sermons weekly for the past fourteen years. The account of the closing scenes and of the funeral services given in this chapter, is for the most part compiled from material sent to us direct from our London house, in answer to cable dispatches.

Him. I hope we are prepared to stand to this rule to-day. If there be ridicule and reproach for the gospel of Christ, let us be willing to be ridiculed and reproached for His sake. Let us gladly share with Him in his humiliation, and never dream of shrinking. This involves a great privilege, since they that are with Him in His humiliation shall be with Him in His glory. If we share His rebuke in the midst of an evil generation, we shall also sit upon His throne, and share His glory in the day of His appearing. Brethren, I hope the most of us can say we are in for it, to sink or swim with Jesus. In life or death, where He is, there will we, His servants, be. We joyfully accept both the cross and the crown which go with our Lord Jesus Christ: we are eager to bear our full share of the blame, that we may partake in His joy.

It frequently happens that when a great disaster occurs to a band of men, a mutiny follows thereupon. However little it may be the leader's fault, the defeated cast the blame of the defeat upon him. If the fight is won, "it was a soldiers' battle"; every man-at-arms claims his share of praise. But if the battle is lost, cashier the commander! It was entirely his fault; if he had been a better general he might have won the day. This is how people talk: fairness is out of the question. So in the great disaster of Ziklag, when the town was burned with fire, and wives and children were carried away captive; then we read that they spoke of stoning David. Why David? Why David more than anybody else, it is hard to see, for he was not there, nor any one of them. They felt so vexed that it would be a relief to stone somebody, and why not David? Brethren, it sometimes happens, even to the servants of Christ, that when they fall into persecution and loss for Christ's sake, the tempter whispers to them to throw up their profession. "Since you have been a Christian you have had nothing but trouble. It seems as if the dogs of hell were snapping at your heels more than ever since you took upon you the name of Christ. Therefore, throw it up, and leave the ways of godliness." Vile suggestion! Mutiny against the Lord Jesus? Dare you do so? Some of us cannot do so, for when He asks us, "Will ye also go away?" we can only answer, "Lord, to whom should we go? Thou hast the words of eternal life." No other leader is worth following. We must follow the Son of David. Mutiny against Him is out of the question.

Sharing with the Leader.

"Through floods or flames, if Jesus lead,
We'll follow where he goes."

When a dog follows a man, we may discover whether the man is his master by seeing what happens when they come to a turn in the road. If the creature keeps close to its master at all turnings, it belongs to him. Every now and then you and I come to turns in the road, and many of us are ready, through grace, to prove our loyalty by following Jesus even when the way is hardest. Though the tears stand in His eyes and ours; though we weep together till we have no more power to weep, we will cling to Him when the many turn aside, and witness that He hath the living Word, and none upon earth beside. God grant us grace to be faithful unto death!

If we thus follow our Leader and bear His reproach, the end and issue will be glorious victory. It was a piteous sight to see David leaving two hundred men behind him, and marching with his much-diminished forces after an enemy who had gone, he scarce knew where, who might be ten times stronger than his little band, and might slay those who pursued them. It was a melancholy spectacle for those left behind to see their leader a broken man, worn and weary like themselves, hastening after the cruel Amalekite. How very different was the scene when he came back to the brook Besor more than a conqueror! Do you not hear the song of them that make merry? A host of men in the front are driving vast herds of cattle and flocks of sheep, and singing as they march, "This is David's spoil!" Then you see armed men, with David in the midst of them, all laden with spoil, and you hear them singing yet another song; those that bring up the rear are shouting exultingly, "David recovered all! David recovered all!" They, the worn-out ones that stayed at the brook Besor, hear the mingled song, and join first in the one shout, and then in the other; singing, "That is David's spoil! David recovered all!"

Yes, we have no doubt about the result of our warfare. He that is faithful to Christ shall be glorified with him. That he will divide the spoil with the strong is never a matter of question. "The pleasure of the Lord shall prosper in his hand."

The old truth by which we stand shall never be blotted out.

> " Engraved as in eternal brass
> The mighty promise shines.
> Nor shall the powers of darkness rase
> Those everlasting lines."

We are certain as we live that the exiled truth shall celebrate its joyful return. The faith once for all delivered to the saints may be down-trodden for a season; but rejoice not over us, O our adversaries: though we fall we shall rise again! Wherefore we patiently hope, and quietly wait, and calmly believe. We drink of the brook Besor by the way and lift up our heads.

This morning I want to utter God-given words of comfort to those who are faint and weary in the Lord's army. May the divine Comforter make them so!

I. I shall begin by saying, first, that FAINT ONES OCCUR EVEN IN THE ARMY OF OUR KING. Among the very elect of David's army—heroes who were men of war from their youth up—there were hands that hung down, and feeble knees that needed to be confirmed. There are such in Christ's army at most seasons. We have among us soldiers whose faith is real, and whose love is burning; and yet, for all that, just now their strength is weakened in the way, and they are so depressed in spirit, that they are obliged to stop behind with the baggage.

Possibly some of these weary ones had grown faint because *they had been a good deal perplexed*. David had so wrongfully entangled himself with the Philistine king, that he felt bound to go with Achish to fight against Israel. I dare say these men said to themselves, "How will this end? Will David really lead us to battle against Saul? When he could have killed him in the cave he would not, but declared that he would not lift up his hand against the Lord's anointed; will he now take us to fight against the anointed of God? This David, who was so great an enemy of Philistia, and slew their champion, will he war on their behalf?" They were perplexed with their leader's movements. I do not know whether you agree with me, but I find that half-an-hour's perplexity takes more out of a man than a month's labor. When you cannot see your bearings, and know not what to do, it is most trying. When to be true to God it seems that you must break faith with man, and when to fulfill your unhappy covenant with evil would make you false to your Christian professions, things are perplexing.

If you do not walk carefully, you can easily get into a snarl. If Christians walk in a straight line, it is comparatively easy going, for it is easy to find your way along a straight road; but when good men take to the new cut, that by-path across the meadow, then they often get into ditches that are not in the map, and fall into thickets and sloughs that they never reckoned upon. Then is the time for heart-sickness to come on. These warriors may very well have been perplexed; and perhaps they feared that God was against them and that now their cause would be put to shame; and when they came to Ziklag, and found it burned with fire, the perplexity of their minds added intense bitterness to their sorrow, and they felt bowed into the dust. They did not pretend to be faint, but they were really so; for the mind can soon act upon the body, and the body fails sadly when the spirits are worried with questions and fears. This is one reason why certain of our Lord's loyal-hearted ones are on the sick list, and must keep in the trenches for a while.

Perhaps, also, *the pace was killing to these men.* They made forced marches for three days from the city of Achish to Ziklag. These men could do a good day's march with anybody; but they could not foot it at the double-quick march all day long. There are a great many Christians of that sort—good, staying men who can keep on under ordinary pressure, doing daily duty well, and resisting ordinary temptations bravely; but at a push they fare badly: who among us does not? To us there may come multiplied labors, and we faint because our strength is small.

Worst of all, *their grief came in just then.* Their wives were gone. Although, as it turned out, they were neither killed nor otherwise harmed; yet they could not tell this, and they feared the worse. For a man to know that his wife is in the hands of robbers, and that he may never see her again, is no small trouble. Their sons and daughters also were gone: no prattlers climbed their father's knee, no gentle daughters came forth to bid them "Welcome home." Their homes were still burning, their goods were consumed, and they lifted up their voice and wept: is it at all wonderful that some of them were faint after performing that doleful *miserere?* Where would you be if you went home this morning, and found your home burned, and your family gone, you knew not where? I know many Christians who get very faint under extraordinary troubles. They should not, but they do. We have reason to thank God that no temptation has happened to us but such as is common to men; and yet it may not seem so; but we may feel as if we were specially tried, like Job. Messenger after messenger has brought us evil tidings, and our hearts are not fixed on the Lord as they ought to be. To those who are faint through grief I speak just now. You may be this, and yet you may be a true follower of the Lamb; and as God has promised to bring you out of your troubles, he will surely keep his word. Remember, he has never promised that you shall have no sorrows, but that he will deliver you out of them all. Ask yon saints in heaven! Ask those to step out of the shining ranks who came thither without trial. Will one of the leaders of the shining host give the word of command that he shall step forward who has washed his robes and made them white in the blood of the Lamb, but who never knew what affliction meant while here below? No one stirs in all that white-robed host. Does not one come forward? Must we wait here forever without response? See! instead of anyone stirring from their ranks, I hear a voice that says, "These are they which came out of great tribulation." All of them have known, not only tribulation, but *great* tribulation. One promise of the New Testament is surely fulfilled before our eyes—"In the world ye shall have tribulation." When trouble came so pressingly on David's men they felt their weakness and needed to halt at the margin of the brook.

Perhaps, also, *the force of the torrent was too much for them*. As I have told you, in all probability the brook Besor was only a hollow place, which in ordinary times was almost dry; but in a season of great rain it filled suddenly with a rushing, muddy stream, against which only strong men could stand. These men might have kept on upon dry land, but the current was too fierce for them, and they feared that it would carry them off their feet and drown them. Therefore, David gave them leave to stop there and guard the stuff. Many there are of our Lord's servants who stop short of certain onerous service; they are not called to do what their stronger comrades undertake with joy. They can do something, but they fail to do more; they can also bear trials, but they are unable to bear more; they faint because they have not yet come to fulness of growth in grace. Their hearts are right in the sight of God, but they are not in condition to surmount some peculiar difficulty. You must not overdrive them, for they are the feeble of the flock. Many are too faint for needful controversy. I have found a great many of that sort about lately: the truth is very important, but they love peace. It is quite necessary that certain o us should stand up for the faith once delivered to the saints; but they are not up to the mark for it. They cannot bear to differ from their fellows; and they hold their tongues rather than contend for the truth. There are true hearts that, nevertheless, cannot defend the gospel. They wish well to the champions; but they seek the rear rank for themselves. And some cannot advance any further with regard to knowledge; they know the fundamentals, and feel as if they could master nothing more. It is a great blessing that they know the gospel, and feel that it will save them; but the glorious mysteries of the everlasting covenant, of the sovereignty of God, of his eternal love and distinguishing grace, they cannot compass— these are a brook Besor which as yet they cannot swim. It would do them a world of good if they could venture in; but, still, they are not to be tempted into these blessed deeps. To hear of these things rather wearies them than instructs them: they have not streugth enough of mind for the deep things of God. I would have every Christian wish to know all that he can know of revealed truth. Somebody whispers that the secret things belong not to us. You may be sure you will never know them if they are secret; but all that is revealed you ought to know, for these things belong to you and to your children. Take care you know what the Holy Ghost teaches. Do not give way to a fainthearted ignorance, lest you be great losers thereby. That which is fit food for babes should not be enough for young men and fathers: we should eat strong meat, and leave milk to the little ones.

Yet these fainting ones were, after all, in David's army. Their names were in their Captain's Register as much as the names of the strong. And they did not desert the colors. They had the same captain as the stoutest-hearted men in the whole regiment; they could call David " Master " and " Lord " as truly as the most lion-like man amongst them. They were in for the same dangers; for if the men in front had been beaten and had retreated, the enemy would have fallen on those who guarded the stuff. If the Amalekites had slain the four hundred, they would have made short work of the two hundred. They had work to do as needful as that of the others. Though they had not to fight, they had to take care of the stuff; and this eased the minds of the fighting men. I will be bound to say it was a great trial to them not to be allowed to march into the fight. For a brave man to see the troops go past him, and hear the last footfall of his comrades, must have been sickening. Who could pleasantly say, " I am left out of it. There is a glorious day coming, and I shall be away. I shall, until I die, think myself accursed I was not there, and hold my manhood cheap that I fought not with them on that day"? It is hard to brave men to be confined to hospital, and have no drive at the foe. The weary one wishes he could be to the front, where his Captain's eye would be upon him. He pants to smite down the enemies, and win back the spoil for his comrades.

Enough of this. I will only repeat my first point: fainting ones do occur even in the army of our King.

II. Secondly, THESE FAINTING ONES REJOICE TO SEE THEIR LEADER RETURN. Do you see, when David went back, they went to meet him, and the people that were with him. I feel very much like this myself. That was one reason why I took this text. I felt, after my illness, most happy to come forth and meet my Lord in public. I hoped he would be here; and so he is. I am glad also to meet with you, my comrades. We are still spared for the war. Though laid aside a while, we are again among our brethren. Thank God! It is a great joy to meet you. I am sorry to miss so many of our church-members who are laid aside by this sickness; but it is a choice blessing to meet so many of our kindred in Christ. We are never happier than when we are in fellowship with one another and with our Lord.

David saluted the stay-at-homes. Oh, that he might salute each one of us this morning, especially those who have been laid aside! Our King's salutations are wonderful for their heartiness. He uses no empty compliments nor vain words. Every syllable from his lips is a benediction. Every glance of his eye is an inspiration. When the

The Leader's Return.

King himself comes near, it is always a feast-day to us! It is a high day and a holiday, even with the faintest of us, when we hear his voice. So they went to meet David, and he came to meet them, and there was great joy. Yes, I venture to mend that, and say there is great joy among us now. Glory be to His holy name, the Lord is here! We see him, and rejoice with joy unspeakable.

David's courtesy was as free as it was true. Possibly those who remained behind were half afraid that their leader might say, " See here, you idle fellows, what we have been doing for you!" No; he saluted them, but did not scold them. Perhaps they thought, " He will upbraid us that we did not manage to creep into the fray." But no; " He giveth liberally, and upbraideth not." He speaks not a word of upbraiding, for his heart pities them, and therefore he salutes them—" My brethren, God has been gracious to us. All hail!" David would have them rejoice together; and give praise unto the most High. He will not dash their cup with a drop of bitter. Oh, for a salutation from our Lord at this good hour! When Christ comes into a company His presence makes a heavenly difference. Have you never seen an assembly listening to an orator, all unmoved and stolid? Suddenly the Holy Ghost has fallen on the speaker, and the King Himself has been visibly set forth among them in the midst of the assembly, and all have felt as if they could leap to their feet and cry, " Hallelujah, hallelujah ! " Then hearts beat fast, and souls leap high ; for where Jesus is found His presence fills the place with delight. Now, then, you weary ones, if you be here, any of you, may you rejoice as you now meet your Leader, and your Leader reveals Himself to you! If no one else has a sonnet, I have mine. He must, He shall be praised. " Thou art the King of Glory, O Christ ! All heaven and earth adores Thee. Thou shalt reign for ever and ever."

III. Thirdly, FAINT ONES HAVE THEIR LEADER FOR THEIR ADVOCATE. Listen to those foul-mouthed men of Belial, these wicked men : how they rail against those whom God has afflicted! They came up to David and began blustering—" These weaklings who were not in the fight, they shall not share the spoil. Let them take their wives and children and begone." These fellows spoke with loud, harsh voices, and greatly grieved the feebler ones. Who was to speak up for them? Their leader became their advocate.

First, do you notice, *he pleads their unity?* The followers of the son of Jesse are one and inseparable. David said, "Ye shall not do so, my brethren, with that which the Lord hath given *us*, who hath preserved *us*." "We are all one," says David. "God has given the spoil, not to you alone, but to *us* all. We are all one company of brothers." The unity of saints is the consolation of the feeble. Brethren, our Lord Jesus Christ would refresh His wearied ones by the reflection that we are all one in Him. I may be the foot, all dusty and travel-stained; and you may be the hand, holding forth some precious gem; but we are still one body. Yonder friend is the brow of holy thought, and another is the lip of persuasion, and a third is the eye of watchfulness; but still we are one body in Christ. We cannot do, anyone of us, without his fellow; each one ministers to the benefit of all. The eye cannot say to the hand, "I have no need of thee." We are all one in Christ Jesus. Surely this ought to comfort those of you who, by reason of feebleness, are made to feel as if you were very inferior members of the body: you are still living members of the mystical body of Jesus Christ your Lord, and let this suffice you. One life is ours, one love is ours, one heaven shall be ours in our one Saviour.

David further *pleaded free grace,* for he said to them, "Ye shall not do so, my brethren, with that which the Lord hath given us." He did not say, "With that which you have conquered, and fairly earned in battle," but "that which the Lord hath given us." Look upon every blessing as a gift, and you will not think anyone shut out from it, not even yourself. The gift of God is eternal life; why should you not have it? Deny not to anyone of your brethren any comfort of the covenant of grace. Think not of any man, "He ought not to have so much joy." It is all of free grace; and if free grace rules the hour, the least may have it as well as the greatest. If it is all of free grace, then, my poor struggling brother, who can hardly feel assured that you are saved, yet if you are a believer, you may claim every blessing of the Lord's gracious covenant. God freely gives to you as well as to me the provisions of His love; therefore, let us be glad, and not judge ourselves after the manner of the law of condemnation.

Then he pleaded *their needfulness.* He said, "These men abided by the stuff." No army fights well when its camp is unguarded. It is a great thing for a church to know that

The Law of Reward.

its stores are well guarded by a praying band. While some of us are teaching in the school or preaching in the street, we have great comfort in knowing that a certain number of our friends are praying for us. To me it is a boundless solace that I live in the prayers of thousands. I will not say which does the better service—the man that preaches, or the man that prays; but I know this, that we can do better without the voice that preaches than without the heart that prays. The petitions of our bed-ridden sisters are the wealth of the church. The kind of service which seems most commonplace among men is often the most precious unto God. Therefore, as for those who cannot come into the front places of warfare, deny them not seats of honor, since, after all, they may be doing the greater good. Remember the statute, " They shall part alike."

Notice that David *adds to his pleading a statute*. I like to think of our great Commander, the Lord Jesus, making statutes. For whom does He legislate? For the first three? For the captains of thousands? No. He makes a statute for those who are forced to stay at home because they are faint. Blessed be the name of our Lord Jesus, He is always looking to the interests of those who have nobody else to care for them! If you can look after your own cause, you may do so; but if you are so happy as to be weak in yourself, you shall be strong in Christ. Those who have Christ to care for them are better off than if they took care of themselves. He that can leave his concerns with Christ has left them in good hands. Vain is the help of self, but all-sufficient is the aid of Jesus.

To sum up what I mean: I believe the Lord will give to the sick and the suffering an equal reward with the active and energetic, if they are equally concerned for His glory. The Lord will also make a fair division to the obscure and unknown as well as to the renowned and honored, if they are equally earnest. Oh, tell me not that she who rears her boy for Christ shall miss her reward from Him by whom an apostle is recompensed! Tell me not that the woman who so conducts her household that her servants come to fear God, shall be forgotten in the day when the " Well dones " are distributed to the faithful! Homely and unnoticed service shall have honor as surely as that with which the world is ringing.

Some of God's people are illiterate, and they have but little native talent. But if they serve the Lord as best they can, with all their heart, they shall take their part with those that are the most learned and accomplished. He that is faithful over a little shall have his full reward of grace. It is accepted according to what a man hath. We may possess no more than two mites, but if we cast them into the treasury, our Lord will think much of them.

Some dear servants of God seem always to be defeated. They seem sent to a people whose hearts are made gross and their ears dull of hearing. Still, if they have truthfully proclaimed the Word of the Lord, their reward will not be according to their apparent success, but according to their fidelity.

Some saints are constitutionally depressed and sad; they are like certain lovely ferns, which grow best under a constant drip. Well, well, the Lord will gather these beautiful ferns of the shade as well as the roses of the sun; they shall share His notice as much as the blazing sunflowers, and the saddest shall rejoice with the gladdest. You Little-Faiths, you Despondencies, you Much-Afraids, you Feeble-Minds, you that sigh more than you sing, you that would but cannot, you that have a great heart for holiness, but feel beaten back in your struggles, the Lord shall give you His love, His grace his favor, as surely as He gives it to those who can do great things in His name. Certain of you have but a scant experience of the higher joys and deeper insights of the kingdom, and it may be that you are in part faulty because you are so backward; and yet, if true to your Lord, your infirmities shall not be reckoned as iniquities. If lawfully detained from the field of active labor this statute stands fast for ever, for you as well as for others: "As his part is that goeth down to the battle, so shall his part be that tarrieth by the stuff: they shall part alike."

IV. Now, fourthly, FAINT ONES FIND JESUS TO BE THEIR GOOD LORD IN EVERY WAY. Was he not a good Lord when he first took us into his army of salvation? What a curious crew they were that enlisted under David! "Every one that was in debt, and every one that was discontented, gathered themselves unto him, and he became a captain over them." He was a captain of ragamuffins; but our Lord had not a better following. I was a poor wretch when I came to Christ; and I should not wonder if that word is near enough to the truth to describe *you*. I was a good-for-nothing, over head and ears in debt, and without a penny to pay. I came to Jesus so utterly down at the heel, that no one else would have owned me. He might well have said,—" No, I have not come to this—to march at the head of such vagrant beggars as these." Yet He received us graciously, according to His promise, " Him that cometh to me I will in no wise cast out." Since then, how graciously has He borne with us! We are not among those self-praising ones who have wrought such wonders of holiness; but we mourn our shortcomings and transgressions, and yet He hath not cast away the people whom He did foreknow. When we look back upon our character as soldiers of Christ, we feel ashamed of ourselves, and amazed at His grace. If anybody had told us that we should have been such poor soldiers as we have been, we should not have believed them. We do not excuse ourselves: we are greatly grieved to have been such failures. Yet our gracious Lord has never turned us out of the ranks. He might have drummed us out of the regiment long ago; but here we are still, enrolled, upheld, and smiled upon, What a Captain we have! None can compare with Him for gentleness. He still owns us, and He declares, " They shall be mine in that day when I make up my jewels."

Brethren, let us exalt the name of our Captain. There is none like Him. We have been in distress since then: and He has been in distress with us. Ziklag smoked for Him as well as for us. In all their affliction He was afflicted. Have you not found it so? When we have come to a great difficulty like the brook Besor He has gently eased His commands, and has not required of us what we were unable to yield. He has not made some of you pastors and teachers, for you could not have borne the burden. He hath abounded towards us in all wisdom and prudence. He has suited the the march to the foot, or the foot to the march. How sweetly He has smiled on what we have done! Have you not wondered to see how He has accepted your works and your prayers? You have been startled to find that He did answer your feeble petitions. When you have spoken a word for Jesus, and God has blessed it, why you have thought, "Surely there is a mistake about this! How could my feeble word have a blessing on it?" Beloved, we follow a noble Prince. Jesus is the chief among ten thousand for tenderness as well as for everything else. How tenderly considerate He is! How gentle and generous! He has never said a stinging word to us ever since we knew him. He is that riches which has no sorrow added to it. He has rebuked us; but His rebukes have been like an excellent oil, which has never broken our heads. When we have left Him, He has turned and looked upon us, and so He has cut us to the quick; but He has never wounded us with any sword except that which cometh out of His mouth, whose edge is love. When He goes away from us, as David did from those two hundred who could not keep up with him, yet He always comes back again in mercy, and salutes us with favor. We wonder to ourselves that we did not hold him, and vow that we would never let him go; but we wonder still more that He should came back so speedily, so heartily, leaping over the mountains, hastening like a roe or a young hart over the hills of division. Lo! He has come to us. He has come to us, and He makes our hearts glad at His coming. Let us indulge our hearts this morning as we take our share in the precious spoil of His immeasurable love. He loves the great and the small with like love; let us be joyful all round.

There is one choice thing which He will do, that should make us love Him beyond measure. David, after a while, went up to Hebron to be made king over Judah. Shall I read you in the second book of Samuel, the second chapter, and the third verse? "And his men that were with him" (and among the rest these weak ones who could not pass over the brook Besor), "and his men that were with him did David bring up, every man with his household: and they dwelt in the cities of Hebron." Yes, He will bring me up, even me! He will bring you up, you faintest and weakest of the band. There is a Hebron wherein Jesus reigns as anointed King, and He will not be there and leave one of us behind. There is no kingdom for Jesus without His brethren, no heaven for Jesus without His disciples. His poor people who have been with Him in faintness and weariness shall be with Him in glory, *and their households*. Hold on to that additional blessing. I pray you, hold on to it. Do not let slip that word —"*and their households.*" I fear we often lose a blessing on our household through clipping the promise. When the jailer asked what he must do to be saved, what was the answer? "Believe on the Lord Jesus Christ, and thou shalt be saved." You have heard that answer hundreds of times, have you not? Did you ever hear the rest of it? Why do preachers and quoters snip off corners from gospel promises? It runs thus; " Thou shalt be saved, *and thy house.*" Lay hold of that blessed enlargement of grace, "and thy house." Why leave out the wives and the children? Will you let the Amalekites have them? Do not be satisfied without household salvation. Let us plead this word of the Lord this morning: O thou blessed David, whom we have desired to follow, who hast helped us so graciously even unto this day, when thou art in thy kingdom graciously remember us, and let it be said of us, "and David went up thither, and his men that were with him David brought up (they did not go up of themselves) every man with his household; and they dwelt' in the cities of Hebron;" "*Every man with his household.*" I commend that word to your careful notice. Fathers, have you yet seen your children saved? Mothers, are all those daughters brought in yet? Never cease to pray until it is so, for this is the crown of it all, "Every man with his household."

What I have to say lastly is this: how greatly I desire that you who are not yet enlisted in my Lord's band would come to Him because you see what a kind and gracious Lord He is! Young men, if you could see our Captain, you would down on your knees and beg Him to let you enter the ranks of those who follow Him. It is heaven to serve Jesus. I am a recruiting sergeant, and I would fain find a few recruits at this moment. Every man must serve somebody: we have no choice as to that fact. Those who have no master are slaves to themselves. Depend upon it, you will either serve Satan or Christ, either self or the Saviour. You will find sin, self, Satan, and the world to be hard masters; but if you wear the livery of Christ, you will find Him so meek and lowly of heart that you will find rest unto your souls. He is the most magnanimous of captains. There never was His like among the choicest of princes. He is always to be found in the thickest part of the battle. When the wind blows cold He always takes the bleak side of the hill. The heaviest end of the cross lies ever on His shoulders. If He bids us carry a burden, He carries it also. If there is anything that is gracious, generous, kind, and tender, yea lavish and superabundant in love, you always find it in Him. These forty years and more have I served Him, blessed be His name! and I have had nothing but love from Him. I would be glad to continue yet another forty years in the same dear service here below if so it pleased Him. His service is life, peace, joy. Oh, that you would enter on it at once! God help you to enlist under the banner of Jesus even this day! Amen.

THE LAST SERMON.

According to *The Sword and The Trowel*, Mr. Spurgeon delivered two addresses to the friends assembled at Mentone—one on the last evening of 1891 by way of retrospect, and the other on the first morning of the present year by way of prospect. Both discourses were delivered sitting, and the following is that for the New Year :

"Passing at this hour over the threshold of the New Year, we look forward, and what do we see? Could we procure a telescope which would enable us to see to the end of the year, should we be wise to use it? I think not. We know nothing of the events which lie before us—of life or death to ourselves or to our friends, or of changes of position, or of sickness or health. What a mercy that these things are hidden from us! If we foresaw our best blessings, they would lose their freshness and sweetness while we impatiently waited for them. Anticipation would sour into weariness, and familiarity would breed contempt. If we could forsee our troubles, we should worry ourselves about them long before they came, and in that fretfulness we should miss the joy of our present blessings. Great mercy has hung up a veil between us and the future; and there let it hang!

"Still, all is not concealed. Some things we clearly see. I say, 'we'; but I mean those whose eyes have been opened, for it is not everyone who can see in the truest sense. A lady said to Mr. Turner, 'I have often looked upon that prospect, but I have never seen what you have put into your picture.' The great artist simply replied, 'Don't you wish you could see it?' Looking into the future with the eye of faith, believers can see much that is hidden from those who have no faith. Let me tell you, in a few words, what I see as I look into the new year.

" I see a pathway made from this Jan. 1, 1892, to Jan. 1, 1893. I see a highway cast up by the foreknowledge and predestination of God. Nothing of the future is left to chance; nay, not the falling of a sparrow, nor the losing of a hair is left to haphazard; but all the events of life are arranged and appointed. Not only is every turn in the road marked in the divine map, but every stone on the road, and every drop of morning dew or evening mist that falls upon the grass which grows at the roadside. We are not to cross a trackless desert; the Lord has ordained our path in His infallible wisdom and infinite love. 'The steps of a good man are ordered by the Lord; and he delighteth in his way.'

"I see, next, a Guide provided, as our companion along the way. To Him we gladly say, 'Thou shalt guide me with Thy counsel.' He is waiting to go with us through every portion of the road. 'The Lord, He it is that doth go before thee; He will be with thee, He will not fail thee.' We are not left to pass through life as though it were a lone wilderness, a place of dragons and owls; for Jesus says, 'I will not leave you comfortless; I will come to you.'

"Though we should lose father and mother, and the dearest friends, there is One who wears our nature, who will never quit our side. One like unto the Son of Man is still treading the life-ways of believing hearts, and each true believer cometh up from the wilderness, leaning upon the Beloved. We feel the presence of the Lord Jesus even now, in this room, where two or three are gathered in His name, and I trust we shall feel it through all the months of the year, whether it be the time of the singing of birds, or the season of ripe fruits, or the dark months when the clods are frozen into iron. In this Riviera we ought the more readily to realise our Lord's presence, because the country is so like 'Thy land, O Immanuel!' Here is the land of oil-olive, and of figs, and of the clusters of Eshcol. By such a blue sea He walked, and up such rocky hills He climbed. But, whether here or elsewhere, let us look for Him to abide with us, to make this year truly to be 'a year of our Lord.'

"Besides the way and the Guide, I perceive very clearly, by the eye of faith, *strength for the journey provided*. Throughout the whole distance of the year, we shall find halting-places, where we may rest and take refreshment, and then go on our way singing, 'He restoreth my soul.' We shall have strength enough, but none to spare; and that strength will come when it is needed, and not before. When saints imagine that they have strength to spare, they turn sinners, and are apt to have their locks shorn by the Philistines. The Lord of the way will find the pilgrims with sufficient spending-money for the road; but He may not think it wise to burden them with superfluous funds.

"God all-sufficient will not fail those who trust Him. When we come to the place for shouldering the burden, we shall reach the place for receiving the strength. If it pleases the Lord to multiply our troubles from one to ten, He will increase our strength in the same proportion. To each believer the Lord still says, 'As thy days, so shall thy strength be.' You do not yet feel that you have grace to die with: what of that? You are not yet dying. While you have yet to deal with the business and duty of life, look to God for the grace which these require; and when life is ebbing out, and your only thought is about landing on the eternal shore, then look to God your Saviour for dying grace in dying moments. We may expect an inrush of divine strength when human strength is failing, and a daily impartation of energy as daily need requires. Our lamps shall be trimmed as long as they shall need to burn. Let not our present weakness tempt us to limit the Holy One of Israel. There is a hospice on every pass over the Alps of life, and a bridge across every river of trial, which crosses our way to the Celestial City. Holy angels are as numerous to guard us as fallen ones to tempt us. We shall never have a need for which our gracious Father has furnished no supply.

"I see, most plainly, a Power overruling all things which occur in the way we tread. I see an alembic in which all things are transformed. 'All things work together for good to them that love God, to them that are the called according to His purpose.' I see a wonder-working hand which turns for us the swords of disease into the ploughshares of correction, and the spears of trial into the pruning-hooks of discipline. By this divine skill, bitters are made sweet, and poisons turned to medicines. 'Nothing shall by any means harm you,' is a promise too strong for feeble faith; but full assurance finds it true. Since God is for us, who can be against us? What a joy to see Jehovah Himself as our banner, and God himself with us as our Captain? Forward then into the New Year, 'for there shall no evil befall you.'

"One thing more, and this is the brightness itself: this year we trust we shall see God glorified by us and in us. If we realize our chief end, we reach our highest enjoyment. It is the delight of the renewed heart to think that God can get glory out of such poor creatures as we are. 'God is light.' We cannot aid to His brightness, but we may act as reflectors, which, though they have no light of their own, yet, when the sun shines upon them, reflect His beams, and send them where, without such reflection, they might not have come. When the Lord shines upon us, we will cast that light upon dark places, and make those who sit in the shadow of death to rejoice in Jesus our Lord. We hope that God has been in some measure glorified in some of us during the past year, but we trust He will be glorified by us far more in the year which now begins. We will be content to glorify God either actively or passively. We would have it so happen that, when our life's history is written, whoever reads it will not think of us as 'self-made men,' but as the handiwork of God, in whom His grace is magnified. Not in us may men see the clay, but the Potter's hand. They said of one, 'He is a fine preacher'; but of another they said, 'We never notice how he preaches, but we feel that God is great.' We wish our whole life to be a sacrifice; an altar of incense continually smoking with sweet perfume unto the Most High. Oh, to be borne through the year on the wings of praise to God; to mount from year to year, and raise at each ascent a loftier and yet lowlier song unto the God of our life! The vista of a praiseful life will never close, but continue throughout eternity. From psalm to psalm, from hallelujah to hallelujah, we will ascend the hill of the Lord, until we come into the holiest of all, where, with veiled faces, we will bow before the Divine Majesty in the bliss of endless adoration. Throughout this year may the Lord be with you! Amen."

www.ingramcontent.com/pod-product-compliance
Lightning Source LLC
Chambersburg PA
CBHW030605300426
44111CB00009B/1104